Unmothering Autism

Ethical Disruptions and Affirming Care

PATTY DOUGLAS

I0011032

UBCPress · Vancouver

Printed in Canada on FSC-certified ancient-forest-free paper (100% post-consumer recycled) that is processed chlorine- and acid-free.

UBC Press is a Benetech Global Certified Accessible™ publisher. The epub version of this book meets stringent accessibility standards, ensuring it is available to people with diverse needs.

Library and Archives Canada Cataloguing in Publication

Title: Unmothering autism : ethical disruptions and affirming care / Patty Douglas.
Names: Douglas, Patty, author.
Series: Disability culture and politics.
Description: Series statement: Disability culture and politics | Includes bibliographical references and index.
Identifiers: Canadiana 20240492242 | ISBN 9780774869737 (softcover)
Subjects: LCSH: Autistic children – Care. | LCSH: Autistic children – Family relationships. | LCSH: Mothers of autistic children.
Classification: LCC HQ773.8.D68 2025 | DDC 305.9/084083—dc23

Canadä

Canada Council   Conseil des arts
for the Arts   du Canada

BRITISH COLUMBIA
ARTS COUNCIL

BRITISH
COLUMBIA

UBC Press gratefully acknowledges the financial support for our publishing program of the Government of Canada, the Canada Council for the Arts, and the British Columbia Arts Council.

This book has been published with the help of a grant from the Canadian Federation for the Humanities and Social Sciences, through the Scholarly Book Awards, using funds provided by the Social Sciences and Humanities Research Council of Canada.

UBC Press is situated on the traditional, ancestral, and unceded territory of the xʷməθkʷəy̓əm (Musqueam) people. This land has always been a place of learning for the xʷməθkʷəy̓əm, who have passed on their culture, history, and traditions for millennia, from one generation to the next.

Printed and bound in Canada
Set in Zurich, Univers, and Minion by Apex CoVantage, LLC
Copy editor: Robert Lewis
Proofreader: Sophie Pouyanne
Indexer: Patti Phillips
Cover designer: Alexa Love
Cover image: Katrissa Singer, *Superior Mom* (crochet sculpture, 2018)

UBC Press
The University of British Columbia
www.ubcpress.ca

For Brennan and Jesse

Contents

Acknowledgments

This book would not have been possible without the generosity and encouragement of my wonderful friends, mentors, family, disability community, and (m)other co-researchers. As a result of my decision almost twenty years ago to "disrupt" my life as a teacher and solo (m)other to attend graduate school, this book represents the incredible journey taken pursuing a deeper understanding of our family's experiences of autism and "care." What began as a feeling of unease first became the basis of my doctoral research, and is now a book greatly deepened by the generosity and insight of my reviewers, UBC Press editors, and many brilliant thinkers in disability justice, critical autism studies, Indigenous disability studies, and more. I am delighted that this book is out in the world.

First and foremost, I would like to acknowledge and thank my sons, Brennan and Jesse – their love, encouragement, and faith have been unwavering. During the time it took to finish this book, my sons have grown into amazing young people and thinkers. They have engaged my ideas along the way, read excerpts and taught me deeply about love, life, and living well in difference. May this book do justice to our journey together. My family and extended family, too, have helped in more ways than they know, through encouragement, excitement, support, and sharing the journey. Thank you to my mom, sister, brother, stepdad, Aunty Patty and Gerry, cousins, Grandma and Grandpa, Chris, and the rest of my beautiful family. Your support means the world to me.

I am deeply grateful to my many incredible mentors and interlocutors along the way who, each in their own way, have challenged me and added depth to my thinking. While almost too many to mention, a special and heartfelt thank you to Carla Rice, John Portelli, Kari Dehli, Katherine Runswick-Cole, Megan Boler, Roger Simon, Tanya Titchkosky, Tom Reynolds, and many others who have been sources of support, inspiration, and encouragement along the way.

Thank you to colleagues, too, who have been a source of both inspiration and provocation: Anne McGuire, Chris Chapman, Christine Kelly, Dorothy Taare-Smith, Elizabeth Harrison, Jacqui Getfield, Katie Aubrecht, Meg Gibson, Steacy Easton, and others too numerous to list here. To my many wonderful and encouraging friends, old and new, thank you for your wisdom, understanding, and support: Alyson, Andrea, Anita, Chris, Melinda, my choir, Peter, Susanne, teacher friends and mentors, and many others.

I also could not have navigated the many twists and turns of writing this book without the intellectual and financial support of the Social Justice Education Program at the University of Toronto. I would also like to acknowledge the support of the Social Sciences and Humanities Research Council of Canada. I am truly thankful.

I am grateful to Katrissa Singer for giving me permission to feature their art on the cover. I first saw this piece in 2019 and am thrilled it is now part of the book!

Finally, I am tremendously grateful to all the (m)others who agreed to take part in my focus groups. Their thoughtfulness and enthusiasm, practice of affirming care, and willingness to share and reflect on their knowledge and experience integrally shaped how I proceeded, and how I came to pursue the meaning of care. I am deeply appreciative.

Artist Statement[1]

The artwork that appears on the front cover of this book, *Super(ior) Mom*, was created in 2017. The title was inspired by the so-called Autism Mom stereotype, and my own experiences growing up with a mother whose identity was so closely tied to her role as caregiver to an "unusual" or "difficult" child. The piece alludes to the popular perception of motherhood as heroic. *Super(ior) Mom* exposes the paradox of a mother's love: while it can nurture and support, it can also confine and suffocate.

– Katrissa Singer

Unmothering Autism

Introduction

Toward Ethical Disruptions and Affirming Care

My son is trapped inside this label called autism and I'm gonna get him out.

— Jenny McCarthy, *Louder Than Words* (2007, 7)

In 2007, actor Jenny McCarthy published *Louder Than Words: A Mother's Journey in Healing Autism,* a *New York Times* bestseller in which McCarthy recounts her desperate journey as a mother to discover what was wrong with her son, Evan. Since infancy, Evan had displayed odd behaviours such as "hand-flapping," "toe walking," "playing with door hinges" and "lining up toys" – traits that McCarthy had once thought beautiful but that were now signs associated in the public imagination with the tragedy of autism and with autism and mothering. In her memoir, McCarthy narrates her grief and hero's journey to heal her son from autism after receiving his diagnosis, including her fight against childhood vaccines, which she identifies as causing autism, and against the incompetent medical professionals administering them.[1] McCarthy's memoir and public anti-vaccine campaign, along with other campaigns against autism by powerful parent advocacy organizations like Autism Speaks (McGuire 2016), have etched into public discourse the now ubiquitous figure of autism's warrior mother, who tirelessly advocates for her child, undertakes research, educates herself and others, and does much more to recover her child from autism against all odds (Douglas 2013). I use the term "autism mother" to describe this new form of maternal subjectivity as a socio-cultural production rather than a natural given, one that emerged, as we shall see, through shifting

biomedical and popular understandings of autism and through the recruitment of mothers into care regimes that aim to fix autism. I also use the
term "(m)others" to acknowledge the constructed nature of motherhood
as well as "the multiple care-givers in disabled children's [and adults'] lives ...
[and] the continuing gendered nature of care" (Douglas et al., "Making
Memories," 2022, 3). When I write about autism mothers or about other
work or individuals that do not acknowledge its constructed nature, I use
the term "mothers."

McCarthy would go on to write a second book, *Mother Warriors: A
Nation of Parents Healing Autism against All Odds* in 2008, bringing to life
the success stories of other autism mothers across North America and
beyond warring against autism and advocating to heal their child through
every day (often dangerous) interventions such as special diets, chelation
(or heavy metal) therapy, vitamin therapies, early intensive behaviour
therapy, and more. McCarthy's views are extreme. Indeed, as the work of
disability studies scholar Tanya Titchkosky (2003, 236) suggests, she might
be understood as overconforming to a world that "has almost no interest
in, and sometimes would rather kill, alternative ways of being-in-the-
world," including autism. McCarthy's description of how an autism "label"
remade her son's unique way of being into something to be feared and
fought against captures a common sense about autism still circulating in
popular media, parent advocacy organizations, autism services, education,
and health systems in the Global North (Douglas et al., "Re-storying
Autism," 2021).[2] This understanding is now globally exported through
health initiatives and North American parent advocacy organizations
(Douglas 2013; McGuire 2016); autism is a problem to be eliminated, and
autism mothers have a duty to reshape their love and to fight against this
enemy at all costs (literally by going into massive debt to fight autism).

I know something about McCarthy's warrior mother story, something
that is familiar. I, too, am the (m)other of a son who attracted the label of
autism. I, too, watched my son's unique and beautiful characteristics –
lining up cars, spinning objects, rocking and finger-flapping – remade
into red flags in the pages of parenting magazines, in the disturbed (and
disturbing) glances of other parents, and in the language of psychology
and childhood pathology that became our lexicon as my son entered
daycare and school. I include this narrative and others with the permission

of my sons, Brennan and Jesse. At the time my son was diagnosed in 2005, understandings of autism readily available in schools, doctors' offices, and autism agencies in Toronto were saturated with understandings of autism as disorder and tragedy. (Today, in large part due to the work of autistic self-advocates, critical allies, and the neurodiversity movement, representation is more diverse,[3] but deficit narratives arguably continue to prevail.) For example, one of the first articles that I read about autism – clipped and saved for me by a family member who was also trying to understand the diagnosis – appeared in *Time* magazine and was entitled "Inside the Autistic Mind" (Wallis 2006). It rehearsed the now-familiar story: autism is an alarming neurodevelopmental disorder located and locatable in brains, environmental triggers play an important role in the disorder, researchers are beginning to find answers through genetic research, behavioural therapies are urgently needed to reshape (or normalize) autistic behaviour, and autistic people are finding ways to communicate despite their "unusual" and "odd" brains – which is, states the author, reason for hope (Wallis 2006, 46).

My search to reconcile such contradictory experiences as a (m)other – the beauty of our everyday versus dominant understandings of autism as an alarming disorder in need of a solution – first took place during late night Internet excursions when the physical labour of (m)othering and medical appointments had abated. Here again, I quickly encountered a clamor of troubling representations of autism and research on causes and cures on websites of various autism organizations alongside disconcerting popular media portrayals. Almost always a variation of the same tale, the story is told of the tragic loss of a normally developing child, disordered brains, maternal grief, family stress, the need for more biomedical research and more services, and most important of all, maternal heroism (or defeat) in treating and recovering a child through a mother's love as framed by biomedical or professional care (see Clarke 2012; and S. Jones and Harwood 2009). A *Redbook* magazine article entitled "What Autism Does to a Mother," for example, begins this way: "Nicole Kalkowski knows that beyond the stress, fear, and family turmoil that come with learning that your child has this devastating disorder, there is also a devastating aloneness ... We follow this mother of three as she struggles to save her son" (Rones 2008, n.p.). Here, mother Nicole Kalkowski, her son, and family are the devastated, isolated victims of autistic disorder, and being a mother means struggling to "save" your child (and family) from such a fate. The article details how such a rescue might take place. This mom found hope in online advocacy organizations and found recovery through individual biomedical interventions, such as a gluten-free, casein-free diet.

Within such dominant narratives, I have found myself and my sons made over. At various junctures, because I embraced my son's difference and advocated for acceptance and inclusion, I was cast as the "mad," possibly dangerous, and sometimes heroic mother who had to be educated about the need to reshape my son's so-called autistic behaviour (see Douglas et al., "Mad Mothering," 2021). My younger son was cast as the innocent sibling victim. We were a family coping with autism. And my autistic son's so-called brain disorder was the problem. This critique of the dominant narrative is not meant to suggest that life in disability is without struggle or that there is not an urgent need for more help. For some families, as disability and social inclusion scholar Stacy Clifford Simplican (2015, 219) argues, a model of "complex dependency" is needed if we are to systemically address the difficult knowledge that some individuals "can be both vulnerable and aggressive" without reinscribing reductive understandings of disability or stigma. Autistic self-advocacy organizations like Autistics United Canada also assert the dire need for supports grounded in the affirmation of autistic people rather than in the quest for a cure. However, as Titchkosky (2007) reminds us, rarely questioned is the seductive effect of tragedy narratives that locate the trouble of autism solely within disordered individual brains and behaviour rather than within disordered systems and stigmatizing representations.

I have found myself both compelled and angered by popular and biomedical narratives of autism and mothering. The certainty and control promised by biomedical research can be enticing. More than once, our family found ourselves trying to decipher computer images of autistic minds/brains, pondering who might have passed down the autism gene in our family and trying to identify what the environmental triggers might have been. Was the culprit my landlord's removal of lead paint when my son was a baby? Was it the medicine that I took when I was pregnant? At times, too, these cultural tales became vehicles for expressing love and concern for my son, as well as for organizing the work of the maternal subjectivity thrust upon my everyday life, that of autism mother. My family and I, too, lived the search for recovery: gluten-free, casein-free diets, supplements (we all took them), behavioural consultants, alternative therapies (magnetism!), medication, auditory processing, and sensory integration therapy – the list goes on.

More often, however, such narratives pathologized and eclipsed the tenderness and beauty as well as the struggle and violence (see Kelly 2017; and Rich 1986) of our lived experiences. Whether owing to the surprise of "the stim," such as flapping hands, to the "jarring transition," or to interludes of rapture, including long periods watching water drip or objects spin, our journey exceeded and disrupted any easy way of being together or any easy meaning of care.[4] The rupture between the private world that I inhabited with my sons, Brennan and Jesse, as a family and the public world where we encountered professionals in schools, doctors' offices, and autism agencies seemed irreconcilable. Rather than mimicking dominant narratives of autism as tragedy and alarm and (m)othering as a fight against autism, our rhythm as a family was more often sculpted in unique and lovely ways by the "disruption" of my son's ways of being, identified as autistic. Whereas other (m)others, for example, might scoop up their sometimes screaming young child or might shout, "Time to go!" when leaving the park, our world was shaped differently. My son's unique connections to the sensory world and time meant instead that together we visited each flowerbed, in turn, as part of an oft-repeated ritual as we slowly made our way out of the park. Along with other such troubling family behaviours, these untimely transitions and rituals that marked my son's body as autistic disrupted the everyday realities of (m)othering, schools, and autism agencies, where we sometimes met with professional and public concern and even violence. Bullying, exclusions, and negative remarks about my (bad) mothering and my (bad) son by teachers, parents, and school administrators were commonplace. Particularly salient was the day that my younger son and I walked in on the scene of the school's principal restraining my then eight-year-old autistic son, who lay spread-eagled and face down on the carpet, the culmination of my son's forcible removal from a washroom stall, where he had retreated to calm down after an upsetting event in the classroom.[5] This same principal had also called the police on different occasions to escort children in the same class – other unruly (disabled) eight year olds – out of the school in handcuffs (see Hune-Brown 2016). In the face of such violence, it was not for cures or for more behavioural therapies that I fought.

Rather, I wanted to understand more deeply – even somehow to reconcile – the contradictions between beauty and violence that we experienced as a family surrounding the embodied difference of autism (see Arendt [1954] 1994, 307–27; and Titchkosky 2003, 236).[6] Such everyday encounters were impossible for me to turn away from or to forget. They told a story about autism and (m)othering that differed from McCarthy's account and became an ethical and political call for the cultivation of a deeper and more complex social and political understanding of how such occurrences could be possible at all – an understanding and public dialogue that this book invites. I pause here to note that violence – physical, psychological, and ethical, as discussed below – against autistic children, adults, and mothers appears in many of the book's storylines. I pause for two reasons. First, I want to summon a practice of care. I invite my reader to take up these passages in whatever way is needed to care for yourself, whether that means skipping over certain passages, talking with someone you love and trust, reading passages together with others, having a comfort item close by, stimming, or picking up and putting down the book (see Kafer 2016; Price n.d.; and Re•Storying Autism Writing Collective 2022). This care-full, ethical approach to witnessing (Levinas 1989) is one that I also took up in writing this book. Indeed, there were times when I paused, cried, raged, talked with others, read and reread news items, or watched and rewatched videos and films, and there were times when I put the book down. Second, I pause to describe the place of violence in the book. The book traces shifting forms of autism mother subjectivity and power (including tactics of violence); for example, in Chapter 2 I trace representations of the refrigerator mother and of mother blame, to which both mothers and their children were subject, including in the form of forceful psychoanalytic treatment and through the separation of children from mothers. The book also investigates deeply held cultural assumptions about embodied difference as threatening and about women as natural caregivers, assumptions that normalize violence and the imperative to fix autism through a mother's love in the mother-child dyad. Violence is, in other words, a complex part of the normalizing maternal care regime in which the book intervenes (see Chapter 1 for more on violence). I return to the topic of violence at several points in the book. For now, I note that I join other critical scholars and activists who seek to transform our world, one that includes exclusion as an ordinary practice (Titchkosky 2007, 149–52) and one that just as ordinarily commits violence against those who are perceived as different – women and femme folks as well as autistic, (m)othering, Black, queer, Indigenous, "Mad," and other nonconforming bodies (see also Brown, Ashkenazy, and Onaiwu 2017; Douglas et al., "Mad Mothering," 2021, 2024; Hodge et al. 2023; Schalk and Kim 2020; and L. Simpson 2017). Autistic people and the neurodiversity movement have been calling for a valuing of autistic difference as a fundamental part of being human together for some thirty years (Sinclair 1993; Singer 2017; Walker 2012, 2021). This book is written in solidarity.

The glimpses that I offer of loving a different son in a world calling for sameness and identity with non-autistic ways of being spotlight deep cultural contradictions within Global North relationships to embodied difference about who and what is valued – and cared for and about – under late modernity.[7] Inspired by concepts in feminist, disability, and critical autism studies, this book investigates these cultural contradictions – what I call the paradox of care. To mother a different child is a paradox, at once meaning love and violence, constraint and possibility, intimacy and rupture (see Douglas, Rice, and Kelly 2017; and Kelly 2016, 2017). I argue for an ethic of disruption in everyday text, talk, and knowledge production about autism, (m)othering, and care, an ethic that centres the previously marginalized perspectives of (m)others/carers and autistic people while unsettling what it means to (m)other and care. By an ethic of disruption, I mean a stance of perpetual questioning about matters presumed to be settled, such as the shape of a mother's love. A stance of perpetual questioning insists on a new quality of attention in knowledge production and care, one that affirms autistic difference and care relationships – hereafter called affirming care (see below). This ethic of disruption reveals not only the taken-for-granted assumptions about difference that seduce autism mothers, and perhaps all (m)others, to care about autism through curative or remedial labour but also new possibilities for being human together that affirm and celebrate difference. Everyday talk and text – hereafter called text or popular media and science (on text, see Titchkosky 2007, 26–28) – means popular science, mass media, and the popular culture in which autism and autism mothers make an appearance as well as insights from focus group conversations that I held with (m)others of autistic offspring in southwestern Ontario. I describe how I went about gathering my archive later in this introduction and share snippets from popular media and focus groups along the way.

The book aims to reveal new insights about power and subjectivity that continue to capture us in our contemporary moment, and it seeks to insert new possibilities for critique and creative resistance into knowledge production about (m)othering and care. As Chapter 1 describes, I pay particular attention to governmentality – meaning, as philosopher Michel Foucault (1982, 221) puts it, the "conduct of conduct" – as a seductive form of late-modern power that invites autism mothers to care through cure or remediation. The book offers (m)others, family, kin, and others new possibilities to affirm autism in all its beauty and struggle – indeed, all embodied difference – as a fundamental, valuable, and even desirable part of being human together. This book is thus written in solidarity with the disability justice movement. Disability justice author and activist Leah Lakshmi Piepzna-Samarasinha (2018, 21) describes disability justice as an intellectual, political, and creative movement founded and led by disabled, queer, Indigenous, Black, and other people of colour "visioning a world where we flourish, that values and celebrates us in all our myriad beauty."[8] In this post-COVID-19 moment, when less valued people – autistic, Black, older, disabled, working-class, and Indigenous – are either targeted and murdered by police or left to die within inadequate care systems and under worse conditions (see Alexiou 2020; Cheung 2020; Piepzna-Samarasinha 2018; and Walcott 2020), such work, following cultural studies scholar Stuart Hall (1997, 220), is "deadly political," being entangled with life-and-death questions of power, violence, and human possibility.

Toward Ethical Narration

Narrating stories of lived experience as a (m)other of an autistic son is nothing new. Since the 1960s at least, parents and mothers have been writing their stories of life together with their autistic child (see Axline

1964; Junker 1964; and C. Park 1967). I aim to narrate differently, turning to my experience and encounters with everyday text neither as repeated stories of grief, heroism, and defeat nor as true stories about autism or about my sons and family but as important starting points for releasing new stories into the world about difference. Cherokee and Greek author Thomas King (2003, 2) says, "The truth about stories is that that's all we are." Stories create and therefore can re-create worlds. Narrating anew is thus an urgent interpretive, critical, and creative task in our moment. How might life with an autistic child or adult not only be a site of struggle and even violence but also offer new possibilities to reimagine ordinary life together outside of such constraints?

Given the oppressive histories of autism research and parent memoirs, I am keenly aware of the ethical dangers involved in my choice to write this book. Including glimpses of my narrative has the potential to participate in histories of disability as spectacle (Garland-Thomson 1997), to reinscribe the "unacknowledged whiteness" (Schalk and Kim 2020, 33) of feminist disability studies, and to eclipse my sons' own stories. Positioned complexly, I write as a white-settler academic. I also write as an invisibly disabled, neurodivergent academic and solo mother of two neurodivergent sons, one of whom has attracted the label of autism.[9] In my approach to centring previously marginalized knowledge and experience, I am indebted to the disability justice movement and to the legacies of feminist thought that have shown the power and necessity of theorizing from the margins (see hooks 1984; and Schalk and Kim 2020, 32). Although it remains an impossible task, I attempt to narrate ethically – to disrupt, as philosopher Emmanuel Levinas (1989, 82) invokes, "my place in the sun" or the innocence of my subjectivity (see also Simon 2000). I also maintain that a careful engagement by disabled and nondisabled (m)others, parents, and carers across and between disability and non-disability is imperative in the project of telling new stories and transforming disability oppression, a key challenge being taken up by disability studies, critical autism, and feminist scholars alike, a challenge of which this book is a part.[10]

I have lived the disquieting but very ordinary demand that I remedy my son's autism, to borrow a phrase from Canadian feminist sociologist Dorothy Smith (1987, 49–60), as a "line of fault" or rupture between the personal and the political. In this lived site of contradiction, I am situated between living with and loving my son and contending with an ableist world that cannot yet imagine forms of social life and identity that integrally include and affirm life together with autistic individuals. Ableism means dominant discourses and systems that vest power in bodies and minds considered normal and therefore desirable and good, including those identified as productive, autonomous, ordered, nondisabled, white, male, straight, and middle-class (see Campbell 2009; and Goodley 2014). Ableism also intersects with other systems of oppression such as sexism and racism (Erevelles 2011; Schalk and Kim 2020; see also Chapter 1). For my family, the demand to remedy autism has often meant public praise when we got the work of advocacy or behavioural therapies right (or when my son appeared "normal"), and it meant public blame and exclusion when my son's different behaviour appeared to others as alarmingly autistic or, sometimes, as not autistic enough. I forward the concept of rupture between lived experience and everyday text to open room for critical and creative inquiry about such lived contradiction. Feminist disability studies scholar Rosemarie Garland-Thomson (1997, 10–12) also opens this space of critical inquiry by paying attention to "the gap between disabled people and their representations" (10) or to the "misfit" (Garland-Thomson 2011) between disabled bodies and ableist worlds. Tanya Titchkosky (2003, 2007, 2011), whose work in disability studies draws from interpretive, critical race/ Blackness, feminist, and cultural studies approaches, opens this critical and creative space to rethink ordinary exclusions within our life together by attending to "between-ness" (2007, 21), whether as marginality (2003, 236), liminality (2007, 21), or the gap between "received stories of justified exclusion and the possession of disquiet" (2011, 76). I situate my analysis in what I call the space of rupture between body and world, personal and political, material and discursive where autism and (m)othering might become something new. This space of rupture is marked by power even as it is a potential site of resistance that is lived, intimate, relational, and fleshy (see also Douglas, Rice, and Kelly 2017). Situating my work in this space of rupture is my own attempt to reconcile, on the one hand, the dominant culture's curative demand that I remedy autism through my love for my son and, on the other hand, the surprising disruption and beauty of autism in our everyday life.

An Ethic of Disruption

I innovate an ethic of disruption in order to proceed in knowledge production in a way that fosters new possibilities – new stories and practices – for being human together. This section describes my ethic in philosophical terms and then offers an example based in Ontario, Canada. An ethic of disruption means bracketing the question of the real meaning of autism and orienting instead to autism as a kind of commotion or disruption within what Titchkosky (2007, 164) calls the ordinary and expected "movements of [everyday] life" (see also Foucault 1980a, 25). Rather than treating autism as a biomedical problem or tragedy that requires a mother's care to remedy, I attend to the disruption of autism as a lived, embodied, and culturally produced phenomenon that also reveals not only the Western cultural desire for identity but also the possibility of living otherwise. Despite gains made in autism acceptance and affirmation by autistic self-advocates and critical allies, including family and kin, the prevailing understanding of autism remains a biomedical one and is woven through with moral undercurrents that cast autism is an undesirable, tragic, and even dangerous neurodevelopmental disorder on the rise globally (Douglas et al., "Re-storying Autism," 2021).[11] A normal life, presumed to be a social good, as feminist philosopher Anita Silvers (1998) articulates it, thus excludes the disorder of autism. Within this predominant view, a mother's care in the form of a mother-child dyad is implicated, steeped in what disability studies scholar Rod Michalko (2002, 99) calls the "biomedical ethics of remedy," what autistic disability studies and rhetoric scholar M. Remi Yergeau (2018, 4) refers to as the "critical exigence" to stop autism, and what autistic scholars Alicia Broderick and Robin Roscigno (2021, 79) describe as the "cultural logic of intervention" (see also Bumiller 2008, 2009; and E. Kim 2017). Autism needs fixing, the dominant cultural story goes, and mothers, given their nurturing feminine nature, proximity as primary caregivers, and close ties to autistic life, are integrally involved.

Reorienting to knowledge production about autism and (m)others through an ethic of disruption means, first, adopting the philosophical stance of the skeptic. This stance understands knowledge production as a site of perpetual questions about how different lives have come to matter, who we have become in our contemporary moment, and how we in Western culture have come to practise care as cure, and failing that, as remedy (see

Butler 2004; Clare 2017; E. Kim 2017; and Rabinow and Rose 2003, xx–xxi). Here, I am influenced by Foucault's (2000, 448) ethic of discomfort and by his formulation of philosophy's task (borrowed from phenomenologist Maurice Merleau-Ponty) as entailing an agreement "never to consent to being completely comfortable with one's own presuppositions." Like Foucault, I do not seek comfortable answers but new questions that keep in play a constantly shifting ground, one that is "always unexplored" (448).

Compelled by my own experiences and by those of the (m)others of autistic offspring with whom I spoke in focus groups, I offer an ethic of disruption that goes beyond Foucault's discomfort by also adopting a creative philosophical stance and by exploring disruption as a site to imagine new generative possibilities for a life together in difference (Runswick-Cole and Goodley 2018; Douglas, Rice, and Siddiqui 2020; Douglas et al., "Re-storying Autism," 2021). This is a creative and hopeful stance in knowledge production, one that requires a shift in how we – researchers, memoirists, parents, family and kin, practitioners, policy makers, educators, and others – care about or pay attention to the disruption of autism. I call this new form of attention in knowledge production and everyday life affirming care. I am helped in this work, first, by phenomenological sociologist Alfred Schutz's exploration of attention as a form of perception. Schutz (1970, 74) says that although we belong to this world together, the ways that we configure meaning are "concealed" from us within already accomplished and taken-for-granted "interpretive schemes" that nevertheless direct our attention, understanding, and action in some ways and not others (see also Husserl [1954] 1970, 104). In research and everyday life, disruption "hangs together" (phenomenologist Edmund Husserl, quoted in Schutz 1967, 82) without much ado since the very recognition of disruption presumes and is configured through the same interpretive schemes (Schutz 1967, 82–83; Natanson 1970, 63). The Global North's interpretive schemes, for example, conceal the prestige of science and its assumptions about normal human development as non-autistic and about autism as a disordered, tragic, undesired disruption that must be remedied. Orienting toward care that is affirming, as opposed to curative or remedial, shifts the attention in research and everyday life away from assumptions about "unruly" autistic bodies being in need (rather than not) "of further analysis" (Schutz 1967, 74). Within an ethic of disruption, affirming care offers the quality of attention necessary to learn anew from relationships with difference and to imagine other possible worlds together.

It is important to note that the objective of an ethic of disruption is not to moralize or to prescribe "better" ways (Rabinow and Rose 2003, xxviii) to understand autism, mothering, and care. Rather, an ethic of disruption aims to disrupt and remake the ground of a world where both the exclusion, marginalization, and violence toward bodies marked as different and the individualizing of maternal care within a mother-child dyad are marked as ordinary (Titchkosky 2007, 149–52; see also Goodley and Runswick-Cole 2018). An ethic of disruption is a creative, caring, and relational philosophical stance that pays attention to the questions and lessons that emerge in the surprise of a life together in disability, one that disrupts what have come to be regarded as the normal and possible ways of being in the world together. An ethic of disruption, guided by affirming care, gestures to something beyond dominant regimes of care as fixing and beyond understandings of being human as non-autistic.

Given the persistence of Western biomedical understandings of autism as a problem and the prevalence of parent memoirs and other popular media that forward this understanding (e.g., see Cooper 2016), narrating the story of autism and (m)othering differently is a serious task. As an aside, it is interesting to note that a dash of autism has become almost desirable, as seen with the television series characters Sheldon in *The Big Bang Theory* and Shaun in *The Good Doctor,* and also that affirming representations of autism and (m)othering are emerging (e.g., see Ashburn and Edwards 2023; Hammond 2023; and Studies in Social Justice special issue Autism_Media_Social Justice 2021). Arguably, however, autism tropes such as savantism, dangerousness, otherworldliness, and computer-like characters continue to haunt popular media and science. Any quirk of autism must ultimately be only a self-styling and cannot intrude upon the narrow confines of performing the neoliberal consumer subject as autonomous, productive, and self-entrepreneurial. Neoliberalism means the marketization of every aspect of life through forms of government (e.g., surveillance and invitation), ideology, and policy making (see Larner 2000; and Vandenbeld Giles 2014) that emphasize hyper-individualism, freedom of choice, shrinking public supports, and deregulation, on the one hand, and competitive global-capitalist economic and moral demands for hyper-productivity and adaptability, on the other hand (Goodley 2014; Erevelles 2011; Larner 2000; D. Richardson 2005). For example, in the television series *Atypical*, the main character, Sam, is self-motivated to overcome his sensory and social struggles and to attend college, work part-time, live on his own, and travel; he is also played by a non-autistic actor. However, Sam's life does not reflect reality for all autistic people (nor for their families and kin), who may not have access to supports or who cannot (or do not wish to) perform normatively (Douglas et al., "Beyond 'Inclusionism,'" forthcoming; Re•Storying Autism Writing Collective 2022).

Black feminist scholar Audre Lorde (2007, 36) articulates the vital need for an ethic of disruption or an alternative way of producing knowledge (for Lorde, a poetic way) that enfolds embodied difference and what I have called affirming care: "The quality of light by which we scrutinize our lives has direct bearing upon the product which we live, and upon the changes which we hope to bring about through those lives." *Unmothering Autism* raises ethical tensions about autism, (m)othering, and care to underscore that a different way of researching and narrating (m)othering and autism is needed – one that is in solidarity with feminist and critical autism studies, with disability studies and disability justice, and with autistic self-advocacy (see Davidson and Orsini 2013; Milton 2014; Re•Storying Autism Writing Collective 2022; Schalk and Kim 2020; and Waltz 2020). Through an ethic of disruption and affirming care, the aim of this book is to move knowledge production (including memoirs, popular media, and science), parent advocacy, and care beyond the usual exclusion, stigma, and violence experienced by those perceived and marked as different.

An Example from Ontario, Canada

Consider, for example, how together an ethic of disruption and affirming care make room for something new within the public controversy in Ontario surrounding the rebranded Ontario Autism Program. Although parent advocacy for publicly funded autism services in Ontario has been ongoing since at least the 1990s, parent protest and anger erupted in the media, in provincial legislature, at rallies across Ontario, and via Twitter hashtags such as #AutismDoesntEndat5 when changes were announced in 2016 that limited access to funded Intensive Behavioural Intervention (IBI) to children under the age of five (Kirby-McIntosh n.d.; Klar, Douglas, and McGuire 2016). As described by parent advocate Laura Kirby-McIntosh (n.d., para. 5), a news release on March 29, 2016, by the Ontario Ministry of Children, Community and Social Services limited public funding of IBI services to children aged two to four in order to ensure that IBI is offered during "appropriate developmental windows," with a significant reduction in hours of funded therapy after age five. This change meant that many families previously put on lengthy waitlists for IBI would no longer be eligible for funding for their autistic child. During the intense advocacy campaigns that would follow, opposition parties joined upset parents to "sound the alarm" (Klar, Douglas, and McGuire 2016, para. 4), marking public debates about age cut-offs for IBI with a rhetoric of "lost potential, sacrificed lives, condemned children and compromised futures" (para. 9). Pressure from parent advocates and opposition parties resulted in an announcement on June 28, 2016, by the Liberal government that the age cut-off for funded IBI would be removed (A. Jones 2016). Following the 2018 election of a Conservative government in Ontario (which would be re-elected in June 2022), protests once again erupted when a flat-rate funding model was proposed regardless of individual support needs. Beginning in May 2019, a twenty-member advisory panel consisting of clinicians, autism researchers, parent advocates, and two autistic self-advocates held province-wide consultations. The report of the panel, *Recommendations for a New Needs-Based Ontario Autism Program: The Ontario Autism Program Advisory Panel Report* (Government of Ontario 2019), was released in October and recommended a new "needs-based" Ontario Autism Program (Kirby-McIntosh n.d.). Although the program now incorporates some of the recommendations of parent advocates and autistic self-advocates, since the COVID-19 health pandemic and the writing of this book, its implementation has been further delayed.

What is most notable about the ongoing debate and protests surrounding the Ontario Autism Program is not the glaring need for more public support for families and autistic individuals in Ontario and Canada – indeed, for all disabled people and families. This need has been well established (see Autistics for Autistics n.d.; Klar, Douglas, and McGuire 2016; and Stoddart 2005). Rather, it is the rhetoric of hopelessness surrounding the debate taken up by parent advocates and political opposition parties alike that continues to be most striking. One of the debate's key focal points has been opening access to often intensive and early behavioural therapies as the only hope for autistic children's futures. Behavioural therapy, also referred to as Early Intensive Behavioural Intervention (EIBI) and Applied Behaviour Analysis (ABA), is a set of therapies that attempts to reduce autistic behaviours and to increase normative and "functional" ones, such as spoken language or making eye contact, through up to forty hours per week of therapies beginning at age two, alongside classroom and home practice. ABA and EIBI have their beginnings in the behaviourist philosophy and experiments of Ole Ivar Lovaas and George Rekers at the University of California, Los Angeles, in the 1960s and '70s, among others. Lovaas used rewards and aversives (e.g., electrified floors or withdrawal of a mother's affection) to shape so-called desirable (or normative) behaviour in autistic and gender-nonconforming children (see Dawson 2004; Gibson and Douglas 2018; Gruson-Wood 2016; Re•Storying Autism Writing Collective 2022; and Sequenzia 2016). Despite some thirty years of contestation by autistic people and scholars about the legacy of behavioural therapies as part of broader injustices against disabled and gender-nonconforming people, as well as accruing evidence about the normalizing aims and intensity of behavioural therapies as potentially damaging,[12] ABA and EIBI continue to be forwarded as the most evidence-based, effective (and funded) autism interventions both in Ontario and in many other regions of North America.

Together, an ethic of disruption and attention through affirming care take us deeper into understanding the assumptions about the human that drive the rhetoric of hopelessness and intensive advocacy for ABA and EIBI within the Ontario autism debates. M. Remi Yergeau (2018, 12) is helpful here. Yergeau describes the autism science underpinning ABA as "god theories" animated by normative standards of the human as nonautistic: "What [god theories] share in common is a persistent disbelief in the capacities of autistic people to be volitional, to be social, and to be selves. Given autism's classification as a disorder of social communication, these (dis)beliefs about autism are ... theories that privilege restrictive notions of what it means to interact and interrelate." Within such logics, different ways of being human – ticcing, flapping, rocking, an averted gaze – become understood as deficient, avolitional, and even nonhuman. For example, one such "god theory" within cognitive neuropsychology underpinning the perceived urgency for ABA and EIBI is Theory of Mind (ToM). As autism researcher Baron-Cohen (1995) describes, ToM is understood to be the capacity to read the thoughts, intentions, and feelings of others and is posited as the neurological seat of empathy (locatable within brains), the very trait that makes us human. Within ToM, autistic behaviour becomes meaningless and nonhuman, the involuntary effect of disordered neurology (Yergeau 2018). Critical autism scholar Damian Milton (2012) proposes "double empathy" to disrupt such deficit views of autism. Milton asserts that autistic people do not lack empathy. Instead, communication difficulties stem from a failure of empathy on the part of both non-autistic and autistic people. However, based on a biomedical view, intensive, often around-the-clock behavioural intervention such as EIBI or ABA – practised at school, in the clinic, and through a mother's or carer's labour in the home – becomes the only hope to recover an autistic child's potential humanity and future until a cure is found. The ever-growing, shocking, and lengthy list of mothers, parents, and other care-givers who have murdered their autistic child (Autistics for Autistics n.d.; McGuire 2016, 195–201; see also Chapter 7) attests to the dire need for both an ethic of disruption and affirming care to trouble stories of hope-lessness and to open space for new approaches and supports that embrace and affirm difference as fundamental and valuable.

Everyday Text

The socio-cultural location of this book is everyday text. Within Global North societies where written language and literacy, rather than oral or other language, are key values and demands, everyday text such as news-paper articles, blogs, and medical forms occupy a central place in our lives (D. Smith 1999, 135; Titchkosky 2007, 26–28). How text enters our lives as (m)others in the space of rupture between the embodied, interpreting, creative subject and abstract "ruling relations" (D. Smith 1999) or textual modes of power is the tangle that I explore in this book.[13] We come to conduct ourselves, and our relationships with others, through text. An article on the "signs" of autism in a parenting magazine, for example, organizes how we, (m)others, watch our child for signs of autism. I recall the re-education of my gaze, for example, through everyday text. What I once thought (and still do think) beautiful and unique – lining up cars in the same order every day but not playing with them – was written over by medical discourses about warning signs of autism and pathology (e.g., see Autism Canada n.d.). Such texts are difficult to unsee. Text is identity-shaping in this way, an identity that is lived intimately and governed bodily – in our case, within everyday relationships between (m)other and autistic child/adult. This is to say, with Merleau-Ponty (1962), that texts carry with them the cultural ground of the world from which they emanate, including taken-for-granted assumptions about normative human development, mothering, and care. Indeed, each utterance, Merleau-Ponty tells us, contains just this world of unarticulated yet "ready-made meanings" (213). He says that a "word is a gesture, and its meaning, a world" (214). Text thusly orients us to shared (and exclusionary) meanings of autism, as well as to one another in relationships of care. Another way to articulate this circumstance is to say that text is a site of social action, which is not only constrained by power and by the taken-for-granted assumptions of our social world but also, more hopefully, open to "modification" (D. Smith 1999, 145) through our everyday actions (see Titchkosky 2007, 27). It is the social location of text to which I turn in order to interrogate how power inheres, identity comes to be lived and resisted, and meaning is accomplished. Through such an interrogation, we might begin to insert something new.

Through countless sites, texts enter our lives and shape our identities and embodied practice. Indeed, being the (m)other of an autistic child means encountering multiple everyday texts – from the red flags of autism to diagnostic checklists in magazines, doctors' offices, and more – and also encountering the meanings, constraints, and possibilities that these everyday texts impart for our life together with our autistic offspring. I have come to understand these lived encounters as composing a kind of autism (m)other network, one that shapes similar (although not identical) movements through a social world organized and coordinated by text. For this book, although text has often seemed to refer to anything that can be read for meaning (e.g., see Barthes 1977), text means everyday text by or about autism mothers drawn from popular culture, popular science, and the mass media between 1940 and 2022, as well as from focus group conversations that I had with (m)others of autistic offspring in southwestern Ontario. The archive that I compiled is thus part of a larger social and intertextual organization of autism and (m)othering that includes other sites such as schools or health care settings (D. Smith 1999, 134; Foucault 1972). My choice to focus on texts from popular media and science, as well as on my own and (m)others' experiences of and responses to them, acknowledges the reach of popular texts through shared autism (m)other networks, as well as the intimate and lived salience of text in (m)others' and autistic people's everyday lives.

Composing an Archive: Gathering Texts

Compelled by troubling representations of autism and autism mothers, I began to gather an archive. I watched – and rewatched – autism mother videos, clipped articles from newspapers and popular science magazines, viewed motion pictures, television shows, and documentaries, spent copious amounts of time in the archives of University of Toronto Libraries, read popular books by autism experts, and reviewed parent memoirs, government reports, autistic writers' blogs, and more. I wanted to understand the cultural obsession with fixing autism and blaming mothers, many renditions of which are powerfully depicted. I do this work of tracing understandings of autism mothers and autism in the midst of what Foucault (1980a, 7–8) calls a "discursive explosion" – a bringing into discourse – of autism in our time (see also Hacking 2010). To bound an otherwise unwieldly archive, I focused my search on texts available to a Toronto audience; however, my findings are relevant to a broader audience, as these texts have always crossed borders and boundaries. My archive begins in the 1940s with the emergence of autism as a so-called new medical disorder in North America and concludes in 2022, when I wrote the final draft of this book.

Rather than a catalogue or quantification, my archive traces discontinuous shifts in the interpretation of autism and autism mothers as depicted in everyday text – from the refrigerator mother to the mother therapist and autism's warrior mother. I borrow from Foucault (1972, 127), who describes the archive as "the general system of the formation and transformation of statements." This approach means that I focus on the "general system," or conditions of possibility, out of which shifting truths about autism and autism mothers emerge, including how the Global North has come to understand mothering and care as intensive maternal labour toward remediation or a cure, as though this orientation is only natural. I approach shifting truths about autism mothers both as interpretive utterances that are "representative of the cultural grounds of possibility from which they emanate" (Titchkosky 2011, 97) and as traces of power or historical struggles of domination and resistance around the meaning of autism, difference, care, and being human together (Foucault 1984, 83–86).

Composing a Living Archive: Focus Groups

Unique to my project, I include in my archive focus group conversations that I had with (m)others in southwestern Ontario about popular media and science that depict autism and autism mothers. Although focus groups have obvious differences from archived historical texts, participating in research about autism has arguably become an ordinary part of everyday talk for (m)others of autistic children. This participation suggests the relevance and importance of my decision to include focus group conversations. Foucault (1972, 130) identifies the difficulty, perhaps even the impossibility, of identifying the ground animating our own archive, one that we inhabit, including the ways that we still "speak" from within its rules. Departing from Foucault, I proceed from the contention that both the critical interrogation of the grounds of our own living archive and its documentation are vital activities if we are to imagine different possibilities for being together. Although these activities, to borrow from feminist-of-colour scholar Jasbir Puar (2007, xix), may contain yet unknown ways that "the present is still unrecognizable to us," they also provide an "alternative historical record, archive and documentation of our contemporary moments" (xv). This is an orientation to focus group conversations not only as empirical data about, for example, (m)others' experiences but also as an interrogation of the cultural ground out of which dominant conceptions of autism and autism mother identity emerge – including how these ideas are taken up, lived, negotiated, and importantly, resisted within (m)others' lives. I briefly introduce my focus groups below to provide context for these conversations, glimpses of which are woven throughout the chapters to come.

In flyers that I circulated via autism (m)other networks in Toronto, I invited (m)others to speak about and to push back against popular and scientific representations of both autism and autism mothers and to reflect on their experiences of loving an autistic child or adult offspring.[14] As a basis for our conversations, I shared two collages that I had made using images from my archive (alongside some homemade banana bread!) as well as a number of contemporary autism mother books.[15] Collages were homemade on blue poster board, and included cut-out snippets of headlines and articles from popular magazines and newspapers on the themes of "Extremes: Love and Violence" as well as "Popular Science." They included, for example, journalist Nancy Rones's (2008) *Today's Parent* article, "What Autism Does to a Mother," a photograph from *The Autism File Magazine* (O'Brien 2009) of a group of mother warriors dressed in black evening gowns fighting against autism, as well as headlines and articles about the signs of autism, diet, depression, murder, the limits of love, and more affirming depictions of autism and (m)othering, all of which I take up in detail in the book.

(M)others who took part in focus groups self-identified as single or partnered, as birth or adoptive, and as immigrant and/or white, Jewish, or Asian. They described autistic offspring ranging from eight to twenty-eight who over their lifespans had attracted labels such as high-functioning autism, Pervasive Developmental Disorder – Not Otherwise Specified (PDD-NOS), autism, Asperger's syndrome, and regressive autism. (M)others also described children and adult offspring who communicated through speaking, music, and typing and who went to public school, worked at sheltered workshops, attended university, and lived at home or on their own. My own experience as a (m)other of an autistic son meant that I had insider status. I also acknowledge my power as a university-based researcher to set the terms of the research. I join other feminist and disability studies scholars (Re•Storying Autism Writing Collective 2022; see also Kirby, Greaves, and Reid 2010; Matthews 1983; Milton et al. 2020; and Rice et al. 2020) who work to flatten hierarchies between participants and researchers by centring and valuing participants' lived experience and knowledge and by challenging the problematic notion of disinterested objectivity in research. As a form of member checking, I invited (m)others to a public (anonymized) talk that I gave on my focus group analysis. I was astonished as the room filled with (m)others, grandmothers, siblings, kin, and friends from my own and other (m)others' lives. Caring about autism, autistic people, and ways of (m)othering that differ from those proposed by the dominant scientific sense of care as remedy was catching. I continue to be in touch with some of the (m)others with whom I spoke in focus groups.

Working interpretively and critically, I understand focus groups as sites of collective social action, power, and resistance mediated by text. This perspective departs from social-scientific research on autism grounded in taken-for-granted (humanist) assumptions about the subject/participant as a source of "truth" about an objectively knowable social world (e.g., see Morgan 1997, 4–6; also St. Pierre 2014).[16] Instead, (m)others and I pursued the meaning of autism, (m)othering, difference, and care in everyday text and everyday lives, traced how power and resistance operate, and co-constituted alternatives grounded in affirming care, difference, love, and extended (chosen) networks and relationships. My focus group conversations with (m)others have similarities to what disability studies scholars Katherine Runswick-Cole and Daniel Goodley (2018) call the "maternal" or "disability commons" – a form of (m)othering, disability, and care that is collective and dispersed rather than individualized within the mother-child dyad – and what second-wave feminists like bell hooks (2000, 8) called consciousness-raising groups comprised of "women examining sexist thinking and creating strategies where we would change our attitudes and belief via a conversion to feminist thinking and a commitment to feminist politics."

My approach to focus groups also opens them beyond their particularity into a site from which we can glean future research directions and recommendations about what is necessary for more ethical representations and practices around autism, (m)othering, and care. The point becomes that some (m)others some of the time resist and respond differently from within the constraints and exclusions of neoliberal, ableist, patriarchal, capitalist care regimes. Education scholar Max Van Manen (1990, 23) articulates the tension between particularity and universality by suggesting that research can be oriented toward "mediating in a personal way the antinomy of particularity (being interested in concreteness, difference and what is unique) and universality (being interested in the essential, in difference that makes a difference)." From this orientation, my focus groups are a way to disrupt the ground of a shared social world that devalues autism as well as (m)others and, at the same time, to hold onto what Van Manen calls the "uniqueness" of the meaning that we make of our lives (5). This approach disrupts what feminist scholar Donna Haraway (1991, 191) calls the "gaze from nowhere" in reference to the Cartesian subject and resists its opposite, the "god-trick" of relativism (Haraway 2018, 15–16), which imbues lived experience with truth (see also Scott 1991). It also remains open to how embodied difference always exceeds identity categories, gesturing to the fundamental alterity of us all and to the ethical call to respond to the other without doing the violence of making others identical (see Boler 1999; Levinas 1969).

In the chapters to come, I share reflections about my experiences in focus groups as well as some of the "secrets and intimacies" (Van Manen 1990, 5) about being in relationship with difference and about resisting power shared by (m)others in the groups. By that, I mean snippets of conversation that show not only the neoliberal, ableist, white supremacist, and patriarchal regimes of care that constrain (m)others but also the ones that outline different, reciprocal, affirming ways to care about being human together – those that disrupt the dominant sense of care as remediation. My way of proceeding thus reveals glimpses of the ordinary surprises that remain so seamlessly concealed from us in our everyday lives even though they are, to borrow Van Manen's words, "constitutive of the world" and "bring the world as world into being for us and in us" (5). My focus group discussions open clear beginnings, especially as these beginnings relate to how (m)others are represented and to how they feel compelled to make something out of these representations that moves beyond problem-saturated understandings of autism and autism mothers.

Where Are the Autism Fathers?

Although the central pursuit of this book is a deeper understanding and disruption of autism, autism mothers, and care, the reader will also meet several autism fathers along the way (see also Jack 2014; and McGuire 2016). Autism fathers hold a prominent place in the birth of autism as a clinical disorder as well as in histories of autism treatment and care. Among others, the reader will meet benevolent patriarch Bruno Bettelheim, a well-known psychologist at Chicago's Orthogenic School in the 1960s, who removed "psychotic" children from their mothers' so-called disordered love by prescribing residential treatment; popular hero Bernard Rimland, the father of an autistic son and the psychologist who spearheaded the parent advocacy movement in the United States and popularized pseudo-scientific biomedical remedies like vitamin treatments; and Ole Ivar Lovaas, a clinical psychologist and authoritarian father figure who disciplined – often violently – autistic children's "disordered" behaviour and recruited mothers' intensive care. The book traces and disrupts these "expert" paternalistic ways of knowing and treating autism that eschew (m)others' and autistic people's lived experiences of difference, love, and care.

Autism fathers also appear in the book as they go about their everyday lives, whether seeking diagnosis for their child, taking part in research studies, appearing in popular media, advocating for services, or loving their autistic offspring. Autism fathers, however, have not been captured by power in quite the same way as mothers. Within early research studies and popular media, for example, fathers were described, like mothers, as cold, overly rational, and distant (see Kanner 1943; and *Time* 1948). Yet fathers' chilly love did not come under public scrutiny and governance in quite the same way. Rather, autism's cause and cure (including undertaking intensive care regimens) remained "naturally" assigned to mothers in the shape of the mother-child dyad. Beginning in the 1970s, fathers, alongside mothers, also wrote memoirs about their experiences of living with and loving their autistic child or adult offspring (e.g., see Greenfeld 1972). Rhetoric scholar Jordyn Jack (2014) describes how parent memoirs are often conventionally gendered. Narratives by fathers tend to be individual quests for deeper understanding of their autistic offspring in relation to a father's own identity, whereas memoirs written by (m)others centre meditations on the kinds of care prevalent in my own and other (m)others' narratives in this book. Autism fathers have also earned the reputation of absconding from their spouses, families, and autistic children. The stress of having an autistic child, according to this view, is a destroyer of marriage and families (McGuire 2016). Although it may indeed be the case that parenting an autistic child in an ableist world with few supports is stressful for parents, children, families, and kin, scholars like Jack (2014) and others (e.g., see Saini et al. 2015) have cast doubt on the verity of sharply higher divorce rates and numbers of absent fathers that circulate in popular media and research. Despite this doubt and although twenty-first-century shifts in parental leave and gender ideology in the Global North have opened the role of primary caregiver or (m)other to many men (see Doucet 2006), it remains predominately women who are tasked with the intensive care of autistic and disabled offspring (Douglas et al., "Mad Mothering," 2021). This reality is a compelling reason for a book like this one to pursue a deeper understanding and unsettling of the so-called natural arrangement that requires mothers to remedy autism.

The Social Construction of Mothering

The Paradox of Care

Central to the work of disrupting scientifically governed maternal care as autism's remedy and installing new understandings in knowledge production and everyday life is framing autism and (m)othering not as a biological imperative but as a paradox, one that tasks (m)others and autistic offspring with identity making. This is to say that mothering (the practice) and motherhood (the institution) are social constructions.[17] In this section, I briefly unpack autism's paradox of care as a key aspect of the social construction of (m)othering not typically considered by feminist or disability studies. Below and at key points in the chapters to come, I also address the social construction of (m)otherhood as a patriarchal, ableist institution more broadly.

To unpack the paradox of care, sociologist Zygmunt Bauman (2004a) is helpful. He suggests that under modernity, identity has become our most "pressing" "problem" and "task" (18–19, 20, 32). In our case, under the guise of a mother's love, care paradoxically contains "a duty and an urge" (20; see also Broderick and Roscigno 2021; Michalko 2002; and Yergeau 2018) to achieve a self-same (non-autistic) identity for our different autistic child, whether through intensive behavioural therapies, alternative biomedical remedies like vitamin or chelation therapy, or taking part in genetic research intended to find a cure. Some "quirks" or "strengths" of autism may now be tolerated and even desired by capitalist markets, but as we have seen, the prevailing idea is that a narrow identity and selfhood circumscribe the only life worth living – one that closely approximates an autonomous, economically productive life of self-mastery. This normative identity has been extended to all life and care, I suggest, through new "naturally" loving (and instrumentally calculative) intensive autism mother subjectivities (see also Douglas 2013; Douglas, Rice, and Siddiqui 2020;

and Titchkosky and Michalko 2012). Popular parenting magazines and newspaper articles, for example, feature autism mothers and intensive care regimens as a cautionary tale for *all* parents, particularly mothers, about the dire consequences to be expected – the "stress," "fear," and "aloneness" – if our identity-making care work fails (see Rones 2008, n.p.). The ongoing advocacy of the Ontario Autism Coalition is another case in point. The political rhetoric of hopelessness, burden, and stress to be ameliorated by intensive normalizing therapies, ones predominately taken up by mothers, surrounds these campaigns.

The paradox of care raises late modernity's compulsion for sameness to a new level of hyperbole and requires all mothers to practise what feminist scholar Sharon Hays (1996) calls intensive mothering– a Western, white, neoliberal, marketized, self-entrepreneurial, patriarchal, capitalist version of mothering (Runswick-Cole and Goodley 2018; Walkerdine and Lucy 1989). Installed at the heart of intensive mothering is the patriarchal ableist demand that mothers expel difference, or at least smooth out any disruption it may cause. Patriarchy is a system that vests power materially and ideologically in cisgender white men while devaluing so-called feminine traits like vulnerability and interdependency alongside labour such as care, typically performed by women, especially women of colour (e.g., see hooks 2004). Recent recruitment campaigns by parent advocacy organizations in the Global North (e.g., see *Autism File Magazine* 2009a) extend the duty to achieve a self-same identity globally, issuing seductive calls for mothers in the Global South to join the war against autism and to ascribe to Global North versions of mothering and care that aim to fix autism, understood as a biomedical problem. In this way, (m)othering, autism, and care are shaped into an impossible and irremediable ethical paradox, what feminist philosopher Susan Bordo (2003) calls a cultural contradiction, one that must be brokered daily. To engage in mothering and caring means both to love our autistic children in all their uniqueness as they appear in our everyday lives and simultaneously to remedy or eliminate the difference of autism by practising the ethical and other violences of making our children identical.

The emergence of autism mother subjectivity and care as an ethical paradox has everything to do with what and who is valued, hoped for, and imagined as possible in late-modern life. Underpinning the paradox of care is the spectre of the normative (humanist) human, grounded in Western Enlightenment philosophies of "human perfectibility; scientific hierarchies of gender, race and disability; and survival-of-the-fittest logics of neoliberal capitalism," casting those who are non-normatively embodied/ enminded as "not quite, lesser than or disqualified from the fully human" (Douglas, Rice, and Siddiqui 2020, 398; see also Braidotti 2013). This mythical human is nondisabled, hyper-independent, intensively product-ive, and fit, as well as white, male, cisgender, and heterosexual. Based on this view, what we elide are alternative ways of being human, such as the neurodiversity movement's understanding of autism as a valid and valuable way of being (see Sinclair 1993; Singer 2017; Walker 2012, 2021; and Waltz 2013) and the Māori understanding of autism (and all diversity and life) as a gift to be shared communally; the Māori phrase for autism is *tōnā anō takiwātanga,* meaning *a life in their/his/her own space and time* (see Opai 2017; also Douglas et al. "Beyond 'Inclusionism,'" forthcoming). Indeed, autism – as diagnosis, as socially constructed disorder and disease, as field of medical research and biotechnology, as identity – is a product of the Global North (Bevan-Brown 2013; McGuire 2016; Nadesan 2005). Additionally elided are more collective ways of (m)othering and caring for and about autistic offspring (beyond the mother-child dyad) that often align with self-articulated Black, Indigenous, neurodiversity, Global South, disability justice, feminist, and other communities (e.g., see Chataika and McKenzie 2013; Collins 1987, 1990, 2015; de Sousa Santos 2018; Runswick-Cole and Goodley 2018; and Schalk and Kim 2020).

The Social Construction of Motherhood
The paradox of care reveals that there is nothing "natural" about the mean-ing and practice of mothering as intensive curative labour assigned to women. Motherhood is, rather, a social construction (see Collins 1987; E. Kim 2017; O'Reilly 2007; and Rich 1986). For mothers of disabled children in particular, motherhood is shaped and constrained by patriarchal, ableist, white supremacist systems of power that assign the primary labour of care to women as "natural" caregivers who must produce offspring who can, at the very least, approximate normalcy in the service of neoliberal capitalism (see Broderick and Roscigno 2021; McGuire 2018; and Yergeau 2018). Indeed, when (child) development goes awry, it is mothers, guided by the

dominant biomedical sense of normal child development, who must remedy their individual child so that they do not become a drain on already strained political, education, and economic systems (Runswick-Cole and Goodley 2018). (M)others who advocate for access within systems on behalf of their autistic child risk being labelled as difficult and even "mad" (Douglas et al., "Making Memories," 2022). Further, what (m)othering can be and who can (m)other are constrained by enduring structures of neoliberal capitalism that presume the economic unit of the nuclear family as natural and normative – that is, a cisgender woman and man and their biological offspring who live together in one household, often with a gendered division of labour (see Douglas et al., "Mad Mothering," 2021; and Gibson 2014). These structures devalue and pathologize alternative practices of care, as we have seen above.

Although part of the aim of this book, then, is to trace, recuperate, and revalue the disruptive and affirming practices of the care and activism of (m)others of autistic offspring living and loving under the constraints of neoliberal capitalism in the Global North, as well as to trouble deficient understandings of autism and autism mother, the aim of the book is broader. I also aim to unsettle the social construction of mothering a disabled child and the dominant sense that mothering naturally means intensive curative or remedial labour performed by individual women on the bodies, hearts, and minds of their autistic and disabled children/offspring within the mother-child dyad. This form of motherhood is an oppressive, patriarchal, ableist social arrangement produced through the material structures and ideologies of late modernity, such as the nuclear family. It is based on a "god-trick" (Haraway 1991, 191; 2018, 15–16), one that universalizes, essentializes, and reifies a very particular form of mothering that is located in the Global North and identified with all that is white, bourgeois, patriarchal, heteronormative, neoliberal, capitalist, and ableist. This trick also installs the eugenic aim to remediate (and eliminate) autism and disability (and to produce a fit workforce) through maternal care (see E. Kim 2017; and Runswick-Cole and Goodley 2018). Briefly, eugenics is the twentieth-century scientific and social movement that aimed to improve the stock of populations by controlling reproduction (Wilson n.d.) in order to stop those deemed unfit (e.g., disabled, queer, Black, Indigenous, working-class, Jewish, and single mothers) from reproducing and living while incentivizing and supporting those deemed fit and desirable (e.g., white, heterosexual, middle-class, and able-bodied/minded). One of the most extreme and unthinkable examples of eugenics was the pursuit of "racial hygiene" via the Holocaust in Nazi Germany in the 1930s and '40s, in which millions of Jewish, disabled, autistic, queer, Roma, and other "defective" people were subject to involuntary sterilization, scientific experimentation, mass incarceration, and genocide (Snyder and Mitchell 2006a, 2006b; Stote 2015). Within Canada, too, disabled people and Indigenous, Black, and other women and people of colour, understood as biologically inferior, were institutionalized, involuntarily sterilized, prevented from accessing life and love, and more (Malacrida 2019). These practices persist in the form of what disability studies scholar Claudia Malacrida (2019) calls "newgenics," examples being the intensive remedial care assigned to mothers and the scientific search for the cure for autism.

Feminist-of-colour disability studies scholar Eunjung Kim (2017) forwards the concept of "unmothering disability" to describe how Korean culture instilled a eugenic desire for mothers to biologically reproduce nondisabled children. Disability studies scholars Katherine Runswick-Cole and Sara Ryan (2019, 1127) forward a related concept of "unmothering disabled children," by which they mean "shift[ing] responsibility for activism away from mothers alone to call for a community response to social injustice." I borrow from Kim and from Runswick-Cole and Ryan, extending their concept of "unmothering" to the field of critical autism studies. Both the individualization of (m)othering and the eugenic desire to eliminate autism and to biologically reproduce normalcy are certainly part of the paradox of care that I am articulating. In addition, I use the term "unmothering autism" not only to uncouple autism mothers and mothering from the compulsory, intensive, remedial care regime governed by patriarchy and conventional autism science within the mother-child dyad but also, following Runswick-Cole and Ryan (2019), to reclaim alternative, collectivized, and activist practices of care and of (m)othering autistic offspring. These alternative practices, as we shall see, were hinted at in my focus group discussions with (m)others and include (m)others creating collective care networks (whether chosen or other family and kin relations), advocating for access, affirming and celebrating autistic difference, attending to uniqueness, and practising care as a form of resistance to the patriarchal, ableist institution of motherhood and practices of remedial care (see also Chapter 8). Runswick-Cole and Goodley (2018, 231) similarly propose "re-thinking mothering through disability to call for a coming together of the 'disability commons' to campaign for the rights of disabled children and young people." And so I call for the "coming together" of a feminist, (m)othering, critical autism and disability commons that can collectively work to affirm care and gender as well as racial and autistic justice.

At the heart of the book, then, is the contention that the meaning and shape of autism, (m)othering, and care are made within everyday worlds and knowledge production and therefore *can be remade* between us, even if just fleetingly. This is to say, with Titchkosky (2003, 237), that disability and care "embody alternative ways of being-in-the-world and act as living depictions of the possibility that things could be otherwise." In addition to recuperating and revaluing the previously marginalized knowledge of (m)others of autistic offspring, I trace alternative, affirming, and disruptive practices of care and constructions of (m)othering and care in the space between (m)other and autistic child/offspring, body, and world. Consequently, the book questions and disrupts some of our most intimately experienced, felt, and sometimes ineffable ways of being together as (m)other and child, including those that are not only personal or natural experiences of love, care, and disability but also political and ethical sites of lived power, subjugated/marginalized knowledge, resistance, and possibly, the insertion of something new (see also Boler 1999, 20–21).

Organization of *Unmothering Autism: Ethical Disruptions and Affirming Care*

Interspersed with glimpses of my own story and the stories of (m)others with whom I spoke in focus groups along the way, this book describes how autism mother subjectivity emerged as an ethical paradox on the scene of everyday text in southwestern Ontario, Canada. Although I centre locally circulating storylines, they are broadly applicable to North America and other contexts where similar storylines have circulated. Chapter 1, "Disruption as a Place to Begin," sets the stage for the disruptive knowledge of the book. I first show how all knowledge production is situated and contextual in order to trouble Western science's often unquestioned depiction of autism as a tragic brain disorder in need of mothers' curative or remedial care. Reworking critical and interpretive approaches in sociology, feminist and critical autism, and disability studies, I centre the experience of (m)others (who may also identify as autistic or neurodivergent) who care for and about an autistic child or adult. This focus provides a generative way to take up questions of power and subjectivity, along with questions of resistance, disruption, and difference, as possible gestures toward living otherwise. I then describe how I worked both genealogically and phenomenologically to analyze my archive of text, including focus groups. Briefly, genealogy is a historiological method that is helpful in tracing the emergence of both autism and autism mother subjectivity, and phenomenology is a philosophy of everyday life that is helpful in opening rich descriptions and theorizations of lived experience. Guided by my ethic of disruption and affirming care, I use the tensions and edges between critical and interpretive approaches to (re)value autism and the subjugated, disruptive, and radical knowledge of (m)others. In this way, the book also contributes to what disability studies scholar Dona M. Avery calls the "disability story of parents," one that helped to forge the disability rights movement in Canada (quoted in Ryan and Runswick-Cole 2009, 43).

Part 2 of the book traces the multiple emergences of autism mother subjectivities in popular media – from the heyday of psychoanalysis to the rise of behaviourism, cognitive neuroscience, and present-day biogenomics. I meld this more genealogical approach with interpretive glances of the appearance of autism mothers in everyday text, including insights from focus groups, as well as with my own rereading of texts as its own activity of resistance. The payoff of the chapters in Part 2, which works to unmother autism, is the reclaiming of knowledge production as radically hopeful as well as the recuperation of autism, (m)othering, and care from the pathologizing terms of intensive mothering and Western autism science.

Chapter 2, "Autism's Refrigerator Mothers: The Psychoanalytic Gaze," traces how autism's refrigerator mother – the so-called cold mother understood to cause autism in her child – arrived on the scene in the 1940s, when psychoanalysis prevailed. I trace the emergence of this mother as she is depicted through these new forms of knowledge (i.e., psychoanalysis), technologies of blame, and forms of visibility (e.g., the case study in popular magazines), which brought her into view in new ways and shaped new spaces of governance that turned her gaze inward as she undertook her own self-governance. Chapter 3, "Returning the Psychoanalytic Gaze," works more interpretively to consider how the directing of this mother's gaze inward also, and ironically, became the ground for (m)others' collective resistance. We also meet (m)others from focus groups who were given the label of refrigerator mother and who formed part of this resistance. Taking a "backwards glance" at what might be "behind" (Ahmed 2006a, 570) the appearance of the refrigerator mother also opens interpretive space around this figure since the activity of rereading this mother in everyday text is its own form of resistance, one that is committed to a different kind of knowledge about our human life together.

Chapters 4 and 5 work similarly by melding genealogical analysis with interpretive moments, focus group insights, and my own rereading of texts as an activity of resistance. In Chapter 4, "Autism's Mother Therapists: Behaviourism's Gaze," I trace how cognitive psychology and behaviourism became dominant and how autism mothers emerged as at-home therapists and cultural heroes whose skilled techniques were required to normalize their autistic child. Chapter 5, "Retraining Behaviourism," takes a second look at autism's mother therapist from a different angle, pursuing moments when autism and affirming care glimmer, both in popular representation and focus groups, as something other than a tragic disorder that must be recovered through a mother's intensive and sometimes violent care. In the critical sense described by philosopher Mary Zournazi (2003), this is hopeful work that engages and adds an ethic of disruption to the "disability story of parents" (Avery, quoted in Ryan and Runswick-Cole 2009, 43) while moving the story of (m)othering, autism, and care beyond a problem-solution binary where mothering and care mean instrumental curative labour (see also E. Kim 2017; Runswick-Cole and Goodley 2018; Runswick-Cole and Ryan 2019).

In the years 2000–22, when biogenomic views of the human arose, autism's "warrior mother" emerged as a new mother expert and figure held responsible for shoring up all of this figure's power in order to care about alarming rates of autism diagnosis after 2000. This figure combines a masculine-coded warring element and a feminine-coded softness, a masculine-coded instrumentality and a mother's love, an acceptance of neurodiversity and a ruthlessness about the need to become an expert and to eliminate difference. Chapter 6, "Autism's Warrior Mothers: The Genomic Gaze," traces the emergence of the mother warrior figure in the midst of the "discursive explosion" (Foucault 1980a, 7–8; see also Hacking 2010) of autism and autism mother texts during our time. In Chapter 7, "Resisting Genomics and War," I include my lived experience of encountering this warrior mother in popular media and offer a phenomenological description. This second look at the warrior mother reveals the cultural ground that produces her as a figure at war against autism. Through this close work, the need for something more emerges beyond the reproduction of a dominant scientific sense of autism as a problem and beyond the expert sense of the solution, which intensively implicates (m)others in the normalization of their child.

Chapter 8, "(M)others Speak Back: Affirming Autism and Care," explores this something more – which is pointed at in the preceding chapters – through a close description of focus group conversations held in Toronto with (m)others of autistic offspring. (M)others spoke together about forms of care that both mirrored dominant cultural representations of autism and autism mother subjectivity and gestured to and creatively constructed something more. This something more – a form of critical, creative, and loving attention in (m)othering and knowledge production that I call affirming care – turns toward the disruption of embodied difference as valuable and transgresses the violence and exclusions of curative care regimes and identity that culturally produce, exclude, and pathologize autism (and indeed, embodied difference) within our late-modern life together. This chapter, beginning as it does with the difference of autism, gestures to what else might be possible for being human together, including uncoupling autism from a mother's compulsory curative care within the mother-child dyad (E. Kim 2017; Runswick-Cole and Ryan 2019) and centring alternative ways to (m)other and care. The conclusion, "Is Neurodiversity's Mother Next?" ties the threads of my chapters together and brings the reader into the contemporary moment of 2023 and into the ever-unfolding story of autism, (m)othering, and care.

This book is an invitation to attend to the layered histories, regimes of power, resistance, suffering, and care that mark our human journey together, as discussed by feminist-of-colour scholar Sara Ahmed (2010, 12). By attending to these factors, all of us might learn something new about difference, care, and the meaning of human flourishing. My aim is to open space for the creation of new and transformative stories about autism, (m)othering, and care that unmother autism and affirm autistic difference, and I consider knowledge production as one such political, pedagogical, and ethical site in which to open this space.

Part 1

Disrupting Autism Mothers

1

Disruption as a Place to Begin

During my graduate studies, I began to think critically about my experiences as the (m)other of a son who had attracted the label of autism. I wanted to understand more deeply the lived contradictions between beauty and violence that marked our everyday life, and for this reason, I had left my job as a special education teacher and returned to school. Within the Social Justice Education Department that became my intellectual home, I found several theoretical and methodological alternatives to Western science and biomedicine that helped me to understand my dissonant lived experiences, as well as the structures of ableism and patriarchy that shaped our lives as a family. Disability studies' depictions of the experience and politics of alternative embodiments, concepts from Black phenomenology like sociologist and civil rights activist W.E.B. Du Bois's ([1903] 1994) "double-consciousness," and feminist accounts like Dorothy Smith's (1987) sociology for women all touched on what I was experiencing. Yet something seemed to be missing in these approaches too. As interdisciplinary or radical as they might be, none of them quite seemed to capture the contradictions that my family was living or how the relationship between mother and child was made compulsory at the centre of such a life in all its beauty, struggle, contradictions, and exclusions. Significant for me, too, (m)others and children rarely appeared in these radical literatures and philosophies or in the department itself, much less (m)others of disabled children – although, happily, they are showing up! I needed to seek out or to create the conversations that were missing from or marginal within dominant approaches and only just emerging within the radical academic literatures that offered such rich alternatives to the Western Enlightenment's scientifically grounded ways of knowing.

It was in this way that I first chose to weave together critical and interpretive sociological thought with feminist and disability studies in an approach that I have come to think of as disruptive knowledge. I needed to understand how exclusion and violence have become ordinary and how the terms "autism" and "autism mother" have acquired meaning such that it seems only natural that autism – understood as a problem – needs the solution of mothers' intensive, scientifically governed care. My aim in developing such an approach was and is emancipatory – to reveal the contingent, lived, and embodied nature of autism mother subjectivity and autism by proceeding with an ethic of disruption and by placing affirming care at the centre of knowledge production. This approach, which I outline in this chapter, opens space for other possibilities of being together beyond curative or remedial care (see also Clare 2017; E. Kim 2017; and Runswick-Cole and Ryan 2019). It is an approach grounded in ways of knowing, being, and caring that move beyond conventional Western scientific ones to include and value the surprise of different bodies and alternative, distributed forms of care – an approach that also "unmothers" autism (E. Kim 2017; Runswick-Cole and Ryan 2019).

Epistemological and ontological commitments – how we know what we know and understand reality and being – arising from my fractured experiences as the (m)other of a son who had attracted the label of autism ground my disruptive approach. I do not seek control over or certainty about autism and care. Rather, I seek understanding based on partial and previously excluded perspectives, what disability studies scholar Rosemarie Garland-Thomson (2002) calls "sitpoints"[1] from which we might proliferate more "promising" (Haraway 2018, 15) and ethical understandings of difference and intervene in systems of domination and exclusion. As Donna Haraway (1991, 196) describes the matter of partiality in knowledge production, "We seek not the knowledges ruled by phallogocentrism (nostalgia for the presence of the one true Word) and disembodied vision, but those ruled by partial sight and limited voice." In invoking Haraway's (2018, 16) metaphor of "partial sight" and "limited voice," I do not wish to set up a "false choice between reality and relativism" or objectivity and subjectivity. Rather, my approach to knowledge production – including attention to the research apparatus itself through an ethic of disruption – challenges the separation of the knower from the known, of body from world. It also challenges the denial of particularity within conventional scientific approaches and instead "embodies vision" (Haraway 1991, 189), recognizing the partiality, contingency, ethical dimension, and political investments of all knowledge. This shift in knowledge production challenges the dominant sense that autism, mothering, and care can be researched as objects in and of themselves and outside of history, thus opening them to historical and ethical investigation. Both an ethic of disruption and attentiveness in knowledge production through affirming care guide my turn to everyday autism and autism mother texts and to (m)others' experiences as sites of critical, interpretive, ethical, political, and embodied knowledge. This is knowledge that might "subvert" or "turn around," as education scholars John Portelli and Christina P. Konecny (2013, 94) put it, the exclusionary, constraining, and sometimes violent scientific and popular ways of knowing and caring about autism and embodied difference under late modernity.[2]

The Partiality of Knowledge: Toward an Embodied Approach

What has counted as universal knowledge about autism, autism mothers, and care – autism as a disorder and scientifically governed care in the shape of the mother-child dyad as the solution – is not universal at all but partial, being representative of a narrow, non-autistic, gendered, Global North, white, bourgeois experience and being rooted in a Western scientific approach, which is historical and located. Philosopher Susan Bordo (1987, 5) describes the western European Enlightenment's search for a philosophy that would yield "truth" and "certainty" to a humanity "naturally" endowed with reason – exemplified in René Descartes's *Meditations on First Philosophy* (1641) – as "an aggressive intellectual 'flight from the feminine' into the modern scientific universe of purity, clarity, and objectivity" (see also Descartes 1985, 111–12). Whether or not we agree that the premodern western European world was more "feminine" than the modern world emerging in Descartes's time, Bordo's thesis underscores that those ways of knowing more typically associated with disabled, feminine, queer, (m)othering, autistic, Indigenous, Black, and other non-normative bodies and minds – the disruptive, affective, sensuous, embodied, practical, situated, and relational – are equally deserving of philosophical status. Sociologist Boaventura de Sousa Santos (2018, 134) puts the matter this way: "Science must be confronted with the need to separate its methodological autonomy from its claim to exclusive epistemological validity (the only valid or rigorous knowledge)." This shift to understanding knowledge as situated and partial troubles the universality and authority of conventional autism science and intensive maternal care and contests their exportation globally.

Troubling Conventional Autism Science

Science, suggests Haraway (1991, 187), is a set of practices and technologies caught up in the "search for translation, convertibility, mobility of meanings and universality – which I call reductionism, when one language (guess who's) must be enforced as the standard for all the translations and conversions." Since the philosophy of Descartes and his followers, instrumental reason has arguably been the "one language" that has been enforced as the standard for translation in scientific knowledge production – instrumental, impersonal, efficient, exhaustive, and relationally detached procedures to be universally applied through autonomous human consciousness (Descartes 1985, 120; de Sousa Santos 2018, 133–34; Lloyd 1993, 39–50). Instrumental reason revolutionized both epistemology and ontology by separating subject from object and imbuing a very particular experience – nondisabled, western European, white, male, bourgeois, rational, autonomous – with both necessity and universality (R. Solomon 1988, 7). Haraway (1991, 188) calls the resultant "view from nowhere" within Enlightenment philosophy and science a "god-trick," "a leap out of the marked body and into a conquering gaze from nowhere … [a gaze] that makes the unmarked category [e.g., a scientist] claim the power to see and not be seen, to represent while escaping representation."

Consider, for example, how the "god-trick" is at play on the website of the Kilee Patchell-Evans Autism Research Group (n.d., para. 3) in a mundane description of an approach to autism science that infuses laboratory rats with proprionic acid (PPA) to test the gut-brain theory of autism:

> PPA infusion immediately produces reversible repetitive dystonic behaviors, hyperactivity, turning, retropulsion, object fixation, perseveration, caudate spiking, the progressive development of limbic kindled seizures,

and the impairment of social behavior, suggesting that this compound has central effects. Examination of brain tissue from PPA treated rats (brain sections, homogenate, ToF-SIMS imaging, gene arrays) reveals an innate neuroinflammatory response. (See also MacFabe 2012)

Further down the page, the research group explains its method, which includes not only studies on laboratory rats but also the extraction of brain tissues, gut tissues, and stool samples from people who have attracted the label of autism.

Within this mundane description of autism research, the objects to be studied – autistic guts, stool, and brains – are separated from actual people as well as from the seemingly bodyless rationality, instrumentality, and objective scientific knowledge represented by the Kilee Patchell-Evans Autism Research Group. On the website, we meet director Dr. Derrick MacFabe and the products of his research group's scientific endeavours. We do not, however, learn of these scientists' everyday lives working, loving, and living as historical embodied beings in the Global North's late-modern, capitalist world, what feminist sociologist Dorothy Smith (1999, 6) describes as "the actual ongoing practices of actual individuals as they go forward in just the everyday/everynight sites in which they happen and in the time they perdure." Are there children, perhaps even autistic children, in these scientists' lives whom they love and leave behind to enter this objectifying realm? Is it in a mother's care that such children are left for the work of science to proceed? What emotional and psychic work is required for this separation of love from instrumental science to occur? What are the material conditions surrounding the "personal and local life" (53) of these scientists that sustain this abstracted realm of scientific knowledge production, including the ways that mothers are directed by conventional autism science to care about and remedy their child as disordered (and thus to subject them to studies)?

Rather than the local and contingent, what the viewer beholds in this research group's description of autism science (Kilee Patchell-Evans Autism Research Group n.d., para. 2) are troubled (autistic) matter – "brain, behavioral, dietary, gut, metabolic and immune factors implicated in ASD [autism spectrum disorders]" – and a lab filled with PPA-injected rats, far removed from everyday/everynight lives. The scientists in this autism research group, like the endeavour of autism science to explain and control difference, remain obscured as the ones invested with the power to "see and not be seen" (Haraway 1991, 188) and as the ones in possession of "the only valid or rigorous knowledge" (de Sousa Santos 2018, 134). Instead, what the reader sees (Kilee Patchell-Evans Autism Research Group n.d., para. 3) are rodents injected with propionic acid and their bizarre behaviours taken as autistic. The leap made by the research group from the behaviour of PPA-injected rats to gut, brain, and stool samples from autistic children and to gut-brain abnormalities that may cause autism is made seamlessly. This an interpretive move that reduces autism to mere matter – stool, brain tissue, and gut tissue from rats and humans – and separates scientific practices from social processes of meaning making, alternative sitpoints on autism, and the everyday/everynight sites of autistic people's lives, together with the lives of those who love and care about them. M. Remi Yergeau (2018, 3) calls autism stories such as this one "shitty narratives ... that author autistic people as victim-captives" of disordered bodies and brains. "In these constructions," Yergeau tells us, "our shit holds more rhetorical power than we do" (3).

Indeed, on the research group's website, autism becomes little more than bizarre behaviour located in defective bodies and brains and in disordered PPA-injected rats offered up for the scientific gaze. Ethnomethodologists like Harold Garfinkel (1967, 3) point out that such accounts are not separate from the "socially organized occasions" when they occur (see also Gill and Maynard 1995; and Maynard 2005). In other words, socially organized scientific practices produce accounts of the natural and normative body and generate particular modes of communication as normative partly through the identification of autism as abnormal and Other (see also Dindar, Lindblom, and Kärnä 2017; and Michalko 2002, 47–48, 56–58).[3] The aim of all this science is to remedy autism – by identifying the link between autistic gut and brain, for example. Although seemingly a benevolent aim, it is one that conceals its implication in the Global North's scientific project to control and vanquish the autistic body as a "body-gone-wrong," to borrow from disability studies scholar Rod Michalko (2002, 12). This scientific project underpins remedial practices such as Applied Behaviour Analysis (see Introduction; and Gibson and Douglas 2018), the institutionalization of autistic and disabled people, medicalized mother blame (for producing and failing to remedy autism), and more, as we shall see (Dolmage 2011; Douglas 2014; Douglas et al., "Mad Mothering," 2021 Douglas et al., "Making Memories," 2022). As explained by Esther, one of the (m)others with whom I spoke in focus groups, she felt "relief" after genetic testing revealed that she was not directly to blame (through her behaviour or choices) for her son's autism. Esther's doctor had advised her to undergo genetic testing while pregnant, advice perhaps compelled by patriarchal, ableist, biomedical logics that assign blame to mothers, albeit now indirectly through their part in inadvertently passing on so-called autism genes.

The scientific practices described here mark and objectify autistic bodies as Other, elide processes of meaning making in which such practices occur, erase the local and particular of (m)others' and autistic people's lives, and leave the gendered, raced, and abled body of science – and scientists – unmarked. These scientific practices also depend on a particular understanding of evidence as empirical (Portelli and Konecny 2013, 93) – as that which can be seen, measured, and quantified through the senses – an understanding of knowledge production that I am troubling here. Recent critiques by Global South scholars (Bevan-Brown 2013), autistic and disability justice activists (e.g., Brown, Ashkenazy, and Onaiwu 2017), and scholars within critical autism studies (Milton 2012; Re•Storying Autism Writing Collective 2022; Walker 2021; Yergeau 2018) not only offer alternative sitpoints that affirm autism as a fundamental way of being human but also disrupt the Global North's scientific reduction of autism and autistic people to defective guts, genes, and brains. Other critical autism scholars draw attention to the failure of science to locate any causal biological or genetic mechanism for autism at all (Runswick-Cole, Mallett, and Timimi 2016; Singh 2016). Questioning the "god-trick" in conventional autism science, positioned as the "one language" (Haraway 1991, 187) for understanding autism and autism mothers, is a central task of this book.

Toward an Embodied View of Knowledge Production

The "god-trick" in science is not innocent but is historically implicated in expelling alter embodiments not only from Western canons of knowledge about autism but also from what is possible in terms of our human life together. Through conventional autism science, autistic bodies join the

Western Enlightenment's Others (e.g., mothers as well as Indigenous, Black, disabled, gender-nonconforming, and working-class people) as abnormal and outside the human, and a mother's care in the shape of the mother-child dyad is implicated. Consequently, working toward new stories about autism, (m)othering, and care cannot simply be a matter of doing better science to reflect excluded experiences. As Haraway (2018, 15) puts it, "Reflexivity is a bad trope for escaping the false choice between realism and relativism in thinking about strong objectivity and situated knowledges." In other words, an additive process that imbues previously excluded sitpoints with value, although a good start, is not enough on its own. Not only have different ways of being human been excluded within the conceptual and practical apparatus of Western Enlightenment philosophical traditions and conventional autism science, but they have also been constituted *as* different and devalued through these very same material-semiotic processes. Those attributes that are normative and considered the standard for the human – reason, maleness, whiteness, abledness, autonomy, productivity, order – rest upon the research apparatus of science as well as upon difference for their very sensibility as the valued and the good within an enduring set of gender, race, class, and disability hierarchies (Lloyd 1993, 106; see also Braidotti 2013; de Sousa Santos 2018; Douglas, Rice, and Siddiqui 2018; and Haraway 1991, 2018). And although it is vital to challenge binaries and exclusions by centring autistic and other alternative ways of knowing and being in the world – a task that I also engage in here – these ways of knowing and being are integrally caught up with and constituted by such histories and hierarchies. In other words, the very practices through which we produce knowledge are implicated in who we are and who we might become together (Haraway 2018; Lorde 2007; D. Smith 1999, 6).

This circumstance suggests the need for a new metaphor in knowledge production about autism, to borrow from Haraway (1991, 188–201), that disrupts the "view from nowhere" and "embodies vision." Haraway (2018, 15) elaborates, "What we need is to make a difference in material-semiotic apparatuses, to diffract the rays of technoscience so that we get more promising interference patterns on the recording films of our lives and our bodies." For my purposes here, this need means taking up an ethic of disruption to "diffract" or bend the "material-semiotic apparatuses" of knowledge production, disrupt the dominant scientific sense of autism as a problem that needs to be solved by autism mothers, and proliferate new understandings of autism, care, and (m)othering that are more "promising."[4]

I accomplish this task through a disruptive reorientation to knowledge production about autism and autism mothers as situated. All knowledge is historically contingent, political, ethical, and located. Although these characteristics imply perspectivism, situated knowledge is not an epistemological position that seeks relativism, nor in my case is it one that seeks to imbue the subjugated experience of (m)others and autistic people with unquestioned authority. As an opposite stance to universality or totalization, relativism is its own kind of "god-trick," one that, following Haraway (1991, 191), tries to be "nowhere while claiming to be everywhere equally." Just like any claim to objective or rational knowledge, arguing for the insertion of alterity in both the *how* and *what* of knowledge production proceeds from the partiality and situatedness of all knowledge, as well as from the recognition that knowledge production is a political, ethical, and embodied endeavour. I agree with Haraway that "it is not enough to show radical historical contingency and modes of construction for everything" (187). Rather, as she states,

> We are also bound to seek perspective from those points of view, which can never be known in advance, which promise something quite extra-ordinary, that is, knowledge potent for constructing worlds less organized by axes of domination. In such a viewpoint, the unmarked category would *really* disappear ... The imaginary and the rational – the visionary and objective vision – hover close together. (192; emphasis in original)

The invitation of ways of being labelled autistic, as well as (m)others' knowledge, love, and care, into the *how* and *what* of knowledge production is a political and ethical act, an insertion of contingency, difference, affect, and disruption – bodies, minds, and senses that disrupt and exceed any easy or certain representation or way of knowing, scientific or otherwise (Michalko 1999; Titchkosky 2007). Such disruptive knowledge, as potentially pedagogical, political, and ethical, opens a space for new questions and for new knowledge about power, resistance, subjectivity, and what it might yet mean to be human together and to care outside of the grip of the Western Enlightenment's scientific, non-autistic gaze. Through this disruptive approach, I make room for an alternative way to produce knowledge that incorporates not only the rational and critical but also the previously marginalized sitpoints of (m)others, the surprise of autistic difference, and the possibility of affirming care beyond that of intensive individual labour toward biomedical remedy by mothers within the mother-child dyad. It is through this disruptive approach that the book works to unmother autism.

Disruptive Knowledge

Critical Approaches to Autism and Unmothering

I engage critical thought – particularly the work of philosopher Michel Foucault on power and the subject – within a feminist and disability studies framework to begin to disrupt and historicize the so-called truths of conventional autism science on mothering and care. Foucault (1982, 208) describes his project as emancipatory, the aim being "to create a history of the different modes by which, in our culture, human beings are made subjects." This undertaking means subjecting some of the Western Enlightenment's most evident and cherished truths to historical investigation and to the philosophical stance of radical skepticism; in other words, it means taking up both an ethic of disruption and the quality of attention in knowledge production that I call affirming care (see Introduction). These truths include troubling not only maternal care and love as natural but also the reification of the category of autism itself (see Runswick-Cole, Mallett, and Timimi 2016) and the universal category of the human as an autonomous, meaning-making subject (Foucault 1982). There are limits to Foucault's work tracing forms of power and the subject, such as disciplinary power and madness. He did not take account of the context of western European colonialism and imperialism, nor did he take account of patriarchy. This book thus extends Foucault's work on power and subjectivity to new areas by tracing previously excluded histories of autism and (m)othering informed by a feminist and disability studies framework (e.g., see Erevelles 2011; Fritsch 2015; Puar 2017; Schalk and Kim 2020; Stoler 1995; and Tremain 2015).

The subject, according to Foucault, is an "effect" and "target" of modern forms of power, including disciplinary power, biopower, and governmental power (e.g., see Foucault 1980a, 1995, 2003). One form of late-modern power salient for understanding the emergence of autism mother subjectivity as a solution to the problem of autism is governmentality (Foucault 1982, 221), which involves the "conduct of conduct," or structuring "the possible field of actions of others." Governmentality is a form of late-modern power that also involves the work of self-governance (Foucault 1994, 87), namely "techniques of the self ... the procedures ... suggested or prescribed to individuals in order to determine their identity, maintain or transform it in terms of a certain number of ends, through relations of self-mastery or self-knowledge." In this way, governmental power (Foucault 1982, 221) is "both an individualizing and a totalizing form of power" that operates not only intimately within our everyday lives but also from a distance, constituting subjects as self-governing as well as objects of dominant forms of knowledge (e.g., psychology, biology, genetics, and psychiatry) at the level of populations (see also Foucault 1991a, 99–100).

Consider, for example, how the language of developmental psychology and the imperative to remedy autism within the mother-child dyad enters mothers' lives in the Global North through parenting magazines, autism advocacy websites, and news features highlighting the "warning signs" of autism alongside normalizing therapies. Seductive images and alarming language populate these everyday texts – red flags, typical developmental milestones, or online quizzes assessing a child's risk for autism – and mark the autistic body as disordered and as part of a targeted population for remedy (e.g., see Autism Speaks n.d.b). Mothers, as the "natural" carers of children, are instructed to adopt a wariness and watchfulness for any disruption of typical development and to intervene early, urgently orienting their/our caring labour, or conduct, toward achieving Western norms of development for their child, norms governed by the "psy" disciplines: psychology, psychiatry, and education (see Douglas 2013; and Douglas et al., "Mad Mothering," 2021). Any deviation from so-called normal development as autonomy and economic productivity – what is troubled in the Introduction as an ableist, patriarchal, neoliberal, capitalist, Western scientific understanding of the human exported worldwide by the Global North – is subject to early, intensive, scientifically (and sometimes pseudo-scientifically) guided intervention that recruits mothers' intimate participation in remedying a troublesome population by governing their/ our own conduct. During a focus group exchange about different autism "treatments," for example, Anna, (m)other of twenty-nine-year-old David, a nonspeaking autistic adult, described an intensive form of therapy, based on the Son-Rise Program (see Jordan 1979), that she took up when he was young, compelled by its promise of remedy: "I never left him longer than fifteen minutes, so when he was playing ... I would just kind of pull him back." Here, Anna describes the intensive maternal labour that she took up, briefly, to "cure" her son. Following the Son-Rise Program meant that Anna rarely left David's side and would "pull him back" from what were considered non-normative ways of playing.

By these seductions (e.g., the promise of remedy and normalcy), governmental power enters our everyday lives as mothers in both intimate and distant technical ways, operating in practice through our freedom and "choice" (to parent this way instead of that) by inviting our participation and extending its reach to our bodies, hearts, and minds. As Foucault (1982, 220) says of governmental power, "It incites, it induces, it seduces, it makes easier or more difficult; in the extreme it constrains or forbids absolutely; it is nevertheless always a way of acting upon an acting subject or acting subjects by virtue of their acting or being capable of action" (see also Tremain 2015). Understanding governmentality as a productive, rather than coercive, form of power constitutive of opportunities – albeit constrained ones – for acting and imagining who we might be together within our everyday lives helps to reveal how some ways of being are made possible. Examples include the good (white, bourgeois) autism mother as the watcher of development and as the intensive interventionist (Douglas 2013) and the good (compliant, white) autistic child as the docile subject of intervention (Yergeau 2018), whereas other ways of being, such as those focused on Māori *whāuna* (family and kin) and on collective care both for and about all children and all human and nonhuman kin, remain unimaginable and even "forbidden" (Foucault 1980a, 94–95; 1982, 220–21; see also, for examples, Bevan-Brown 2013; Haraway 2016).

Given the stubborn persistence and disruption of alternative embodiments – indeed, of life and its refusal to be categorized or made identical – autism mothers perpetually fail to "fix" their/our autistic offspring. The promise of Western science to achieve developmental norms and to deliver normalcy through working on the bodies of autistic children is ever elusive. In cultural theorist Lauren Berlant's (2011) formulation, this promise produces a kind of "cruel optimism" through its seductive assurance of a remedy and admission to the good life as non-autistic, both of which are impossible to achieve (see also McGuire 2016). Foucault (1982, 1991a, 2003) describes how the inevitable failure of power to contain us also subjects us – in this case, mothers and autistic people – to direct, illiberal forms of power that cooperate with governmentality to compel normalcy or to stop deviance through sovereign tactics and through violent practices or tactics (see also Dean 2002; and Dehli 2008). For example, among other tactics of bodily containment and punishment, unruly autistic bodies are subject to intensive state-sanctioned normalizing regimes such as Early Intensive Behavioural Intervention (see Introduction; and Gibson and Douglas 2018); physical restraint, seclusion, and isolation (Bartlett and Ellis 2020; Roscigno 2020); and, too often, physical and other violence, including assault, murder, and neglect, at the hands of care providers, parents, and police (McGuire 2016; Ryan 2021). Mothers are also subject to violent and exclusionary practices such as gaslighting by systems that employ covert tactics to dismiss their advocacy on behalf of their child as "mad" (Douglas et al., "Mad Mothering," 2021; Douglas et al., "Making Memories," 2022; Runswick-Cole, Fogg, and Douglas forthcoming). Ableist and racist logics collude in the case of Indigenous, Black, and other autistic people, families, and kin of colour. Until very recently, these groups have been excluded from autism diagnosis and supports – for example, Indigenous children have more often been labelled with fetal alcohol spectrum disorder (see L. Graham 2012; Lindblom 2014; and Roy and Balaratnasingam 2010) – and they continue to face heightened state surveillance and violence by colonialist, white supremacist systems, including high rates of appre-hension of disabled and autistic children by child welfare systems as well as overpolicing and incarceration of disabled Black and brown bodies (see Underwood, Haché, and Douglas 2021; also Bailey and Mobley 2018; Ben-Moshe and Magaña 2014; and Watts and Erevelles 2004).

Thus a critical genealogical approach within a feminist and disability studies frame helps me to trace not only liberal forms of power that govern autism mothers and autistic individuals through freedom and choice but also illiberal forms of power – tactics and practices of unfreedom and violence that stop, contain, or forbid alternative ways of being. This disruptive knowledge, alongside the interpretive approach that I describe below, also reveals the conditions necessary for creating other possible ways to care about autism and (m)othering that embrace and affirm difference.

Interpretive Approaches to Autism and Unmothering

As helpful as critical approaches are in tracing power and opening taken-for-granted truths to historical scrutiny, they cannot address the ways that power and violence are lived, felt, embodied, made meaningful, and resisted by (m)others and autistic people in their everyday life. This section describes how I pursue questions of lived power to unsettle the paradox of care – the curative demand to "fix" autistic difference within the mother-child dyad by working on our autistic offspring to achieve identity with the so-called normal human while also loving them in all their difference and uniqueness (see E. Kim 2017; McGuire 2016; Runswick-Cole and Ryan 2019; and Yergeau 2018). Such questions are close to me as the (m)other of a son who has attracted the label of autism and as a neurodivergent and invisibly disabled (m)other. Living under and resisting patriarchal, neo-liberal, ableist care systems in our everyday life is exhausting, sometimes distressing, and "maddening" work (see Douglas, et al., "Mad Mothering," 2021; Douglas et al., "Making Memories,"2022; and Runswick-Cole et al. forthcoming).

I rethink interpretive approaches in sociology through both an ethic of disruption and the quality of attention that I call affirming care as informed by feminist and disability studies in order to understand (m)others' experiences of lived power more deeply. Although often born of the same scientific turn to certainty that characterizes Western Enlightenment philosophies of the subject (see Natanson 1970; and D. Smith 1987), interpretive approaches, particularly ones that interrogate the space of rupture between body and world, are a radical edge in sociology that challenge Western philosophical underpinnings of the discipline's positivist beginnings.[5] These approaches pay attention to interpretive acts of consciousness in order to understand how enduring forms of power are felt and experienced. For example, Du Bois ([1903] 1994, 2) captures the "double consciousness" of lived experiences of power when he says, "It is a peculiar sensation, this double consciousness, the sense of always looking at oneself through the eyes of others, of measuring one's soul by the tape of a world that looks on in amused contempt and pity." Interpretive approaches attuned to power help to reveal how enduring forms of power come into being over and over again in the here and now of everyday life and suggest ways that we might begin to resist power and might attend to disruption anew.

First, I rethink some of the radical provocations around identity, difference, disruption, and the performance of the ordinary within the sociology of deviance – the go-to approach to research on disability and autism in medical sociology – in order to interpretively engage disability anew. Sociologist Erving Goffman's (1959, 1963) notion of the self, for example, as a socially negotiated performance within stable yet tenuous social situations is replete with the potential for disruption. The performance of selves, according to Goffman (1963, 128), is not only verbal but also includes nonverbal gestures, bodily movements, facial expressions, and emotions, all to "impress" others and manage potential disruptions to one's desired effect – that is, to achieve or perform identity. Goffman's accounts of stigma, too, emphasize a process of identity construction that occurs in interactional contexts involving both an "undesired" attribute and stereotypes (or norms and ideals) that he himself identifies as fictions rather than somehow natural attributes of individual bodies. The phenomenon of "masking" or "camouflaging" – such as suppressing the repeated movements, or stimming, that many autistic people describe as both helpful and enjoyable – is one example of how ableist power is lived bodily (see Anderson 2022; and Felepchuk 2021).

Sociologists concerned with disability, however, do not typically study the ordinary processes of social interaction that accomplish the meaning of autism and difference. Nor are the damaging effects of ableism, misogyny, and patriarchy often regarded as sources of stress for families (see Douglas et al., "Mad Mothering," 2021; Douglas et al., "Making Memories," 2022). David E. Gray's (1993, 2002, 2003) work in medical sociology, for example, begins with an understanding of so-called high-functioning autism (formerly Asperger's syndrome) that is exemplary of the unremarked "view from nowhere" (Haraway 1991, 188). At no point does Gray either query the everyday accomplishment of the ordinary fact of autism as deviance or ponder "restorative measures" (Goffman 1963, 128) such as biomedical treatment and coping. Rather, Gray's work moves quickly to the measurement and management of parental levels of stress (presumably caused by autism), to lay conceptions of autism, or to correlations between the severity of autism and stigma. The disruption of alter identities may indeed be a part of ordinary life, but ableist, non-autistic modes of managing disruption and stigma need not be, despite Goffman's statement that "it can be assumed that a necessary condition for social life is the sharing of a single set of normative expectations" (127). Indeed, borrowing from Tanya Titchkosky (2003, 19), disruption "can be reconfigured into a place where the ordinary of ordinary life can be thought about in a new way," including revealing the grounds of a world where autism appears as a problem and where the intensive labour of autism mothers appears as the solution (e.g., see Anderson 2022).

Second, I rethink interpretive phenomenology within sociology – a philosophy of everyday life that pursues the inarticulate background or interpretive schemes of the shared world that we accomplish together – as a disruptive and embodied approach (see Ahmed 2006a, 2006b; Husserl [1954] 1970; and Schutz 1970). I am particularly influenced by Dorothy Smith's (1992) sociology for women and by Sara Ahmed's (2006a, 2006b) queer phenomenology (see below). Smith (1992, 49) addresses the problematic of exclusion and difference in sociology, whose subject must "neglect her particular local existence" to take part in objectifying practices that "forget" (54) the gendered material relations and practices of textuality that organize social domains such as sociology, disability studies, and care. Smith begins from the vantage of what she calls women's lived "actualities" – the felt, embodied, and particular of a local here and now in social relations with others – which she understands as previously excluded "standpoints" (88–91) in and beyond sociology. This starting point "shifts the ground of knowing, the place where inquiry begins" (91). For my project, this approach shifts the ground of knowing away from the detachedness of conventional sociology and Western science, with their "view from nowhere" (Haraway 1991, 188), and places it practically and actually within the realm of (m)others' lived experiences of disruption and difference in relationship with their autistic child/adult. Based on this view, experience is not knowledge (Scott 1991) but a place – a sitpoint – from which we might seek knowledge and understanding.

Reworking critical and interpretive approaches is a hopeful way to shift knowledge production about autism and (m)othering, one that will help me, ultimately, to unmother autism. Although at times in tension around underlying assumptions about subjectivity, working the edges of critical and interpretive approaches opens space to perceive how we pay attention to disruption and to the configuration of the ordinary – to interpretive and potentially creative acts of consciousness that have everything to do with the accomplishment of power and possibility. Thus critical and interpretive approaches provoked by feminist and disability studies open ways to attend to disruption anew that reject a repetition of the same restrictive "good" (see Husserl, [1954] 1970; Schutz 1967; D. Smith 1987; and Titchkosky and Michalko 2012).

The How of Disruption: Methodology

Methodologically, I wanted to think through how to pursue a deeper understanding of those fleeting but suggestive moments when autistic difference disrupts the normal sense of everyday life. In *Queer Phenomenology: Orientations, Objects, Others,* Sara Ahmed (2006b, 106) describes such a methodological move beautifully, stating that her task as philosopher is not to pursue certainty or foundational knowledge but to "listen to the sound of the 'what' that fleets." I needed methods that could help me to pursue new knowledge and modes of knowledge production beyond dominant Western autism science, an approach from which alterity "fleets." The questions that I had were less empirical and more investigative: What subjugated knowledges might dwell within or emerge from disruptive moments and in the space of rupture between (m)other and child/offspring, lived experience and world? What might these knowledges reveal about the shape of the late-modern world in which we live together? How might such an approach reimagine care and the meaning of being human together?

To get at these questions, I use Ahmed's (2006a, 2006b) metaphor of the queer sideways or backward "glance" as a methodological orientation device with which to follow the "what" that "fleets" within everyday moments of disruption. Ahmed uses the metaphor of the backward or sideways glance to disrupt our everyday straight, white, and masculine-coded orientation to the world. For my project, turning around, taking a backward glance, and averting the analytic gaze away from dominant approaches in autism research and toward disruptive autistic and (m)othering bodies are moves that help me to pursue critically and interpretively what else might be behind – perceptually and historically – the identities autism mother and autism as they appear in everyday text. This context includes, to be sure, assumptions about both the normal human and normal development as white, straight, male, Western, productive, bourgeois, and non-autistic. This new methodological orientation also challenges the metaphor of vision in science and everyday vernacular that equates the physicality of sightedness and making eye contact with universal philosophical and scientific knowledge and with normal, desirable ways of being social (see Yergeau 2018). Instead, I pursue what Haraway (1991, 196) calls "partial sight" – in my case, of the disruptive (averted) autistic gaze and of the alterity of bodies marked autistic, alongside the "bad" (m)others who turn toward such aversions (and who resist ableist power) as something of value. The evidence that I gather through my disruptive methods thus moves beyond the empirical – the observable, measurable evidence gathered through the senses – to locate rich sites of critical and interpretative knowledge in other realms of evidence-based science, including, to borrow from Portelli and Konecny (2013, 93), the "moral, critical, spiritual, artistic and philosophical" as well as lived experience (see also Scott 1991; and Van Manen 1990). To do this work, I use both genealogy and phenomenological bracketing, which are described briefly below.

Disruptive Methods: Genealogy

To trace histories of governmentality, illiberal power, and subjugated knowledges around autism (m)other subjectivities, I use a genealogical method as informed by feminist and disability studies. A feminist and disability studies framework means that I pay critical attention to forms of power missing in Foucault's work, such as ableism and patriarchy, that shape autism and autism mother as white, middle-class, and Western identities (see Cosquer 2019; and Stoler 1995). Genealogy is a historiological method that traces the emergence of truth claims and identities as they are produced and naturalized through late-modern modes of power (e.g., disciplinary power, biopower, and governmental power). This work includes tracing forces of domination and subordination, histories of struggle, and forms of knowledge that target the body (Foucault 1984, 76; 1991b; Tamboukou 1999). To state this concretely, I document the histories of claims to truth circulating in popular media and science about autism as a problem and about a mother's scientifically guided love and care within the mother-child dyad as the solution. I also trace forms of resistance.

Foucault (1984, 86) states that the "development of humanity is a series of interpretations" and that the "role of genealogy is to record its history: the history of morals, ideals and metaphysical concepts, the history of the concept of liberty or of the ascetic life; as they stand for the emergence of different interpretations." Rather than "writing a history of the past in terms of the present," a genealogy performs a "history of the present" (Foucault [1975] 1995, 31; see also Bordo 1987, 5; Gibson and Douglas 2018; and Tamboukou 1999, 205). In other words, genealogy pursues the questions "Why this version of the human?" and "Why now?" to reveal the conditions of possibility for the emergence of interpretations, truths, and identities. To give an example, (m)others in my focus groups, as we shall see in Chapter 8, offered intimate descriptions of how they both lived (or were made to live) and resisted the "different interpretations" of autism mother identity across time – from the refrigerator mother blamed for causing autism by her disordered love to the mother therapist intensively labouring to save her child and the warrior mother fighting to "fix" both genes and science. Anna, (m)other of David (mentioned above), who was labelled by doctors as "mentally retarded," might be understood as temporarily occupying autism's mother therapist. Anna eventually abandoned her search for remedial therapies that promised to "cure" her son and shifted instead to affirming autism as fully human (see Chapter 8). As a critical historiological method, genealogy helps to reveal the fiction of cultural interpretations of autism as nonhuman and of autism mothers as compulsory, intensive labourers ushering in normalcy.

Rather than seeking "lofty" origins, "immobile" causes, or static essences such as human progress and perfectibility as accounts of the history of interpretations, genealogy descends to "cultivate the details and accidents that accompany every beginning" (Foucault 1971, 80), proceeding in a manner different from the "god-trick" found in dominant Western scientific studies of autism and mothering. For example, in Chapter 2, I trace the emergence of the case study as one of these "details and accidents." Case studies were widely reported in popular science magazines and books beginning in 1940s North America and brought intimate details of autistic people's and mothers' lives into public view in pathologizing ways (e.g., see Bettelheim 1959). Here, we can glimpse some of the beginnings not only of the category of autism as nonhuman, bizarre, and tragic but also of a (white, middle-class) mother's scientifically guided love and care as the "natural" remedy (Douglas 2013; E. Kim 2017; Runswick-Cole and Ryan 2019; Yergeau 2018). We can also glimpse the beginnings of both the social construction of intensive mothering (Hays 1999) and the neoliberal capitalist regime of remedial or curative care (Broderick and Roscigno 2021). In seeking the beginnings of "truth" in descent, then, Foucault (1984, 76) points us to a grounding in "the most unpromising of places, in what we tend to feel is without history – in sentiments, love, conscience, instincts."

According to Foucault (1980b, 83), the aim of genealogy is emancipatory: "Let us give the term *genealogy* to the union of erudite knowledge and local memories which allows us to establish a historical knowledge of struggles and to make use of this knowledge tactically today." Genealogy helps me attend to the disqualified knowledges at the edges of everyday text – the surprises of autistic and (m)othering bodies – that disrupt the foundations of who we have come to imagine ourselves to be and of how we care about our life together in our contemporary moment (81–82).

Disruptive Methods: Phenomenology

Genealogy does not, however, address questions of subjective meaning and lived power. To address these questions and to bring perception into my "backwards glance" (Ahmed 2006a, 2006b) at autism, (m)othering, and care, I use the phenomenological method of bracketing. Rather than proceeding from the "natural attitude," or the taken-for-granted assumptions about everyday life, phenomenology "brackets" the natural attitude and instead takes what Maurice Merleau-Ponty (1962, xv) describes as the hopeful and wonder-filled stance of a "perpetual beginner." This approach is not an attempt to separate subject and world but an embrace of open curiosity about the ordinary of everyday life, or as scholar Jeanne LeVasseur

(2003, 417) puts it, "a kind of astonishment before the world that disrupts habitual patterns of thinking." Informed by feminist and disability studies, I use bracketing to reveal the cultural ground, or taken-for-granted assumptions, of everyday life as autism and autism mother appear in acts of interpretive consciousness. To extend the example above from my focus groups, Anna's temporary occupation of autism's mother therapist identity involves a particular interpretation of mothering and the human based on the ground of a particular culture – a Western scientific sense that the normative human is non-autistic, that mothers are "naturally" nurturing, and that maternal care means intensive curative or remedial labour toward making our autistic child identical (Yergeau 2018). Here, interpretive consciousness is embodied, briefly, in Anna's temporary focus on practices of recovering her son; indeed, the tie between (m)other and child, interpretive consciousness, and world is intimate and close (Merleau-Ponty 1962, vii; 1968). Bracketing the natural attitude helps to tease out the embedded taken-for-granted assumptions in such practices and opens space for something new.

Bracketing is also a commitment to a rigorous kind of description rather than to an explanation more typical of scientific knowledge production. Through phenomenological description, the philosopher attempts to get close to the essence of phenomena – such as the tie that binds (m)other and autistic child – even as she acknowledges an excess of meaning that shimmers in an always open horizon of phenomenal experience (see Butler 1998, xi; Gerwitsch 1966, 89–96; and Schutz 1970, 96). The commitment to description rather than to scientific explanation is less a matter of making mental images, as philosophers Judith Butler (1998, x) and Merleau-Ponty (1962, xv) describe, although it may include this process, than a creative act of embodied, interpretive consciousness intimately tied to a world of which it is a part. This tie is so close, says Merleau-Ponty (1968), that we might think of the entanglement between body and world – what I am calling the space of rupture – as a space where body and world meld (see also Douglas, Rice, and Siddiqui 2018; Garland-Thomson 2011; and Grosz 2005). Self and other, autism and world, (m)other and autistic child/adult enfold and come to be together in relation.

Bracketing the natural attitude, with its taken-for-granted assumptions, that surrounds autism and autism mother appearances in everyday text is difficult work. Autism and (m)othering are lived and experienced in a deeply affective register, and biomedical understandings saturate (m)others' and autistic people's sense of the lifeworld, the everyday world that we inhabit together. In today's context, it appears almost beyond question (and almost cruel to suggest otherwise) that *because of* her loss – the loss of her child's normal development – a mother is grieving. Similarly, stories about mothers fighting against autism make sense: mothers must do so, and do so out of love, *in order to* give their child future happiness, survival, and success. Here, in what phenomenological sociologist Alfred Schutz (1967, 86–96) calls the pragmatic use of "because-of" and "in-order-to motives," the near totalizing frame of the biomedical – animated by the unquestioned prestige of Western scientific sensibilities in the natural attitude – remains concealed. Bracketing the natural attitude in order to perform close descriptions reveals how dominant understandings of autism and the sense that a mother should grieve and work for a cure are possible at all. The method exposes what Titchkosky (2011, 273–76) calls the "sayable" and "sensible" world – a world animated by objectivizing biomedical terms that regimes of knowledge and power govern. Revealing the processes and ground of interpretation that govern how meanings are produced will be the payoff of this method. Thus the question of the real meaning of autism will remain both unasked and unanswered here. Uncoupling the presumed real link between autism as biomedical and experiences of meaning and (m)othering allows for the emergence of possibilities for new interpretations, disruption, and ways of being human together.

At the Intersection of Feminist and Disability Studies

Disability Studies: A Brief Background

I also draw from, pose new questions within, and advance conversations about (m)othering, autism, and care at the intersection of feminist and disability studies. My approach is informed by interpretive and critical sociological thought and modes of inquiry. I also include critical autism studies as a field that has more recently emerged in close conversation with disability studies. Briefly, disability studies scholars raise critical questions about and pose alternatives to geopolitical, historical, economic, social, cultural, and material processes that marginalize and devalue alter

embodiments.[6] Approaching fifty years ago, the social model of disability –
a radical understanding of disability as a socio-political, rather than an
individual and tragic, phenomenon located in bodies – erupted on the
political scene in the United Kingdom as the rallying call of the Union of
the Physically Impaired Against Segregation (UPIAS 1975, 14): "In our
view, it is society which disables physically impaired people. Disability is
something imposed on top of our impairments by the way we are unneces-
sarily isolated and excluded from full participation in society. Disabled
people are therefore an oppressed group in society." As for other socially
oppressed groups, proponents of the social model of disability interrogate
the oppression of disabled people as the result of exclusionary socio-
political and economic arrangements and dominant ideologies (see Abberley 1987; and Hunt 1998). It is not individual broken bodies or minds that
disable and exclude but inaccessible physical, economic, social, sensory,
and ideological environments. That the autistic self-advocacy movement's
activism does not focus on a cure or normalizing treatments but instead
confronts inaccessible environments that exclude autistic people from life
is an example of the social model in action (e.g., see Autistic Self Advocacy
Network, autisticadvocacy.org). Indeed, the social model and its activist
beginnings (Davis 2006; Goodley 2011 xii, 2) owe much to and advance
the radical political movements of the 1960s and the work of feminist,
queer, disability rights, neurodiversity, anti-racist, and working-class
scholars.

In bringing together feminist and disability studies, I also attend to
lived bodies that push back, as it were (see Douglas, Rice, and Siddiqui
2020; Garland-Thomson 2011; Paterson and Hughes 1999; and Yergeau
2018). My topic of autism, (m)othering, and care as a site of political,
embodied, and ethical disruptions troubles the social model of disability
and its fixed impairment-disability binary (like second-wave feminist
distinctions between sex and gender). Although this binary has been a
successful political strategy in the Global North's autistic self-advocacy,
disability rights, and independent-living movements, one important critique, articulated here by feminist philosopher Iris Marion Young (2002,
xiii), is that the social model "continues to presume a certain fixity to these
bodies" (see also Yergeau 2018, 108). M. Remi Yergeau adds that none of
the autistic self-advocacy organizations (such as the Autistic Self Advocacy

Network and the Autism Women and Nonbinary Network) that "agitate for neurodiversity and radical social acceptance, believe that autism is immaterial, or is merely a matter of linguistic fiction" (108). In other words, whereas initial articulations of the social model left the matter of disabled bodies (understood as impairment) in all their/our struggle, pain, desire, and joy as unremarked or a matter for medicine, critical attention is now being given to the materiality of bodies within disability and critical autism studies, a movement of which my work is a part.

Poet, essayist, and disability justice activist Eli Clare (2001, 364), for example, rather than regarding different bodies as somehow outside of history, philosophy, social inquiry, relationships, or embodied experience, calls for a reclaiming and valuing of different bodies – queer, shaky, and unsteady bodies: "I am asking that we pay attention to our bodies – our stolen bodies and our reclaimed bodies. To the wisdom that tells us the causes of the injustice we face lie outside our bodies, and to the profound relationships our bodies have to that injustice, to the ways our identities are inextricably linked to our bodies." Bodies taken as autistic – flapping hands, "disconnected" bodies, rocking bodies – are never fixed in this way but slip, disrupt, and exceed any easy distinction between impairment and disability (Yergeau 2018, 108). For this book, paying attention to lived bodies means incorporating critical and interpretive insights about autism/disability neither as an individual problem in need of fixing through remedial care within the mother-child dyad, nor as solely a "social pathology" (Goodley 2011, xi), nor again as an essential identity (whether positive or negative) grounded in different brains. Instead, it means incorporating insights about autism/disability as a relationship where body and world, self and other enfold and where any certain ground about difference and identity is always slipping (see Butler 1993; Corker 1998; Corker and Shakespeare 2002; Douglas, Rice, and Siddiqui 2019; Fritsch 2016, 52; and Re•Storying Autism Writing Collective 2022). This approach holds onto the hope that there may be a different way of caring about autism, (m)othering, and care that moves beyond the normal body of biomedicine and beyond "fixing" autism, as well as beyond the social model's tendency to forget lived bodies.

Critical autism studies is also helpful in theorizing lived experience and power in the space between body and world in nonreductive and nonessentialist ways. Critical autism studies is an interdisciplinary field that emerged during the 2000s in conversation with disability studies, provoked by autistic self-advocates and the emergence of autistic culture as valid and valuable (see Yergeau 2018, 108–9). Autistic scholar Mitzi Waltz (2014, 1337), in reviewing scholars Joyce Davidson and Michael Orsini's (2013) description of critical autism studies in *Worlds of Autism: Across the Spectrum of Neurological Difference,* summarizes the "criticality" in critical autism studies as "investigating power dynamics that operate in discourses around autism, questioning deficit-based definitions of autism, and being willing to consider the ways in which biology and culture intersect to produce 'disability.'" Rather than a negative (biomedical discourse) or positive (neurodiversity discourse) brain-based difference, this approach orients to autism as constituted at the intersection of different bodies and culture, unfixing autism from any biology-culture binary. Other scholars approach critical autism studies differently, debunking the reification of autism within conventional autism science and, at times, neurodiversity discourse (Runswick-Cole et al. 2017). Still others take up critical autism studies as an occasion to provoke methodological debate and to innovate participatory approaches grounded in autistic people's experiences (Hodge, Douglas, and Byrne forthcoming; Milton et al. 2019; Orsini 2022; Re•Storying Autism Writing Collective 2022). Moreover, vital challenges to the whiteness of critical autism studies and autistic self-advocacy (and to the diagnosis/identity itself) have been made by autistics of colour (e.g., see Brown, Ashkenazy, and Onaiwu 2017; and Onaiwu forthcoming). I embrace the contested and multiple nature of critical autism studies (see also Fletcher-Watson et al. 2019; Milton 2012, 2014; Woods et al. 2018; and Woods and Waldock 2020) and hold open the meaning of autism as a historical, relational, cultural, contextual, material-discursive phenomenon made and remade in the space between body and culture, materiality, and discourse (see Douglas et al., "Re-storying Autism," 2021). I also bring critical conversations about (m)othering and affirming care to critical autism studies (see Douglas et al., "Mad Mothering," 2021; and Runswick-Cole 2014; also below). This is a beginning point from which to challenge the reification of autism, embrace both the joy and struggle of different bodies, challenge white supremacy and ableism, distribute and affirm care, and forge possibilities for solidarity between autistic self-advocates, (m)others, and those who care (see Re•Storying Autism Writing Collective 2022; also Ashburn and Edwards 2023).

Working at the intersection of feminist and disability studies also means, as for critical autism studies, deepening disability studies' engagements with difference. Not only does the diversity of disabled bodies, minds, and senses exceed the UPIAS version of disability as "physical disability," but it also exceeds the Global North's legacy of disability studies as a white, male body of work focused on physical disability (McGuire 2016; see also Schalk and Kim 2020). As disability studies author, activist, and artist Corbett J. O'Toole (2004, 295) describes it, the "myth of the white, straight man in a wheelchair is evident in personal accounts, essays, and in the professional literature of disability scholars" (see also Yergeau 2018, 108). Yet, as recently as 2020, feminist-of-colour disability studies scholars Sami Schalk and Jina B. Kim (2020, 32) could assert, "The insights of feminists of color on disability have largely been excluded as intellectual contributions to feminist disability studies." I am indebted to the legacies of thought and activism that Schalk and Kim reference around disability, including those of Black, Indigenous, and disability justice scholars and activists,[7] particularly insights around theorizing from the margins, disrupting Western ontologies (e.g., scientific worldviews and individualism), and collectivizing care in order to unmother autism (E. Kim 2017; Runswick-Cole and Ryan 2019). I also recognize the limits of my theorizing as a white-settler, cisgender academic and (m)other living in the Global North and the complex rub of my identity as a scholar and (m)other who is also neurodivergent and invisibly disabled and who often writes, teaches, leads research, and engages in activism, as Piepzna-Samarasinha (2018) puts it, from my couch or "sick bed." In these layered ways, I bring (m)othering, disability, and care to the centre of knowledge production and make a similar case to that of Schalk and Kim (2020): the intellectual contributions and experiences of (m)others (who may also be autistic and disabled) who confront and challenge ableist patriarchal systems on behalf of and with their autistic or disabled child or adult offspring have been marginalized and even excluded (and, at times, met with hostility) by feminist, critical autism, and disability studies (see Douglas et al., "Mad Mothering," 2021; Douglas et al., "Making Memories," 2022; and Runswick-Cole 2014).

Working the Edges of Feminist and Disability Studies

I work the edges of feminist and disability studies to bring (m)othering, disability, and care to the centre of knowledge production, to pose new questions, and to push conversations about (m)othering, disability, and care in new directions. Disability studies scholars raise difficult questions about care as oppression (Brown, Ashkenazy, and Onaiwu 2017; Kelly 2016; Nishida 2022). They point to how (m)others have been implicated in histories and legacies of curative or remedial care and even of violence (see below; also Dawson 2004; Gibson and Douglas 2018; Sibley 2017; and Yergeau 2018). At the same time, feminist (m)othering, science, and other critical scholars and activists point to how (m)others, care workers, and parents have, in other instances, been critical allies and activists at the forefront of disabled and autistic people's liberation (see Ashburn and Edwards 2023; Douglas et al., "Mad Mothering," 2021, Douglas et al., "Making Memories," 2022; Nishida 2022; Panitch 2008; Ryan 2021; Ryan and Runswick-Cole 2009; and Silverman 2012). In *Understanding Autism: Parents, Doctors, and the History of a Disorder,* for example, science and technology scholar Chloe Silverman (2012) traces the role of parents in the history of autism as a medical disorder. She takes up an analytic of love to show how current understandings of autism (as a biogenetic versus psychological disorder) and of autism science have been irrevocably shaped by the advocacy and love of parents agitating for support and access to life on behalf of their autistic child or adult offspring. Silverman documents North American histories of advocacy and urges parents, doctors, and others both to rethink autism beyond medical disorder and to engage in ethical decision making around autism treatment grounded in normalizing logics such as Applied Behaviour Analysis (11). Like Silverman, I am interested in the nexus where expert (scientific) and lay knowledge meet and in ethical decision making. I also, like Silverman, navigate the tensions between autistic self-advocacy and parent advocacy and care within the Global North's disability movements. In contrast to Silverman, I innovate an ethic of disruption in knowledge production about autism, (m)othering, and care to trouble dominant representations of autism and autism mothers in popular media and science. I also talk with (m)others about the meaning that they make of representation alongside how they resist these powerful regimes. My aim is to unmother autism by tracing histories of autism and autism mother identity and resistance and by affirming autistic difference and alternative, dispersed ways to (m)other and care. I also intervene in the tension between autistic self-advocacy and parent advocacy that Silverman perhaps leaves somewhat unresolved, offering an alternate way forward that forges solidarity through an ethic of disruption and affirming care.

For this book, then, working the edges of feminist and disability studies means paying attention both to how the dominant scientific sense of care is, at times, taken up by (m)others and to how (m)others resist and disrupt (m)othering and care as an either/or oppression-liberation binary. This approach challenges disability studies not only to rethink Western values such as autonomy embedded in the Global North's independent living, self-advocacy, and disability rights movements but also to grapple with the gendered, classed, and raced political economy of care (see below; also Bailey and Mobley 2018; and Runswick-Cole and Goodley 2018). It also challenges feminist (m)othering, science, and other critical scholars to incorporate critical insights about disability and ableism into their work on (m)othering and care (e.g., see Douglas, Rice, and Kelly 2017; Hughes et al. 2005; Kelly 2016; Kröger 2009; Morris 2001; Murphy 2015; Nishida 2022; Shakespeare 2006; and F. Williams 2001). I work the edges of feminist, critical autism, and disability studies and the tensions at this intersection to unravel histories of disability oppression and struggle, as well as to open new, collective, relational, and potentially transformative understandings of the "disability story of parents" (Dona M. Avery, quoted in Ryan and Runswick-Cole 2009, 43). I provide more background below.

First, conversations about gender, disability, and (m)othering already have a history within both disability and feminist studies. Feminist disability studies scholars, for example, articulate the myriad ways that gender and disability operate both materially and symbolically as intertwined systems of oppression, ascribing inferiority, passivity, deviance, material exclusion, medical control, and Otherness to feminine-coded and disabled bodies (e.g., see Bailey and Mobley 2018; Ben-Moshe and Magaña 2014; Fine and Asch 1988; Garland-Thomson 1991, 2001, 2005; K. Hall 2011; Morris 1991, 1993; O'Toole 2004; C. Thomas 1999, 2006; and Wendell 1989, 1996). White supremacy and patriarchy also intersect, imbuing Indigenous, Black, and other women of colour, as feminist-of-colour disability studies scholar

Moya Bailey (2018, 24) teaches, as "simultaneously hyper able-bodied and disabled" by virtue of their race and sex (see also Battersby 1998; and Garland-Thomson 2001). Examples abound of how disability and femininity are historically and bodily equated in Western culture as "too-much" (Bordo, 2003, 160–61) or alternatively as lack – as, for example, deformed monsters or witches, hypersexualized and "crazy" Black women (Bailey and Mobley 2018), deficient Indigenous (m)others and kin, castrated males, rejecting and disordered mothers, genetically disabled, or madwomen (see Bailey 2018; Douglas et al., "Mad Mothering," 2021; Douglas et al., "Making Memories," 2022; and Garland-Thomson 2001, 6–9). Indeed, disability and feminist scholars, including Simone de Beauvoir ([1949] 2011, 16–17), have long demonstrated how women are understood in Western culture as "immanence" alone, not transcendence, "being pure body, unredeemed by mind or spirit." For disabled women, however, as Rosemarie Garland-Thomson (2001, 5) describes, there is a further denial and devaluation: "Whereas motherhood is often seen as compulsory for women and therefore potentially oppressive, the opposite is true for disabled women, who are denied or discouraged from this reproductive role." Feminist-of-colour disability studies scholars Moya Bailey and Izzeta Autumn Mobley (2018, 32) describe how this is a particularly cruel irony for disabled women of colour given that "Black women and other women of colour do most of the labour in the service of disability despite the impact on their ability to care for themselves or their families" and the debility caused by such racist logics and systems. The issue of genetic motherhood, including the screening and abortion of disabled fetuses, is another complex convergence between these two fields, one that has generated rich and contested dialogue (e.g., see Bumiller 2008, 2009; Keller 1995; Landsman 2009; L. Mitchell 2001; Rapp 2011; Rapp and Ginsburg 2011; and Tremain 2010).

Despite feminist disability studies engagements with disability, (m)othering, and care, these topics arguably continue to be marginalized – even devalued – within disability studies and feminist discourse writ large, including disability justice and critical autism studies (see Ashburn and Edwards 2023; Bailey 2018; Douglas et al., "Mad Mothering," 2021; Douglas et al., "Making Memories," 2022; and Schalk 2018). When (m)others of autistic or disabled children appear at all, it is often the oppressive, paternalistic, or tragic aspects of (m)othering a disabled or autistic child or adult offspring that are emphasized – whether for (m)others or disabled people – as if a natural corollary (Douglas et al., "Mad Mothering," 2021). Political scientist Kristin Bumiller (2008, 967) raises the issue specifically for autism: "Autism is remarkable also for its significance to many issues at the core of women's and gender studies, including gender identification, sexuality, motherhood, and the impact of new reproductive technologies." I concur with Bumiller and others (Runswick-Cole and Goodley 2018) that conversations within and between feminist and disability studies about the activism and contributions of (m)others and autistic people need more consideration given that many (m)others journey with disabled and autistic adults beyond childhood, share aspects of ableist oppression with them, require support as carers, and advance disability rights and justice movements (Ashburn and Edwards 2023; Douglas et al., "Making Memories," 2022; Nishida 2022; Ryan and Runswick-Cole 2008; Silverman 2012). Katherine Runswick-Cole and Daniel Goodley (2018, 232) advance conversations at this intersection when they "invoke the 'disability commons' as a collective and affirming alternative approach to individualising models of parenting that oppress both mothers and disabled children." This more collectivized and dispersed approach to (m)othering has parallels to the collective care work advanced by the disability justice movement (Berne 2015; Brown, Ashkenazy, and Onaiwu 2017; Mingus 2011; Nishida 2022; Piepzna-Samarasinha 2018). Both orient to (m)othering/care as a collective form of resistance and flourishing within the austerity logics of Western ableist, colonialist, white supremacist, patriarchal, and neoliberal capitalist contexts, and both think *with* the disruption of disability to disperse care across a "commons." Disability studies and feminist scholar Akemi Nishida's (2022) *Just Care: Messy Entanglements of Disability, Dependency and Desire* is an important example – one grounded in disability justice – of how care collectives, care work, and "bed activism" can be sites of collective resistance to ableism, white supremacy, and neoliberal capitalism. This work is in stark contrast to the social construction of mothering through the dominant scientific sense that "naturally" contains (m)othering and disability within the bounds of intensive remedial labour performed by individual mothers, often within the constraints of the nuclear family, or in the case of upper- or middle-class families, by paid carers who are often women of colour. I am indebted to scholars like Silverman (2012), Bumiller (2008,

2009), and Nishida (2022) and to disability justice activists (Berne 2015) and disability studies scholars (Runswick-Cole and Goodley 2018) in my formulation of affirming care. I am also indebted to the (m)others with whom I spoke in focus groups, who, as we shall see, affirmed autistic difference, pushed back against negative representations, collectivized care, and "invoke[d] the disability commons" (Runswick-Cole 2018, 231) through the networks that they formed to push for access to education, work, and life with and for their children and adult offspring.

Possibilities for expanding strategic alliances between feminist and disability studies around (m)othering and care are emerging. *I Will Die on This Hill: Autistic Adults, Autism Parents and the Children Who Deserve a Better World*, a much-anticipated book published in 2023 by former rivals Meaghan Ashburn, who is the (m)other of two autistic sons, and Jules Edwards, an autistic (m)other, is one example (see also Re•Storying Autism Writing Collective 2022). At the same time, such alliances often remain fraught. Disability and critical autism studies, feminist, and (m)othering scholars and activists are often at cross-purposes (Carey, Block, and Scotch 2020; Douglas et al., "Mad Mothering," 2021). As a vocation to care, (m)othering embodies intimate, emotional, and dependent aspects of care that represent much of what disability activists and autistic self-advocates have fought against in forging the social model and neurodiversity movement, namely associations between disability and the feminine realm of dependency, passivity, emotions, and bodily need (Hughes et al. 2005; Morris 2001; Sibley 2017; Yergeau 2018). Equally troubling for disability activists and autistic self-advocates is (m)others' and parents' complicity with undeniably oppressive, ableist, white supremacist, violent systems of care and treatment like the institutionalized care and treatments based on Westernized biomedical understandings of autism and disability, such as Applied Behaviour Analysis (e.g., see Brown, Ashkenazy, and Onaiwu 2017; Dawson 2004; Hughes et al. 2005; Kröger 2009; Ryan and Runswick-Cole 2008; Sibley 2017; and Yergeau 2018).

As a political alternative to associations with care, social model and neurodiversity activists and scholars have often emphasized a Western, masculine-coded ethic of equality and justice, forwarding empowerment, independence, autonomy, and equal citizenship rights (Hughes et al. 2005). This undertaking has led to important gains for many disabled and autistic people, forging a social and consumer-led model of care that distances itself from emotional, bodily, or dependency aspects. Instead, independent living, self-advocacy, choice, control, and autonomy in terms of "help," "support," or "assistance" – that is, through personal assistants (see Shakespeare 2006, 139) – are emphasized. Care, for the social model, has been disentangled from love, mothers, family, and the so-called feminine realm of interdependency, support, passivity, and emotion, despite many mothers' often life-long involvement in their disabled and autistic off-spring's lives as advocates, activists, and supporters (see Douglas and Klar 2019; Hughes et al. 2005; Kelly 2013; Kröger 2009; Morris 2001; and F. Williams 2001). As articulated for the disability rights movement by Richard Wood, who was director of the British Council of Disabled People (quoted in C. Thomas 2007, 107), "disabled people have never demanded or asked for care!"

Disability studies critiques of care are vitally important. Biomedical forms of care that seek to normalize, contain, or cure autism, and to normalize mothers' implication in them, have exclusionary, even violent, consequences. For example, disability studies scholar Anne McGuire's (2016) book *War on Autism: On the Cultural Logic of Normative Violence,* which discusses parent advocacy and the cultural production of autism, is a powerful attestation not only of the force of the Global North's white, middle-class parent advocacy, which forwards biomedical versions of autism and care, but also of the need for alternatives. Against a cultural backdrop of Western(izing) scientific versions of autism and violence against autistic people, McGuire traces the productive and powerful force of contemporary advocacy in which mothers and parents are the primary movers. The underlying logic of such advocacy, says McGuire, "casts autism as a pathological threat to normative life, and advocacy as that which must normalize, neutralize or otherwise eliminate this threat" (21). For example, Autism Speaks – what McGuire calls "the largest, the richest, and, so, the most influential autism advocacy organization in operation today" (57) – is spearheaded by families. Autism Speaks forwards a conventional understanding of autism as an undesirable neurodevelopmental disorder – one that threatens us all – and is committed to caring about autism by seeking its cure globally via genomic research and via the promotion of this version of autism. Although Autism Speaks has made some moves to incorporate the language of equity and to include autistic people in leadership roles, these efforts appear to be superficial, and McGuire's book demonstrates the vital need for an ongoing disability studies critique of the many aspects of parenting and care, including advocacy. For my project, McGuire's work is a provocation to work the edges of critical and interpretive disability and feminist studies in order to open new sets of questions about (m)othering, care, advocacy, and activism in generative ways.

Feminist work in political economy, for example, diverges from understanding care as a right or form of disability oppression and instead understands care as a form of gender, race, and class oppression. Although its focus in not limited to (m)othering, feminist political economy demonstrates how informal and formal care work is linked to the Global North's restructuring of social, economic, and political relations with the end of the welfare state (Brodie 1995; Walkerdine and Lucy 1989; F. Williams 2001). Beginning in the 1980s, when middle-class white women were entering the workforce in record numbers in North America, neoliberal economic shifts saw the return of care to the realm of the private family (and marketplace) and the withdrawal of public supports from the community, resulting in what sociologists Pat Armstrong and Hugh Armstrong (1984) called a "double burden" of care for women as both paid workers and primary caregivers (see also Bailey 2018; Brodie 1995; and Vandenbeld Giles 2014). The ideology and practice of "intensive mothering" – what Sharon Hays (1996, 8; emphasis in original) describes as *"child-centred, expert-guided, emotionally absorbing, labor-intensive* and *financially expensive"* – also emerged during this time, cementing care in the form of the mother-child dyad as natural, despite the contradictory figure of the "working mother" committed to her career. It would be women of colour from the Global North and Third World who would fill the gap of underpaid care work in these new economies (notably for middle-class white mothers who worked), including in the social model of care forwarded by disability rights activists (see Meekosha 2011; and F. Williams 2001, 2011). Facing these complex economic and ideological contradictions, feminist scholars and activists can often conceive of disabled family members as an added burden of care within their theories (Hughes et al. 2005; Kelly 2013; Kröger 2009; Morris 2001; F. Williams 2001). Whereas a feminist political economy dislodges straightforward notions of equality within the social model of care, disability studies critiques the ableist view of disability as nothing more than a burden that is often evident within feminist political economy. Bridging the edges between a feminist and disability studies critique of (m)othering and care is difficult.

Disability studies scholars have addressed these complex and intertwining oppressions, as Christine Kelly (2013, 2016, 2017) formulates it, by "building bridges" (see also Carey, Block and Scotch 2020) – tenuous ones that might also easily slip – across and between feminist and disability studies critiques of gender and care, feminist political economy, and a feminist ethic of care, which I touch on briefly below (see also Douglas, Rice, and Kelly 2017; Hughes et al. 2005; Kröger 2009; Morris 2001; Shakespeare 2006; and F. Williams 2001, 2011). Within complex situations of constraint, mothers often simultaneously resist and comply with ableist formulations of care and gender ideologies, both practising remedial or curative therapies and affirming difference in relationship with their disabled offspring, an element of affirming care explored in this book (Douglas, Rice, and Kelly 2017; Douglas et al., "Mad Mothering," 2021; Douglas et al., "Beyond 'Inclusionism,'" forthcoming; Goodley and Runswick-Cole 2017; Ryan and Runswick-Cole 2008). These messy realities of care blur any easy lines between autonomy and dependence, self and other, emotion and reason, and private and public, as well as any romantic notions that evacuate struggle or violence from the feminized realm of care (Kelly 2017). Such slippages, too, suggest that the devalued "feminine" realm of emotion, embodiment, and love that the social model of care wished to circumvent cannot be so easily left behind and may have something of value to add to conversations about (m)othering and care (see also Silverman 2012). Feminist philosophers of an ethic of care have worked to empower and imbue the practical, relational, embodied, and affective aspects of the typically feminine domestic realm with philosophical status, linking women's and (m)others' experiences of care to different modes of thinking, reasoning, and being as distinct from what have been labelled male ones. This work counters views of feminine moral reasoning – the relational, contextual, located, and embodied – as deviant from and lesser than a male "ethic of justice" based on universal Kantian ethics (Held 2006, 63). Such approaches argue that an ethic of care is a radical political challenge to Western rationalized modes of knowledge, identity, and social organization (see Gilligan 1993; Kittay 1999; Noddings 2013; Ruddick 1995; and Tronto 1993). My decision to begin an inquiry into women's sitpoints and to value the difference of autistic bodies and the realm of affect and interdependence in my work is indebted to the work in feminist ethics of Eva Feder Kittay (1999), Audre Lorde (1988), Mia Mingus (2011), Joan Tronto (1993), and others both working in and expanding on a feminist ethic of care.

However, I also pay attention to feminist philosopher Anita Silvers (1995, 40) when she says that a feminist ethic of care has the potential to lead to "an even more oppressive paternalism." A feminist ethic of care may not only romanticize women's and mother's socially constructed domestic roles and disability experience but also essentialize and universalize them, thus erasing difference. This erasure often results in the exclusion of the situated experiences of disabled women as (m)others. It also excludes Indigenous, Black, and other women of colour who articulate philosophies of care forged through ancestral and cultural knowledge (see Bevan-Brown 2013; Collins 1987, 1990, 2015; M. Graham 2007; Hamington 2015; and Hankivsky 2014). Within reclaimed African philosophies, for example, social work scholar Mekada Graham (2007, 203) articulates how the woman-centred Egyptian philosophy of Ma'at holds that "care flows through interconnectedness with others and the universe and is maintained by caring both in the individual sense and as a collective endeavour." Audre Lorde (1988, 132), too, asserts the political import of a Black feminist ethic of self-care in the face of her own journey with cancer and the collective resistance of Black women and (m)others in order to survive and transform racialized gender oppression when she says, "Caring for myself is not self-indulgence, it is self-preservation, and that is an act of political warfare."

I do not wish to homogenize alternative ways of understanding care beyond white-settler, colonialist, and Global North ones, and I recognize the limits of my own positionality and theorizing, yet I do spotlight the tensions at the intersection of feminist and disability studies approaches both to raise questions about and to work for solutions to the ableist, gendered, and white supremacist social construction of (m)othering and disability, along with the overdetermination of Western biomedical approaches to care. Other recent feminist and feminist-of-colour disability studies work of this ilk yields new insights about (m)othering, care, and disability as potentially transformative forms of advocacy, activism, pedagogy, relational ethics, crip futurity (or futures in which disabled and autistic people are desired), and disability experience – insights that also aim to transform state violence and barriers to health care, priorities articulated by Indigenous, Black, Global South, and other scholars of colour (see Bailey 2018; Chapman and Kelly 2015; Douglas, Rice and Kelly 2017; Douglas et al., "Mad Mothering," 2021; Douglas et al., "Making Memories," 2022; Filax and Taylor 2014; Kelly 2018; Lewiecki-Wilson and Cellio 2011; Nishida 2022; Runswick-Cole and Goodley 2017; and Schalk and Kim 2020). Indeed, scholars and activists working at these intersections call for an attention to interdependence and to collectivizing care. Not only can this more complex approach revalue and hold disabled people's and carers' or (m)others' perspectives together with the material realities of political economy and intersecting oppressions (on intersectionality, see Crenshaw 1989; and Rice, Harrison, and Friedman 2019), but it can also work to transform gender, race, and class oppression and the legacy of violence against disabled people in the name of care (Douglas, Rice, and Kelly 2017; Kelly 2016, 2017). Thus my feminist and disability studies approach – as shaped by critical and interpretive sociological approaches and modes of inquiry as well as by critical autism studies and the work of autistic, queer, Indigenous, Black, and other disability justice activists and thinkers – presents an occasion to question, disrupt, and think anew about (m)othering, autism, and care as sites that are not a straightforward matter of disability or women's oppression but replete with lessons about human alterity, justice, difference, and possibility.

I forward a feminist and disability studies approach as informed by interpretive and critical sociological thought through which I analyze shifts in everyday text and talk about autism and autism mothers as both an interactive scene of social action and a site of power. The aim of this work is both to (re)value autism, (m)othering, and care and to unmother autism (E. Kim 2017; Runswick-Cole and Ryan 2019) by troubling the mother-child dyad and the biomedical imperative to fix autism through mothers' intensive remedial care. I forward new conversations and release affirming understandings of (m)othering, autism, and care in solidarity with feminist, autistic self-advocacy, and disability justice movements. Part 2 of the book turns to the treasure trove of my archive and what might be made anew of autism, (m)othering, and care.

Part 2

Pursuing Autism Mothers

2

Autism's Refrigerator Mothers
The Psychoanalytic Gaze

Adding a new element to an age-old adage – that mothers are to blame for their child's and society's ills – this chapter traces the emergence of autism's "refrigerator mother," the so-called chilly mother thought to cause autism in her child through her disordered love. This historical narrative is set in southwestern Ontario. It begins in 1943 when "early infantile autism" emerged as a formal medical diagnosis for the first time. I trace the refrigerator mother's emergence within popular science and parenting magazines, film, popular psychology books, and parent memoirs widely available to a Toronto audience. My use of these sources means that my story features some of the typical actors, like autism fathers, who make a regular appearance in autism history, including psychologist Bruno Bettelheim and psychiatrist Leo Kanner. Chapter 3 also turns to (m)others' narratives of resistance, something that has not been done within histories of autism and (m)othering in quite this way before. In both chapters, I also include insights from focus group discussions with (m)others of autistic children or adult offspring.

I begin *in medias res* – in the middle of an already unfolding story about mother blame and about disciplines in childhood disorder such as child psychiatry that emerged on the scene in the 1940s. Autism mothers were not the only bad mothers during this time (e.g., see Dehli 1994a). Depictions of the so-called rejecting and/or suffocating mother already circulated widely, such as the overprotective Jewish mother, deficient working-class mother, pathological Black mother, and absent working mother (see Caplan 1998; Ehrenreich and English 2005, 292; and

Ladd-Taylor and Umansky 1998). What is unique about the refrigerator mother is how she emerged as an extreme – a kind of cautionary tale for all about the danger of a mother's love left unregulated by the authority of patriarchal scientific expertise. A newly shaped paradox of care – that of a mother's love as both inherently essential and dangerous – redefined what it meant to be a good mother as well as understandings of normal human development as non-autistic, economically productive, white, and middle-class (Bordo 2003; Hays 1996). Examining this history through an ethic of disruption and through a quality of attention in knowledge production and life that I call affirming care also reveals disqualified knowledges about human difference, relationality, and care that dwell at the edges of everyday text but at the centre of these (m)others' lives (Foucault 1980b).

The archive from which I draw for this chapter is not meant to be a catalogue of every appearance of autism mothers. The point is not to conduct a complete survey of popular renderings but to undertake an interpretive and genealogical engagement with the historical emergence of a particular meaning of autism mother, the traces and powers of which we live with today. It is the refrigerator mother and her meanings that I am after, not an exhaustive survey of the number of times that she appears in everyday text. My experience of forays into the archives, alongside the divergent storylines, rewritings, and multiple beginnings of autism mother history that they trace, echoes Michel Foucault's (1984, 76) description of genealogical research: "Genealogy is gray, meticulous, and patiently documentary. It operates on a field of tangled and confused documents that have been scratched over and recopied many times." This chapter, extending sociologist Mitchell Dean's (1999) axes of analysis, performs a genealogy of refrigerator mother identity, including how new "forms of knowledge" (such as child psychology), "visibility" (such as the case study), and "technologies" (such as scientific mother blame) draw new lines between the normal and abnormal by redirecting a mother's gaze ever more deeply inward as she moves toward the governance of her own inner emotional and bodily life (see also Rose 1996, 1999). I consider how, in addition, this inward gaze ironically became the ground for (m)others' resistance. Working more interpretively, I also pause at points along the way to glance at what unquestioned assumptions might be "behind" (Ahmed 2006a, 570) the appearance of this mother and open my activity of rereading this mother as its own form of resistance, one that is committed to a different kind of knowledge about our life together. Consequently, this chapter and the next look back to historicize the very possibility of autism and of autism mother, as well as to rethink forms of resistance.

The Birth of Autism Mothers

In 1943, Leo Kanner – an Austrian psychiatrist who in 1924 emigrated to the United States, where he directed the child psychiatry unit at Johns Hopkins Hospital – published eleven case studies of children whom he had observed over some years in his hospital clinic (Kanner 1943; see also Pollak 1997, 249–50). Here, he described children whose characteristics he thought presented a new disorder distinct from other diagnoses such as childhood schizophrenia. He called this new disorder "early infantile autism." Unlike the symptom of autism in childhood schizophrenia, a disease described by psychiatrist Eugen Bleuler in 1911 as involving an initial relationship of self to world (Nadesan 2005, 39), Kanner wrote that the children he observed never forged a social relationship with their parents, their families, or the social world around them. They were impaired in their ability to communicate, unable to engage in reciprocal social interaction, and engaged in stereotyped behaviours such as rocking or "twiddling." These children were, according to Kanner (1943) and the parents he interviewed, in a world of their own from the start.[1]

Working against the backdrop of both biological psychiatry – psychoanalysis, although dominant in these years, did not completely eclipse alternate views – and the mental hygiene and eugenics movements of the first half of the twentieth century, Kanner (1943) wrote that there must be some biological basis for the disorder (see also Douglas and Klar 2019, 205–7).[2] Interestingly, Kanner also noted the potential influence of parents, who seemed to form their own unique group, and he would go on to study them in more depth as well as to offer his views publicly (Kanner and Eisenberg 1955; C. Park 1967, 126–28; Pollak 1997, 249–51). For example, in a medical feature published by *Time* (1948, n.p.), Kanner, then a leading figure in the emerging field of child psychiatry, is quoted as observing that these parents display a "mechanization of human relationships." In another medical feature twelve years later that summarized Kanner's contributions to child psychiatry, his view seems to have solidified: these were the type of parents "just happening to defrost enough to produce a child" (quoted in C.C. Thomas 1960). Describing them as highly intellectual, successful in their careers, predominantly white and middle-class, oriented to abstraction rather than to people, and even "cold," Kanner (1943, 250) had noted elsewhere, "In the whole group, there are very few really warmhearted fathers and mothers." Most mothers, it was noted, were college graduates, and many worked outside the home. It was not long before this emerging understanding of autism and parents, facilitated by the popular writing of Bettelheim and by new forms of visibility (such as the case study) already seen in Kanner's work, began to regulate the "good" mother in new ways – as both inherently loving and destructive.

Turning the Gaze Ever Inward: New Forms of Visibility

The emerging terrain of child psychiatry and psychology as distinct disciplines during the first half of the twentieth century in North America brought certain – and new – aspects of mothering and child development into view within everyday talk and text. The cleanliness of a mother's home, for example, or the shape of her embodied practices, such as affection, taken as signs of good versus deficient mothering, came under scientific and public scrutiny. Valerie Walkerdine's (1984) critical work in developmental psychology and child-centred pedagogy suggests that the developing field of child psychology depended for its central object – the normal child – on middle-class, white-child-centred pedagogic practices in homes and schools. This focus brought some aspects of children's and mothers' emotional and psychic lives into view as natural and normal, such as the mother-child dyad, and others into view as deficient, producing new truths about normal child development that were deeply classed, raced, and abled (see also Dehli 1994a, 90; and Rose 1999). The production of such truths, Walkerdine (1984, 149; emphasis in original) states, "make[s] possible both *what can be said* and *what can be done.*" Just as (m)others' potential affirmation of the difference of autism as a valuable way of being becomes illegible based on this view, so too did all ways of being other than white, non-autistic, economically productive, individualistic, and middle-class, as regulated by the authority of Western science, become illegible and almost unspeakable possibilities within the emerging logics of child psychiatry and psychology.

Within the political landscape of the years after the Second World War, when there was an emphasis on stability and the heightened governance of childhood (Rose 1999, 123–29), early infantile autism came into view as a kind of warning sign about the dangers of scientifically unregulated mothering. Autism emerged as an extreme pole of a new category of emotionally disturbed child described during this time (alongside other examples like delinquency, psychosis, and shyness), a category now considered distinct both from adult disturbance and from childhood feeblemindedness or mental retardation (Nadesan 2005, 53–79; Kirkwood 1967; Landsberg 1965a, 1965b; Schill 1957a). New treatment facilities for emotionally disturbed children such as the program for autistic children at Thistletown in Toronto reoccupied older custodial institutional space (*Toronto Daily Star* 1958; *Toronto Star* 1960). However, rather than a custodial emphasis, the focus was on rehabilitation through early, short-term, and often residential treatment for children, together with what I call maternal treatment for mothers. As disability historian Henri-Jacques Stiker (1999, 128) says of rehabilitation in general, it "marks the appearance of a culture that attempts to complete the act of identification, of making identical." Within the postwar logics of rehabilitation, the newly emerged autistic population became "improvable" and possibly curable, or at least capable of achieving some degree of normalization (McGuire 2016; Rose 1985, 37, 39–89). It would be the scientific surveillance of mothers brought into view in everyday text in case studies, for example, that would turn the gaze of all ever inward as they took up their/our own self-governance, including governance of their love and their intimate psychic, emotional, and embodied practice. I provide a detailed description of this process below.

Maternal Treatment

One highly influential character in the history of autism and mothering is psychologist Bruno Bettelheim, director of the Chicago Orthogenic school from 1944 to 1973. Bettelheim wrote several popular books about emotional disturbance in children and had a considerable popular following. He was featured regularly in American newspapers, popular magazines (e.g., *Scientific American* and *Time*), and women's magazines (e.g., *Ladies Home Journal*), and he appeared on television talk shows (e.g., *The Dick Cavett Show*) and in a made-for-television movie, most of which were available to a Toronto and North American audience (Bettelheim 1950, 1967; Nadesan 2005, 97–98; Pollak 1997, 249–85; D. Simpson 2002). Through a Ford Foundation grant (1956–62), Bettelheim devoted much of his career to the study and treatment of autism. He believed, following a psychoanalytic approach (Ehrenreich and English 2005, 285–87), that it was by giving autistic children the love at each stage of development damaged by their disordered parents, predominately by the failure of a mother's so-called natural love, that recovery from emotional disturbance might be found (Bettelheim 1967, 7). This meant that mothers, too, required treatment.[3]

For the purposes of analysis, I am less interested in villainizing Bettelheim the person than in understanding the new forms of visibility that were popularized in his writing and speaking and how these new stories about autism and mothering travelled. Warrandale, for example, described in the *Globe and Mail* (1965, n.p.) as a residential treatment school in Rexdale, Ontario, committed to providing emotionally disturbed children with the "love and essential nourishment for growth," was influenced by Bettelheim's psychoanalytic approach. The school was directed by social worker John Brown, who studied at the University of Chicago and worked with others influenced by Bettelheim's approach. Amid much controversy surrounding his psychogenic approach, Brown implemented the holding method, a therapeutic technique layered with Freudian symbolism aimed at correcting the damage of a mother's disordered love. In one scene from the award-winning Allan King (1967) documentary of everyday life at the school entitled *Warrandale,* two female-appearing staff members are featured in what looks to be an example of maternal treatment. The film shows them forcibly restraining – holding – a boy of approximately ten years of age who is physically struggling against them and telling them to "fuck off." When he asks one of them to get her breasts out of his face, this staff member repeatedly asks him (while continuing to push her breasts into his face), "Why don't you like my breasts in your face?" As the boy spits and struggles, a second female-appearing staff member takes over. She straddles him, pinning his hands above his head and yelling, "I don't care what you think about my breasts! I want to know what you're really feeling!" At length, the boy collapses in tears as Brown himself enters the room, adjusts the hold of his staff member, strokes the boy's face, and reassures him that he is being helped.

Viewers are invited to wonder what kind of breakthrough or help they may have just witnessed both in Brown's paternalistic, scientific adjustment of the forceful care and treatment meted out by these staff and in the boy's tears that fall at the end of this primal scene. Has the boy's regressed development vis-à-vis his mother's damaging love been corrected by forcefully being held to the breast of a mother proxy and guided by the male hand of science?[4] Here, the causal link between a mother's disordered love and the deficit of autism (Garland-Thomson 2001) is made bodily through a symbolic mother's breast. The mother's breast also becomes what might recover this damaged autistic child as guided by the authoritative and paternalistic hand of science, which is quietly positioned in this scene as the ground from which we might know autism, mothering, and human development.

While autistic children were being identified within the new category of autism, separated from their mothers, and moved into residential or day treatment, mothers were also being worked on and brought into view anew. In addition to the symbolic maternal treatment described above, Brown also included "disturbed" mothers and families directly in their children's treatment through recreation and support groups (Stapleton 1965). Other treatment centres with a rehabilitative goal also emerged during this time. The Crèche, a day-treatment program for autistic children in Toronto, operated with a pedagogic and therapeutic emphasis. Mothers were invited to observe the professional technique of social workers as they worked with their disturbed child (*Globe and Mail* 1961, 1962; *Toronto Daily Star* 1961). In addition, Thistletown – a traditional residential-therapeutic hospital program for autistic children – involved mothers in counselling (*Toronto Daily Star* 1958; Landsberg 1965b). Such maternal treatment also moved into the home through therapists' visits, where mothers' domestic practices – such as cleanliness, affection, and domestic routines – could be directly observed and scrutinized for signs of compulsivity or disorder (C. Park 1967, 164–65). Ironically, although a mother's love was considered natural – with the result that mothers were urged, as feminist scholars Barbara Ehrenreich and Deirdre English (2005, 287–88) have documented, to "trust their instincts" – mothers required scientific guidance about what these so-called natural instincts looked like, as brought into view through the touch of Brown's hand or through mothers' observations of professionals (see also O'Malley Halley 2007, 52).

The compelling of mothers, families, and indeed, a wider public into autism treatment, whether symbolic or real, represents a new form of visibility emerging alongside new treatment facilities. Indeed, it was often the mother, instead of or in addition to the autistic child, who was prescribed treatment to "properly" interact with her child, and it was often the mother whose domestic and emotional life was brought into view and governed in new ways. In *The Siege: A Family's Journey into the World of an Autistic Child,* one of the first widely published autism mother memoirs, Clara Claiborne Park (1967) describes her initiation into psychoanalytic treatment for her autistic daughter, Elly, at Anna Freud's Hampstead Clinic in England. Although the experience differed markedly from the chilly reception in other clinics that the family had tried in the United States, Park recounts, "The sessions, to my initial surprise, centred not on Elly but on me. It was not until much later that my husband told me the one thing that the Clinic had withheld; that they had thought that it was less with Elly's emotions I would need help than with my own" (158). The guidance, intervention, and expertise of science were needed to put in order mothers' disordered inner emotional life for the benefit of her child, turning a mother's gaze ever inward. The instinctually loving mother of psychoanalysis was to be guided by the "insidiously paternalistic" advice of professionals (Ehrenreich and English 2005, 290). According to this clinic, however, Park (1967, 155) was an "unusual" mother since she had already demonstrated that disordered love could be corrected with her "persistence and energy." Because of Park's attention and proximity in (m)othering Elly, a task now bolstered by professional guidance, "regressions had been kept temporary. 'A massive regression now appears unlikely'" (155).

Through new forms of visibility like maternal treatment, the value and prestige of professionalism and paternalistic Anglo-Western science now bodily inhabited mothers' everyday practices and conceptions of good mothering. This change initiated a remarkable yet ordinary paradox of care for mothers as both the cause of and the cure for autism in a historical moment when disability and femininity intertwined as deviance, pathology, and disorder (Bailey and Mobley 2018; Garland-Thomson 2001). In my focus groups, the reach of such scientific and professional scrutiny into (m)others' intimate emotional and psychic lives was striking. In response to collages that I made of popular media and science, Rosa and Anna both shared that they had been labelled "crazy" by doctors and professionals during these years and, chillingly, that this scrutiny had turned their gaze inward and reordered their intimate thoughts and feelings to the extent that they chose not to have another child. Anna described how the prestige of science and a doctor's devaluing of her autistic child occupied her when contemplating a second child: "I always had it in mind." Rosa described how she was observed by doctors and professionals and labelled a "cold" mother. This is a particularly cruel form of maternal treatment by a system that devalues both (m)others and autistic people. Although this linkage between autism and mothering recalls Erving Goffman's courtesy stigma, it also exceeds his conception of disabled-nondisabled relations. Goffman (1963, 28) describes a courtesy stigma as the "discredit" that is extended to "the 'wise,' namely, persons who are normal but whose special situation has made them intimately privy to the secret life of the stigmatized individual and sympathetic with it." Yet, in our case, mothers were obliged to "share some of the discredit of the stigmatized person to whom they are related" (30) and more since mothers' disordered nature caused the discredit. Mothers were compelled to open their bodily and psychic lives to scientific and professional scrutiny (see Ehrenreich and English 2005; Walkerdine 1984; and Walkerdine and Lucy 1989) and to turn their own gaze inward as they took up the scientific reordering of their disordered emotional and psychic life, including not having more children. In this way, mothers were invited to negotiate their identities within a new paradox of care governed by the paternalistic hand of science *and* driven by natural maternal love, again shaped by science (McGuire 2016, 36–41). These practices, vocabularies, and techniques of what sociologist Nikolas Rose (1999) calls the "psy" disciplines – psychology and psychiatry – brought mothers into view in new ways in this historical moment and enticed mothers into their own self-governance through these same regimes. Not only does this social process exalt bourgeois, white mothering practices like those taken up by Park (1967, 155), who loves her child with "persistence and energy" as she brokers her own self-governance, but it also puts in order and concretely influences what being a good mother can mean (including choosing not to have another child), perhaps for all mothers, in the intimate ordering of our emotional and psychic lives.

The Case Study

A second form of visibility already operating in Kanner's (1943) published study and further developed by Bettelheim – the case study – brought the newly defined autistic population and their mothers into view in new ways. Case studies depend on the expertise and interpretive frames of their author. They include the collection, viewing, and interpretation of in-depth information – often viewed as the facts – about an individual's so-called exceptional life in all its "peculiar and exotic" history,[5] along with information about the individual's family.[6] Among others, the six-teenth-century book *On Monsters and Marvels* by surgeon Ambroise Paré (1982) is an example of how the case study as a form of medical visibility has long captured the intimate movements of mothers in Western culture and linked them to the production of disability. Myriad case studies in Paré's volume document mothers' bodily implication in so-called childhood deformity, including "narrowness, or smallness of the womb," "the imagination," "having received some blow or fall," and "hereditary diseases" (vii–viii). Here, the supernatural weaves together with emerging scientific understandings of biology and heredity to blame mothers and to explain the abnormal. In psychoanalytic vocabularies, the case study also brought mothers' *psychic* lives into view, subjecting the devalued feminine – the emotional, embodied, and domestic – to scientific governance in new ways.[7]

Bettelheim (1967) fleshed out his psychoanalytic theory of the refrigerator mother through case studies described in his popular book *The Empty Fortress: Infantile Autism and the Birth of the Self,* as well as in popular science features like "Joey: A 'Mechanical Boy,'" which appeared in *Scientific American* (Bettelheim 1959). In *The Empty Fortress,* Bettelheim (1967, 158) posited that the rejecting mother initiated an autistic withdrawal in her child through her own emotional disorder:

The mother felt trapped in her marriage, resented husband and child ... Both to earn enough to keep the family going and to forget it all, she went back to nursing ... She chose to work in a setting that matched her own feelings of hopelessness: a hospital dealing mainly with terminal cases. The infant's total care was left to miscellaneous babysitters, some of whom seemed to inspire Marcia [her autistic child] with great fear. What little the mother did do for Marcia "I did in a hurry. I'm a bossy person."

Here, Bettelheim takes us far afield from the autistic child, implying that the mother's disordered desires, intentions, and wishes, and her careless inattention to Marcia, were damaging and initiating factors in her daughter's autism. This is evidenced, according to Bettelheim, by the example of her resentment and her choice to return to "work in a setting that matched her own feelings of hopelessness" (158). Apart from going to lengths to stress that it is the infant who ultimately responds to a mother's coldness by withdrawing, Bettelheim's book is peppered with statements such as the "mother's pathology is often severe" (69) and the "figure of the destructive mother ... has its source in reality, namely the destructive intents of the mothering person" (71). A mother's absence through work, rejection, or unconscious "aggression" toward her child is understood to be catastrophic, resulting in a host of emotional ills, including infantile autism (Ehrenreich and English 2005, 295–97). Through the published case study, a mother's bodily and psychic movements are brought starkly into public view, creating new and intimate spaces in everyday life that arguably entice all (m)others to turn their gaze ever inward as they take up an affective investment in domestic roles and in the scientific self-governance of their love and maternal instinct.

Bettelheim's signature inclusion of strange photographs, paintings, and drawings by autistic children in his published case studies provided another form of visibility or "diagram... of power" (Dean 1999, 30) popularized during this time. They provided further evidence of harmful mothers and of autism as a withdrawal, and they were part of a nascent discourse of "recovery" from autism (Bettelheim 1967, 89–339). In "Joey: A 'Mechanical Boy'" (Bettelheim 1959, 117), for example, we meet Joey, a "schizophrenic" (i.e., autistic) child who "had been robbed of his humanity" by his rejecting, emotionally neglectful parents, who treated him like a machine. The mother was targeted:

How did Joey become a human machine? We learned that the process had begun even before birth. Schizophrenia often results from parental rejection, sometimes combined ambivalently with love. Joey, on the other hand, had been completely ignored ... "I never knew I was pregnant," his mother said, meaning that she had already excluded Joey from her consciousness ... "I did not want to see or nurse him," his mother declared. "I had no feeling of actual dislike. I simply did not want to take care of him" ... We were struck especially by her total indifference as she talked about Joey. This seemed much more remarkable than the actual mistakes she made in handling him. (117–18)

This mother was clearly out of order. Other possible descriptions of her indifference – such as resisting the constraints of patriarchy and the possibility that not wanting to mother is acceptable – never appear. Ehrenreich and English (2005, 248) describe the mother-child relationship during this time: "If anything should go awry in the mother and child relationship or in the child's development the finger of blame would no longer point at the mother's faulty technique, but at her defective instincts." Here, natural motherhood, grounded in a female biology that necessarily harbours a desire to care for one's infant, was deficient and "remarkably" missing. This mother was "indifferent" to her infant. Her bodily "not-enough-ness" (Bordo 2003, 160–61) as a mother who "excluded Joey from her consciousness" (Bettelheim 1959, 117–18) invaded her child as autistic withdrawal.

Bettelheim (1959, 127) documented how, with the Chicago Orthogenic School's help, "Joey at last broke through his prison ... and became a human child," a humanity that excludes the alterity of autism and the "not-enough-ness" (Bordo 2003, 160–61) of indifferent mothers as illegible sitpoints that are not part of the "in-group" or "the good" (Schutz 1962, 13). Bettelheim (1959, 116) documents Joey's journey back from autistic withdrawal through drawings. The earliest, a line drawing self-portrait, shows Joey as a robot formed from coiled wires. This "symbolizes the child's rejection of human feelings" because of parental rejection, says Bettelheim. A series of drawings follow with more complex configurations of robots and machines, which demonstrate, for Bettelheim, Joey's growing self-esteem and efficacy "since he has acquired hands with which he can manipulate his immediate environment" (119). Joey's "intense anxieties," a result of "rigid but also completely impersonal" (122) toilet training by his mother, led to a series of pictures about sewage and Joey's damaged anal stage of psychosexual development. A final drawing in the series shows a "gentle landscape," which, according to Bettelheim, "symbolizes that human emotions had been regained. At 12, having learned to express his feelings, he was no longer a machine" (126). Through the paternalistic guidance of science, Joey was recovered from his rejecting parents. At no point is room made for the possibility of Joey's agency as an imaginative or different autistic child or for the possibility of alternate ontologies that value relationships beyond the human, such as with robots or objects (Douglas et al., "Re-storying Autism," 2021; Re•Storying Autism Writing Collective 2022).

New forms of visibility, such as maternal treatment and the case study, emerged alongside early infantile autism and psychoanalytic views of childhood development and disorder. These new forms of visibility invited *all* (m)others to gaze anxiously inward and evaluate their bodily practices of mothering and psychic life in new ways. This is the paradox of care: a mother's proximity to her child became essential to normal development yet potentially destructive. She needed scientific instruction yet was understood to be naturally loving. New links were forged in everyday text between autism and the moral and scientific governance of the good/bad mother. This was accomplished through enticing her to turn her gaze ever inward.

A Technology of Affect

Indeed, it was in some measure through the psychoanalytic blame of mothers for autism – what I call in this section a technology of affect (Ahmed 2004; Hook 2005) – that mothers were enticed to turn their own gaze ever inward and seek scientific guidance on the conduct of their inner life. During the 1950s and '60s, psychoanalytic approaches eclipsed, although not entirely, the influence of alternate understandings of autism.[8] Francis Ilg and Louise B. Ames (1961, 65) of the Gesell Institute in New Haven, Connecticut, for example, two doctors who appeared regularly in the 1960s in a child behaviour column in the *Toronto Daily Star*, offered a biological understanding of autism and reassurances for mothers:

The viewpoint which lays the blame for neurosis, emotional upset, autism or other differences in children at the doorstep of the parents (especially the mother), has many adherents. And it has its encouraging side as well as its discouraging one ... Most parents would feel more relaxed if they shared our belief that most cases of brain injury, and even such extreme emotional disturbance deviations as autism, are largely determined by genetic factors.

These more relaxing biological paradigms represented an alternative birth for autism within North America, one that arose alongside psychoanalytic views. Both Leo Kanner (1943) and Austrian pediatrician Hans Asperger (1991) also felt that there was some biological aspect to autism. And in 1964, at the same time that Bettelheim's refrigerator mother was enjoying popularity, Bernard Rimland (1964), a psychologist and father of an autistic son in the United States, put forward a counter-theory of autism as a genetic and neurocognitive disorder (see also Nadesan 2005, 148–49). It was not quite yet the time for the rise of biological understandings of being human derived from cognitive psychology and biogenetics, at least not for autism. Indeed, this moment is one in which the emergence of the "truth" about autism and autism mothers can be grasped in Foucault's (1984) genealogical sense by linking it to historical struggles of power, knowledge, domination, and subordination.

In the 1950s and '60s, it was the scene of the mother-child relationship, particularly that of the nursing infant and a mother's intimate responses, through which normal development proceeded or was arrested (Nadesan 2005, 97–99; see also McDonnell 1998). As feminist historian Molly Ladd-Taylor (1998, 14) articulates, much psychological research during these years agreed that normal development now depended on a mother's proximity: "The studies of [John] Bowlby, [Mary D.] Ainsworth and others fueled the claim that children's mental health depended on mother-love – and that mother-love meant being at home with your child" (see also Ehrenreich and English 2005, 251). Bettelheim (1967, 17) expressed this idea regarding autism, doing so in psychoanalytic terms: "Because while the infant can make it clear, through the way he holds his body, whether or not he feels comfortably held, he cannot ensure that this active expression of his feelings will meet with a positive response. That will depend on how the mother reacts." Here, the mother-infant relationship is imagined to be naturally symbiotic. The infant's actions "make it clear" to the mother what her response should be. A mother's negative emotions, her "too-muchness"

(Bordo 2003, 161) or not quite right love, as responses to the stimulus of her infant's "active expression of feelings" cumulate in a "negative" result in her infant – an eventual autistic withdrawal. A mother's love, or natural adjustment to her infant's "active expression of feelings," garners the so-called positive result of normal development. According to Bettelheim (1967, 66), maternal reactions could range from the most subtle, such as a grip that is slightly too firm, to the most extreme: "I believe that the initial cause of withdrawal is rather the child's correct interpretation of the negative emotions with which the most significant figures in his environment approach him." Bettelheim (among others) even went so far as to assert, "The precipitating factor in infantile autism is the parent's wish that his child should not exist" (125–26; see also Austrian American psychiatrist Margaret Mahler, quoted at 43; and D. Simpson 2002).

Bettelheim's theory was echoed in mass media and popular science circulating at the time: "Thwarted or ignored in early childhood by hostile or indifferent parents, victims of autism sense during infancy that their own action cannot shape their lives" (*Time* 1968). The "parent" referred to, of course, was predominately the mother, who harboured "murderous impulses" (Mahler, quoted in Bettelheim 1967, 70) that her child should not exist and whose subtle and extreme bodily and psychic responses initiated autistic withdrawal by extinguishing her infant's humanity – a humanity in the shape of particular stimulus-response patterns rather than others. This deterministic psychological view of being human ties disordered femininity to disability (Bailey and Mobley 2018; Garland-Thomson 2001; Rice 2015) and has no room for autistic difference, interpretive ambiguity within the mother-child relationship (which might include both love and aggression), alternative modes of (m)othering such as adoptive or dispersed, or creative agency on the part of the (m)other or child. This extreme scientific regulation of mothers' so-called natural love as disordered (or unnatural) and toxic diminishes their humanity and attests to what feminist Adrienne Rich (1986, 277) describes as the "invisible violence of the institution of motherhood" and to what others have described elsewhere as gaslighting (Runswick-Cole, Fogg, and Douglas forthcoming), a form of violence that operates through blame, fear, and guilt.

Accomplished through the psychoanalytic scrutiny of a mother's emotional, psychic, and bodily life – a technology of affect – these subtle and extreme forms of scientific blame, which simultaneously required a mother's proximity, were invitational, urging mothers to follow psychoanalysis's gaze inward. As Clara Claiborne Park (1967, 21) describes,

> I could not say that Elly [her autistic daughter], in the give and take of a family ... was getting far more of what she needed than she could in a residential school ... I could not speak these heretical thoughts; I could do no more than allow them to hover at the edges of my mind ... I feared that as soon as a real psychiatrist learned about our games he would recognize them for what they were – a mother fooling around, lucky if in her inexperience and deep involvement she merely escaped doing harm. For how likely was it that she could escape it? Alone, without professional guidance, what possible qualifications could a mother have with her psychotic child herself?

Here, to be a mother has come to mean being "alone, without professional guidance." Although science would eventually confirm for Park that she had indeed helped her child, she describes her fear of harming her child through "fooling around" and through "deep involvement" in her own mothering practices, which she regarded as "games" enacted outside of the gaze of science. In the documentary *Refrigerator Mothers* (D. Simpson 2002), another mother asks, "What have we done that is so awful that would drive a child into such a regression? I was told that I had not connected or bonded with the child because of inability to properly relate to the child." The esteem of science in the natural attitude had psychically and bodily inhabited conceptions of natural mothering, alongside mothers' interpretive processes. As communication and disability studies scholar Majia Holmer Nadesan (2005, 70) has found, the idea that the paternalistic "input of experts" was tantamount to successful mothering had been well established by the mid-twentieth century through the mental hygiene and child guidance movements. Sociologist and motherhood scholar Jean O'Malley Halley (2007, 52) elaborates on the contradictions during this time: "Not only were women to trust the experts before all else; they were to trust themselves in a way that essentialized women, attaching what it meant to be women to biological understandings of femaleness." Mother blame – a mother's damaging nature – now had a scientific basis (Sousa 2011, 222; see also Vicedo 2021).

A mother's proximity to her child alongside the scientific requisite to order her psychic life and desires had become both the cause of autism and the necessary condition for her child's normal development (see McGuire 2016, 36–41; and Rose 1999, 202–4; also Lalvani 2019). As Park (1967, 121) puts it, a mother's "heretical thoughts" outside the guidance of science – trusting her intuition or other (m)others' knowledge about childrearing – turned out to be dangerous. This paradoxical governance of mothers' care as naturally nurturing yet potentially disordered, as necessary to the achievement of normal development yet harmful, and as therefore in need of scientific governance and maternal treatment is also described by feminist and disability studies scholars (Bailey and Mobley 2018; Douglas 2013; Grinker 2007, 86–88; Lalvani 2019; McGuire 2016; Nadesan 2005, 69–70, 82–83, 97–99; Rose 1999; Walkerdine 1984; Walkerdine and Lucy 1989, 29). What seems heightened with the refrigerator mother is how forms of visibility such as maternal treatment and the case study, along with the affective technology of blame and fear, enticed mothers to turn their gaze inward as they took up the governance of their own so-called disordered, suspect, and potentially damaging feminine psyche, bodily movements, and desires. In hyperbolic terms, the new technology of affect compelled autism mothers – and perhaps all (m)others – into their own self-governance within a new paradox of care that was marked, on the one hand, by a contradictory maternal feminine (at once natural and regulated, loving and scientifically guided, damaging and necessary) and, on the one hand, by a scientific understanding of autism and regulation of the good/bad mother. This autism mother's legacy continues. For example, in one of my focus group discussions, Esther – (m)other to autistic son Ryan, born after 2000, when both genetic understandings of autism and the cultural requisite to breastfeed became prominent – shared her struggle with nursing, one that she revisited often as the possible cause of her son's autism: "It's always been in my head … He would get better if I nursed him." Her struggle with nursing haunted her and redirected her gaze inward toward her own self-doubt, fear, and blame. Here, Bettelheim's chilly refrigerator mother and her disordered love as the cause of something "wrong" – difficulty nursing and autistic withdrawal – loom. A technology of affect aligns mothers' desires and bodily practices (e.g., to keep nursing) with scientific, patriarchal mothering as a necessary condition for normal development.

Identity

The new identity of refrigerator mother emerged in North America as part of a larger re-education of the good mother that followed the Second World War. This mother was compelled to put in order her natural love, desires, feelings, and bodily movements through scientific self-governance and to be proximate to her child as well as to normal development. The refrigerator mother was an extreme example – a cautionary tale about what would happen to the children of mothers (and to mothers themselves) who did not, did not want to, or could not comply. Yet despite this extreme paternalistic treatment, the refrigerator mother was an ironically privileged identity (and in large part, continues to be today), available only to those with temporal, financial, and educational resources – in other words, to white, bourgeois, Anglo-Western mothers (on differential access to subject positions, see Dehli 2008, 47). This mother emerged as part of – and perhaps as handmaiden to – the postwar reassertion of traditional gender roles and the push of white, middle-class mothers back into the home (Ladd-Taylor and Umansky 1998, 12–13; Nadesan 2005, 83). Mothers' role in what Nadesan describes as the "heightened import of childhood in relation to the larger project of social engineering" (83) was differentially shaped by the popular reach of psychoanalytic views. Other bad mothers and their children (e.g., working class, unmarried, Black, and/or Indigenous) transgressed the bourgeois and white norm and were subjected to different – racist and classed – forms of regulation that implied natural inferiority through vocabularies of "natural" development (Caplan 1998; Dehli 1994b, 198; Grinker 2007, 86–88; Ladd-Taylor and Umansky 1998; McGuire 2016, 40–41; O'Malley Halley 2007, 5–15; Walkerdine and Lucy 1989). In the documentary *Refrigerator Mothers* (D. Simpson 2002), for example, a Black mother recalls, "According to my doctor, my son could not be autistic. I was not white. It was assumed that I was not educated, and therefore he was labelled emotionally disturbed ... You can't even be a refrigerator mother. The irony of it all."

To put the matter differently, through heteronormative, settler coloni-alist, raced, gendered, and classed logics, ones that included new forms of knowledge (e.g, child psychology), visibility (e.g., the case study), and affective technology (e.g., psychoanalytic mother blame), the identity autism mother emerged as a paradox – privileged yet subject to extreme governance, naturally loving yet increasingly scientifically (self) ordered, proximate and necessary for normal development yet linked to disorder and pathology. The refrigerator mother thus linked the imperative of white, bourgeois, maternal femininity to the gendered postwar political economy. In addition, this new figure linked bourgeois motherhood to the "improve-ment" of an emerging and predominately white, male, and middle-class identity of autism. These processes of racialization and classism excluded non-normative (m)others and (m)othering from even the *possibility* of being good, and their children from being normal (Ladd-Taylor and Umansky 1998, 9–10). It is to the emergence of the identity of autism during this time as anything but normal that I now turn.

Within everyday talk and text in Toronto during the 1950s and '60s, autism was described in the starkest of terms as a terrible problem, one desperately in need of a solution and interesting only as a problem (Abberley 1998, 93; D. Mitchell 2002, 15; Titchkosky and Michalko 2009, 2). Suffering from what journalist Michelle Landsberg (1965a, n.p.), for example, called the most "horrifying and far more hopeless" form of "emotional disturbance," autistic children were "withdrawn to the world ... entirely cut off from reality." These children were, according to journalist Leone Kirkwood (1967, n.p.), "fearful, illogical, uncontrolled." They lived, wrote journalist Wendy Darroch (1966, n.p.), in "fantasies ... out of contact with reality" and, according to the *Toronto Daily Star* (1969, 29), in "lonely little worlds." A "forgotten group," autism was a "relatively rare condition" (*Toronto Daily Star* 1960, 4) that nevertheless meant, wrote journalist Florence Schill (1957b, n.p.), a pressing "problem that is too big" for parents to "solve." Autistic children were, indeed, to return to sociologist Erving Goffman (1963, 5), considered "not quite human," their "differentness" an undesired disruption to the natural mother-child bond. That is, autism emerged as an unwanted and stigmatizing disruption to the Global North's white, bourgeois, individualizing social construction of mothering as intensive labour within the mother-child dyad as natural and normative.

Yet the identity of autism emerged, too, as something other and more than the disruptive production of stigma, which Goffman (1963, 5) describes as an individual "attribute" interacting with stereotypes (or norms) that make a person become "discredited" or discreditable within social processes and relationships. Autism emerged, after Kanner, as a subtraction or lack rather than as an attribute, a *withdrawal/regression* "that incarcerates an otherwise 'normal' or nonautistic self" (McGuire 2016, 39–40) in a prison, state of aloneness, or "empty fortress" (Bettelheim 1967). Within such terms, it is impossible to imagine autism as anything beyond a tragedy, let alone a sitpoint, and thus as a different way of being in the world, a viable form of life, or even an identity to negotiate or perform (Butler 2004). Even the most hopeful voices, like those of Ilg and Ames (1960, n.p.), understood autism as something to be remedied, only this time through the "acceptance of them, and reasonable warmth" shown by mothers who "take part in their rituals, find the clues which are meaningful to them." Autistic children were at best thought "improvable," if not always curable, through the emerging treatment regimens for mothers and children alike that might teach, according to the *Globe and Mail* (1962, n.p.), these "mentally disturbed youngsters how to be children." Indeed, the call for treatment facilities was common in this time.

Bettelheim's work was formative, along with Kanner and others, of the understanding of autism as aloneness and a withdrawal from humanity. As a survivor of the Dachau and Buchenwald concentration camps, Bettelheim (1967, 68) introduced troubling parallels between the trauma responses of prisoners that he witnessed in the camps and the behaviours of autistic children that he observed at his school: "Infantile autism is a state of mind that develops in reaction to feeling oneself in an extreme situation, entirely without hope." He saw similarities between autistic children's and prisoners' manner – their "averted gaze," "withdrawal into fantasy," "self-stimulation," "helpless rages" and "empty rote learning" (67–68). All these things Bettelheim understood as evidence of a child being forced to cope with utterly hopeless and extreme circumstances. Indeed, on *The Dick Cavett Show,* Bettelheim claimed, "This autistic child felt that everybody wants him to be dead as the Nazis indeed wanted all Jews to be dead. And when that cannot in one's own inner feeling be counteracted – Yes, somebody cares terribly much about me! – then one is so hopeless that one has not the energy to fight back" (D. Simpson 2002). Like the camp guards, mothers' neglect and destructive intent perpetrated near murderous harm, initiating a "massive withdrawal" from normal development and the human condition in the form of autism (Bettelheim 1967, 126; McDonnell 1998, 223–26). In a very disturbing and ironic sense, Bettelheim's assertion that the "autistic child felt that everybody wants him to be dead" speaks not to mothers' neglect or violence but to Western culture's violent intolerance of any difference outside of a narrow conception of the human as white, autonomous, rational, masculine, economically productive, and indeed, all grown up. The feminine and other alternative realms that centre interdependence, affirm difference, embrace affect, and hold ambiguity are devalued sitpoints to be excluded from what is regarded as the normative human (Hughes et al. 2005). Understanding how (m)others live with – and therefore both comply with and resist – the paradox of their newly emerging identity calls for a rethinking and revaluing of autism and the feminine not only as culturally produced identities but also as viable, disruptive, and possibly even revelatory differences in the sense of challenging dominant Western Enlightenment understandings of the human, identity, difference, (m)othering, and care.

3

Returning the Psychoanalytic Gaze

Ironically, it was the newly emerged identities – autism and autism mother – together with biological understandings of autism yet to come (e.g., see Rimland 1964) that would compose the terms of (m)others' and parents' growing resistance to overt forms of mother blame. The intense surveillance and blame of mothers through psychoanalysis was particularly heightened for mothers of disabled children (Blum 2007; Douglas and Klar 2019; Douglas et al., "Mad Mothering," 2021; P. Ferguson 2002; Panitch 2008, 19; Ryan and Runswick-Cole 2008, 206; Sousa 2015, 222) after the Second World War. A disabled child was evidence of a mother's deeply defective nature. Such defective mothers posed a threat not only to their child but also to the community and nation, as they disrupted the nature of the good mother role in the domestic realm, a disruption that threatened the patri-archal, white supremacist, bourgeois, and ableist postwar capitalist order and social construction of motherhood (Blum 2007; Ehrenreich and English 2005, 208–15; see also Brodie 1995; and Weusten 2011). Indeed, the prestige of autism science and its translation into text during this time meant that mothers, rather than socially oppressive systems, became the target. As feminist psychologist Paula Caplan (1998, 127) puts the matter, "Blame mom ... for being horrible rather than only human" (see also Sousa 2005).

Within popular media and science – including mothers' own accounts of everyday life with their autistic child – autism mother identity emerged in a complex relationship of both complicity and resistance within dom-inant regimes of mothering and care. Sociologist Nikolas Rose (1999,

153–54), writing on the linkages between governance regimes, expertise, and practices of the self, suggests that "in the space between the behaviours of actual children and the ideals of the norm, new desires and expectations, and new fears and anxieties could be inspired in parents." Although shame, fear, and the imperative to normalize their child may indeed have been among such "new desires and expectations," autism mothers' contradictory experiences caring for their autistic child, as we shall see below, also opened space in which the meaning of autism, (m)othering, and care might be both resisted and imagined anew. Tracing a small glimpse of this story here means that this chapter begins to read everyday text and talk about and by autism mothers a little differently.

Rereading as Resistance

As early as 1957, after the first 150 cases of autism were identified in a survey undertaken by the Hospital for Sick Children in Toronto, (m)others and families began organizing (Schill 1957a, 1957b; see also Panitch 2008). At a time when the governance of so-called abnormal populations was shifting to demarcate so-called emotionally disturbed (including autistic) and mentally retarded children in Ontario, mothers helped to found the Ontario Association for Emotionally Disturbed Children, described by journalist Schill (1957b, 11) as an early advocacy organization that "formed to discuss ways and means of treatment facilities as well as to discuss mutual problems." In addition to engaging in nascent disability activism, this organization produced a newsletter and provided briefs to the provincial government on improving education, health care, and treatment for their children (e.g., see Ontario Association for Emotionally Disturbed Children 1964). Disability studies scholar and activist Melanie Panitch (2008) traces the history of activist mothers during this time, with a focus on mothers of intellectually disabled children. Panitch argues that mothers of disabled children emerged as a "vital force shaping advances in disability policy and providing lifelines of information to other parents" (7). Although no comprehensive scholarly history of autism (m)other activism in Ontario before the 1970s has been written, this small peek into organizing suggests that these (m)others were, from the beginning, part of this larger collective movement – understood as a nascent "disability commons" in action (Runswick-Cole and Goodley 2018, 231; see also Vicedo 2021). Activist (m)others challenged custodial forms of care with short-term or community models, established new treatment facilities that included educational possibilities for their children (albeit in the problematic language of rehabilitation and treatment), and spoke from their experience to reimagine the meaning of autism and (m)othering outside of oppressive and individualizing psychoanalytic vocabularies, thus recuperating autism mothers from more overt forms of blame (McGuire 2016, 42–43; Panitch 2008; Sousa 2005; Vicedo 2021).

These accomplishments are significant. Responding to the patriarchal, ableist governance that composed autism mothers' lives, including psychoanalytic/scientific mother blame and exclusion from the good mother role, (m)others, parents, and families collectively resisted power through new spaces such as the self-help groups that arose in reaction to their encounters with professionals, to the labelling of their children as autistic, and to mothers' so-called natural caring role in the domestic realm (Panitch 2008; Ryan and Runswick-Cole 2009). These roles were complex and included, as disability studies and gender scholar Rannveig Traustadottir (1991, 217) asserts, not only caring work in the home and love for their autistic child but also the extension of "care beyond their own child to broader community or societal concerns."

This complexity came alive when two (m)others in my focus groups, Anna and Rosa, whose sons were in their twenties, articulated their response to being labelled "cold" mothers by doctors. Anna, who resisted the label through her own academic study and advocacy, put it this way: "I mean, I'm sorry, I don't need to be told what to do." Anna was met with quiet and affirming choruses of "Mm-hmm's" and "Ya's" from other (m)others in the group, which turned to raucous and ironic laughter when Esther, whose son was born after 2000, added that those categorized as the "newer version" of (genetic) autism mothers are still implicitly blamed, only this time through their ostensible choices. This is one way to begin to tell the hidden "disability story of parents" a little differently (Dona M. Avery, quoted in Ryan and Runswick-Cole 2009, 43; see also Panitch 2008; Ryan and Runswick-Cole 2008; and T. Thomas 2003). To push my example further, the focus groups can be understood as having invoked a "disability commons" (Runswick-Cole and Goodley 2018, 231) where (m)others built on each other's stories, formed an ad hoc network (Piepzna-Samarasinha

2018), and supported each other in retelling and documenting difficult stories. (M)others also shared what disability studies scholars Aime Hamraie and Kelly Fritsch (2019, 2) call access "hacks" – or "practices of critique, alteration and reinvention of our material-discursive world" – at the level of everyday life for their own and each other's autistic offspring, pooling their knowledge to affirm autistic difference in education, health care, and life, including access to cultural, legal, and other resources.

In some ways, to borrow from Panitch (2008, 2), the work of activist (m)others to "improve the quality of life for people with disabilities and their families" beginning in 1950s and '60s Toronto – animated by the comments of the (m)others labelled refrigerator mothers in my focus groups – aligned with the social model's aspirations around disabled people's right to help and support. For some disability studies scholars, too, mother activism was an important thread within the forming of the disability rights movement in North America (O'Toole 2004; Panitch 2008, 4). Such activism is an indication that as powerful as tactics of governance are, they can never be complete. Difference, like human agency, always exceeds. In the words of disability historian Henri-Jacques Stiker (1999, 51), "We are always other than what society made us and believes us to be." In a sense, mothers' resistance and activism during this time are an example of a different kind of technology of affect formed within the matrices of normalizing scientific and patriarchal regimes – a politicized anger and love as a response to blame and a force of resistance transform- ative of their child's treatment as well as their own. For these mothers, the "personal" had become "political" long before the forging of this 1970s feminist rallying call (see Bailey and Mobely 2018; Boler 1999, 114; and hooks 2000).

At the same time, it is important to notice how mothers' and parents' resistance during this time took place on the same terms as the regimes of scientific, racist, bourgeois, gendered governance discussed in detail above. Constituted as the living paradox of the identity autism mother, mothers were complicit. Although activist mothers and parents pushed the limits of the meaning of autism and care and sought to address larger social structures of exclusion, they also aligned themselves with disability through what sociologist Rosalyn Darling (2003) calls a "crusadership" orientation that seeks systemic change to normalize family life (see also Traustadottir 1991).

Rehabilitative, short-term treatment models, as radical as they were, nevertheless sought to achieve identity and were thus complicit with understandings of autism as an "undesired differentness" (Goffman 1963, 5; Stiker 1999, 128). Moreover, this kind of advocacy and activism involved a new requirement of proximity as well as resources that were accessible only to the most privileged of mothers yet were demanded by all. These contradictory demands, as we shall see, continue to shape the identity of autism mothers today as necessarily proximate yet potentially destructive, loving yet scientifically regulated.

Working at the intersection of interpretive and critical approaches within disability and feminist studies suggests that there is a way to understand (m)others' resistance and complicity in a more radical sense and to revalue mothers and embodiment identified as autistic in the process. Panitch (2008, 12) describes how activist mothers in her study "express themselves in two streams. One is informed by socially conventional expectations and values and the second is informed by their lived experience." It is the disruptive and revelatory possibility of (m)others' complex negotiations within the space between social convention and experience that I am interested in attending to here. In her work on text as a site of social action, Tanya Titchkosky (2007, 21) describes a "liminal space between subject and ground." I understand this space – much like the space of rupture that I encountered as an autism mother, which I have described in my introductory chapters – as a creative, embodied pedagogic space where body and world intertwine. This is a space opened through (m)others' encounters with their/our different child as well as through mothers' bodily and psychic entanglements with both the constraints and incompleteness of power, entanglements that occur because of everyday encounters with text. Disability and mothering researchers Cynthia Lewiecki-Wilson and Jen Cellio (2011, 2) also describe the potential generativity of this liminal space in (m)others' lives: "In liminal space, cultural constructions of the subject and situated, embodied experiences intermix, and from/in this fluid boundary state, resistance to cultural scripts and emergent knowledge can potentially arise." Indeed, (m)others' activism itself suggests that so-called refrigerator mothers did not completely come to experience or conduct themselves through the ever-inward-turning gaze of psychoanalytic regimes (Dean 1999). Discussing the overt mother blame in the mass media, popular science, and autism science at the time, Clara Claiborne Park (1967, 127) states, "These were threatening ideas to confront. Yet somehow they did not take hold." Moreover, says Park, in everyday life with her autistic daughter, Elly, there are "heretical thoughts" that "hover at the edges of my mind" (121). During our focus group discussion on this topic, Rosa also told us of her own "heretical thoughts" that resisted the dominant scientific sense of her nonspeaking daughter, Elizabeth, as asocial and of herself as "cold." Much like Park, in the intimate spaces of her home, far removed from the cold gaze of professionals, Rosa described a relationship with her daughter that was filled with music, love, and warmth and an understanding of her daughter as highly social. It is to the radical potential of the liminal space where dominant ideas do not "take hold" and heretical ones "hover" that I finally now turn.

Writing Back

Using an adaptation of the case study, autism mothers turned the gaze on themselves and began to write back to psychoanalytic power in the form of memoirs and first-person narratives about life together with their autistic child, narratives of a kind that is now proliferating. Many of these memoirs included meticulous documentation of mothers' relationships with their autistic child, but unlike with medical case studies, it was not only so-called disorder that mothers were documenting (Vicedo 2021). An early example was Park's *The Siege: A Family's Journey into the World of an Autistic Child*, published in 1967, the same year as Bruno Bettelheim's *The Empty Fortress: Infantile Autism and the Birth of the Self*. Park's is the story of the author's "siege" upon the solitary world of her autistic daughter, Elly, told in the form of a middle-class, educated, white mother's narrative of their life at home with family and within the maze of professional psychiatry and popular psychology. Trying to understand her daughter's autism and her role as mother, Park (1967, 125) reads (and has a command of) not only all the autism experts (e.g., Bruno Bettelheim, Leo Kanner, and Bernard Rimland) but also other autism mother narratives and mass media accounts as key pedagogical terrains for mothers:

> We hear on every hand that what we do in the first months of life ... may mark our child forever. Who are we to qualify this account of our responsibility? Even the parents of normal children move with a certain know-

ledgeable edginess. What goes through the minds of parents who know they have a child whose development has gone wrong?[1]

Park's response to this central question is complex, being both complicit with and a radical challenge to the psychoanalytic and gendered regimes dominant at the time. She comes quite resoundingly to qualify expert accounts of mother blame and to reclaim maternal expertise in relationship with autistic difference as grounds of knowing and being together differently even while she invokes conventional understandings of autism, advocates for expert guidance, and engages various normalizing therapies. Anthropologist Gail Landsman (2009, 212) and researcher and advocate Amy C. Sousa (2005, 229) also note this tension in their work on contemporary (m)othering and disability. Here, I consider these complex tensions during the heyday of psychoanalysis to pry open space where both autism and autism mothers might be read anew. Consequently, my rereading of Park's well-known and much-cited autism mother narrative is its own site of social action and resistance (see also Douglas 2013; and Vicedo 2021).[2]

In some ways, Park's (1967, 5–6) narrative proceeds on the same terms as those of Kanner (1943), Bettelheim (1967), and popular media accounts – in other words, on the terms of a good mother identity, normal development, and emerging views of autism as bizarre, otherworldly, solitary, and tragic: "Elly's eerie imperviousness, her serene self-sufficiency, belonged to those who, like the fairies, can live somehow untouched by the human experience." Here, Park invokes conventional metaphors of autism as aloneness – a child who exists in our world yet is not touched by the presence of others. Park seems to have no language to describe Elly's difference in familiar terms (Weusten 2011, 66–67). Kanner (1943, 218) helped to forge this understanding of autism as aloneness in his original 1943 article when he set out to newly describe and distinguish this group of children who were "happiest when left alone." As Jordyn Jack (2014) points out, Kanner (1943, 217) also introduced autistic children as "markedly and uniquely" different from other disordered children. Unlike those in the category of so-called mental retardation (a distinction not made by the earlier category of feebleminded), which was emerging in North America during this time, autistic children were thought by Kanner to possess a potentially normal intelligence and therefore to be capable of learning, improvement, and even normalization

(Jack 2014, 52–53). Park (1967, 36–37) makes note of Kanner's distinction and in some ways uses the privileged, white, bourgeois identity of autism and intelligence to drive a hero narrative of trying to break through to the other world and to rescue the presumed normal, intelligent child trapped and aloof inside this seeming fortress. Indeed, Park recounts several moments along the way within her narrative of bourgeois motherhood when she tirelessly experiments with various so-called maternal pedagogies to try and catch glimpses of Elly's intelligence and further her normal development: "Three days after I had made a cross, she made one. Surely, it took more intelligence to copy a figure from memory at a remove of three days than to imitate it immediately afterwards as a normal child would do?" (15–16). Even though "these were lights that flickered and went out" (16), they were, for Park, hopeful signs that there might be potential in Elly for normal development and that good mothering – intensive labour within the mother-child dyad – might unhinge her captivity by autism.

Yet even on these now-familiar and problematic terms (i.e., mothers' love as necessary to normal development, autism as aloneness, and the withdrawal of a normal child), Park's narrative introduces an alternative way to care about autism and autistic people through the disruptive, affirming, and ethical moments that open within her descriptions of her life together with her daughter, Elly. Although her tale parallels the romantic hero's narrative prevalent in the psychoanalytic approaches outlined above (Jack 2014), Park (1967, 261) offers no resolution: "It has been a long siege. As a siege, it has been successful, for we have reached Elly. Whatever else she is, she is no longer walled off from affection. Yet we are not the first to discover that to reach another human being is not in itself to cure." Park does not claim to recover her daughter, Elly, through her love or through her engagement with psychoanalytic approaches and professionals (Jack 2014, 50–56). Rather, she challenges the notion of natural love and the prestige of scientific expertise. First, based on her experiences with Elly, Park suggests that love is more than just an emotion. Consistent with feminist philosopher Sara Ruddick's (2005, 13–27) notion of "maternal thinking," Park (1967, 195) argues that love is also a practical form of intelligence and reflection arising from everyday life together: "Intelligence and love are not natural enemies. Nothing sharpens one's wits for the hints and shadows of another's thinking as love does … There are millions of parents who practice this love daily ... knowing that love is a technique as well as an emotion." "Intelligent love" means that being a good mother involves thoughtful practices and reflection gleaned from everyday life together, as well as from science, rather than from somehow natural practices that flow from a mother's natural love (see also Douglas 2013; and Vicedo 2021). In this way, Park redefines the meaning of being a good mother as thoughtful care, which might also be taught and learned (Weusten 2011, 60). Park (1967, 140; emphasis in original) also confronts professional and psychoanalytic expertise, inverting the terms "cold mothers" and "mother blame" after she and her husband encounter professionals more aptly described by such metaphors: "I think I can guess how we appeared to them – highly intellectual, cool, controlled, well-informed, prime examples of Kanner's parents. We *were* controlled. We had no alternative. Refrigerator professionals create refrigerator parents." Although she fits the description of a refrigerator mother, Park refuses its pathologizing terms. Rather than seeking recovery, Park negotiates the tensions between love and scientific expertise as a form of practical love grounded in experience and in the valuing and affirming of embodied difference identified as autism. This kind of love undermines the age-old reason-nature and mind-body oppositions, as well as the prestige of Western science, and it recuperates the devalued feminine realm from the grip of psychoanalysis.

By subverting scientific expertise and embracing and affirming Elly's unique way of being, Park negotiated the irremediable ethical paradox of what it means to be an autism mother and to care – to love our unique autistic children *and* to scientifically remedy their difference by achieving normative identity. She narrates Elly's "long, slow" progress, during which speech and other skills emerged in their own unique patterns through Park's (1967, 217) recognition that "we must speak to her in her own language." For Park, the factors that might slowly bring shape to her daughter's life were this reclaimed love and this expertise based not only on a mother's caring role in relationship with autistic ways of being as an alternative site of knowledge but also on a critical engagement with scientific theory and with the views of professionals, both of which Park read and challenged. Park writes, "The wise and gentle professionals of the most famous children's clinic in the world had given me the reassurance I could not give myself. They did not think that in my lonely and presumptuous work I had injured my child" (158). Although complicit with normalized, scientific understandings of human development and progress, Park simultaneously shifted the ground of knowing about autism. Expertise grounded in mothers' love and experience – "parents are *there*" (176; emphasis in original) and know the "language" of their children (179) – as an alternative site of knowledge about our world together could now challenge the rational ground of scientific authority and professionals in the understanding and treatment of both autism and autism mothers.

Park's (1967, 83) narrative articulates (albeit in somewhat normalizing language) the possibility of what might be considered a different kind of care, one that is grounded in relationships that affirm the difference of our autistic child to insert new understandings that challenge dominant Western scientific regimes:

> We have always made up little songs to fit recurring situations; like many parents we had a good-night song, and others of which we were scarcely conscious. One of these was a car song; to the simplest of tunes, we sang, "Riding in the car. Riding in the car. Elly and her mama go riding in the car" ... Surprisingly, she sang it first not when riding in the car, but one day after I had merely spoken the words. This was the beginning of a curious and encouraging development; what we came to call Elly's leit-motifs. We became aware that this strange child who could not take in the simplest word could absorb a tune and make it do duty for an idea.

Elly's difference is humanized: she uses music, not spoken language, to interact with her mom and to communicate her ideas. In focus groups, Rosa and Anna, too, described how they came to understand their nonspeaking autistic children as they communicated love and expressed feelings and empathy through music. Anna's son David, for example, who types to communicate (and who gave Anna permission to share) told her that music is "where I am calm and peaceful. It touches every single atom in me and sends me good feelings. I understand this world and people from music." In this more embodied, relational view, autism mothers become something more than disordered. Their engagement intellectually and practically is curious and creative rather than cold and disordered. Moments of what literary scholar Josje Weusten (2011, 62–64) calls "wordless proximity" characterized Park's (1967, 92) experiences of such affirming care and such loving, thoughtful engagement with difference marked as autistic:

> I crouch beside her, ready to enter her world in a way she can appreciate if she will and ignore if she wants to. My finger goes under the blanket, then my hand. No response. My head follows. Elly knows I am there. There are two of us now, withdrawn from the world but near each other. It is very inward, warm and dark – a physical expression for undemanding intimacy. There is nothing difficult here – nothing to do, nothing to say. The only thing you need is time and willingness to spend a lot of it with your head under a blanket.

Like Rosa and Anna, Park engaged a different way of being together with Elly, opening beyond that of the normative demands of communicative language to be near yet not in Elly's world, a moment of warm intimacy and uncertain distance that is perhaps suggestive of the ambivalent togetherness and fundamental alterity of us all (Levinas 1969, 33–52, 72–81; McGuire and Michalko 2011). This kind of affirming care is echoed in other autism mothers' stories of their life together with their different child. "They are whole people," one mother in the documentary *Refrigerator Mothers* (D. Simpson 2002) tells the viewers. "They just have a different culture. A different way of communicating. A different language." Perhaps it is in the (re)turning of our gaze toward these shared yet disqualified knowledges and practices – which "hover" at the edges of scientific discourse (whether in mid-century psychoanalysis or in today's biogenomics) yet dwell at the centre of (m)others' lives together with their/our children – that (m)others might work together with feminist and disability studies scholars and activists across our differences and engage critical forms of resistance grounded in different embodiments and care. It is in this space, too, that we can, with Katherine Runswick-Cole and Daniel Goodley (2018, 231), "invoke the disability commons" and unmother autism (see also E. Kim 2017; and Runswick-Cole and Ryan 2019) by revealing, and dismantling, the paradox of care and (m)othering in the form of intensive remedial labour as its own cruel fiction in the service of neoliberal, ableist, patriarchal capitalism.

4

Autism's Mother Therapists
Behaviourism's Gaze

Beginning in the late 1960s, autism's mother therapists emerged within a newly configured paradox of care that cast mothers into the role of heroes recovering their child from autism. Biological understandings of autism gained popularity during these years, particularly as they came to be articulated within genetic, neurocognitive, and behavioural approaches (Nadesan 2005). These years were also witness to an emerging cultural fascination with autism in the Global North (Murray 2008). Everyday depictions of the horrifying and the exceptional about autism proliferated, now couched in a newly configured story about tragedy, parent advocacy, genetic research, and recovery from autism. Everything from behavioural methods for "training" autistic children to facilitated (or typed) communication, the biology of autistic brains, and so-called autistic savantism became objects for the scientific and popular gaze (e.g., see Bower 1986; Dineen 1991; and Rimland 1978).

The medical classification and diagnostic criteria of autism also changed during these years, reflecting a shift from understanding autism as a rare disorder to understanding autism as a spectrum of disorders that began to be diagnosed somewhat more frequently (see Wing 1981, 1988). Psychologist Uta Frith (1993) estimates that autism diagnosis using broader criteria changed the rate of diagnosis from 1 in 10,000 to 1 or 2 in 1,000. In 1980, "infantile autism" first appeared in the *Diagnostic and Statistical Manual of Mental Disorders III* (*DSM-III*), published by the American Psychiatric Association. A year later, British psychologist and mother Lorna Wing translated the work of Hans Asperger into English. These changes in thinking were reflected in subsequent *DSM-III* and *DSM-IV* revisions that introduced Asperger's disorder, Pervasive Development Disorder – Not Otherwise Specified, and autistic disorder as an autism spectrum ranging from mild to severe (Singh 2016, 24–26). At the same time, autism mother (and father) memoirs followed Clara Claiborne Park's (1967) *The Siege: A Family's Journey into the World of an Autistic Child*, and an emergent neurodiversity movement led by autistic individuals began to articulate autism as a viable and different way of being in the world – a being in neurodiversity (Sinclair 1993; D. Williams 2009).[1]

Autism, however, would still primarily be understood during these years as a tragic disorder, this time with a biological origin that mothers must work to overcome through their intensive love within the mother-child dyad as well as through their heroic embodiment of new approaches to care, most particularly behavioural therapies. Using an ethic of disruption, this chapter traces the emergence of autism's mother therapist genealogically, with interpretive pauses along the way, working to reveal the cultural ground of everyday text during the years when biological views predominated (approximately 1965–99). Although other mothers of disabled children would also emerge as activists, heroes, and mother therapists during this time (Panitch 2008), autism mothers became the hero par excellence of newly (re)emerging Western conventional biological understandings of the human. Alongside these understandings was the rise of neoliberalism and intensifying cultural contradictions in North America between freedom and constraint, love and science, masculine and feminine. Also intriguing is (m)others' complicit resistance within these new biological and intensive mothering regimes, particularly in terms of how (m)others began to challenge the paternalism of scientific authority with the "maternal" and, at certain moments, to narrate the difference of autism and their love for their autistic child in ethical, rather than tragic, ways of being human together, the topic of Chapter 5.

By the 1990s, the number of texts about autism mothers retrievable from online databases and library archives (i.e., newspapers, books, and magazines) had grown from the hundreds to the thousands. This proliferation perhaps marked the beginning of the "discursive explosion" around autism in our own time (Foucault 1980a 17–18; Hacking 2010). However, it is the quality of the shift from psychoanalytic to biological approaches as the new dominant framing of autism and mothering, rather than the quantity, that occupies me here. I draw from my archive, including focus groups, to trace emerging forms of governmental power – new forms of knowledge, visibility, technology, and identity – that reconfigured lines between the abnormal and normal human and reconfigured what constituted a mother's duty to care (Dean 1999, 30–32). It would be through the retraining of autism mothers' gaze and through self-governance based on biological understandings of the human that such lines would be redrawn and that the mother therapist as cultural hero would emerge for all (m)others.

Retraining the "Maternal" Gaze

It would in part be the biological arguments and advocacy of American psychologist Bernard Rimland (1964), together with parents searching for alternatives to institutionalization and condemning psychoanalytic views, that the mother-child relationship would be opened to governance anew during these years. Beginning in the mid-1960s, parents drew on Rimland's biological arguments to disavow the refrigerator mother and to instead educate the public about biological views, fundraise for scientific research, and secure public funding for therapies, services, and respite (Silverman 2012). Local, provincial, and national autism associations were formed in Toronto and elsewhere (*Globe and Mail* 1976; Kirkwood 1972, 12; *Toronto Star* 1972). This was one location of the "birth" of autism advocacy in Canada (see McGuire 2016, 41–44, 82–86).

Although advocacy may be a typical part of many parents' everyday lives together with their child – including calls to the teacher and guidance of a child's friendships – autism advocacy emerged as a complex, heightened form of organizing akin to activism in that it called for systemic change and moved beyond concern for individual children (Ryan and Runswick-Cole 2009; Traustadottir 1991, 217). Parent advocates adopted what Rosalyn Darling (2003, 882–83) calls a "crusadership" orientation to disability during these years, one that pressed for systemic change to achieve normalization for families, namely access to educational placements, medical treatment, financial support, employment, and community living. Toronto parents and (m)others fought to maintain institutional ties that supported initiatives such as educational inclusion within the community (i.e., supports to go to school), and they raised sharp concerns about the lack of community supports (Enright 1989; Galt 1995; Wright 1995). Parents were also involved in innovating alternative modes of communication for autistic children – namely facilitated (or typed) communication (see Dineen 1991) – and advocated for scientific research as well as for services and respite care (Enright 1989). Whereas many parents who adopt a crusadership orientation disengage from their activist work once a level of normalization is achieved for their family, this was not the case for many autism advocates, who continued their activist work on behalf of other families (Darling 2003, 882–83; Ryan and Runswick-Cole 2009). As we have seen for the refrigerator mother, the achievements of mother and parent activists are significant, acting as important sources of information and support for families as well as representing the possible beginnings – ones that go back to the 1950s in Ontario – of the disability rights movement in Canada itself (O'Toole 2004; Panitch 2008, 7; Schill 1957a, 1957b). This work continues the "disability story of parents" (Dona M. Avery, quoted in Ryan and Runswick-Cole 2009, 43) and is a testament to parents' historical involvement in activism and advocacy that "invoke the disability commons" (Runswick-Cole and Goodley 2018, 231) to ameliorate their disabled children's lives (Panitch 2008, 2; Silverman 2012).

With emerging biological views, however, resistance to overt psychoanalytic blame would ironically become the ground of new forms of governance and lived complicity within biological and intensive mothering regimes during this time (Foucault 1980a, 94; Hays 1996). That is, biomedical remediation and the achievement of normal behaviour and identity for autistic children also became a key goal – perhaps the overriding goal – of autism advocacy. Breaking away from the earlier Ontario Association for Emotionally Disturbed Children, autism advocacy recast lines in Ontario between those labelled "autistic," "emotionally disturbed," or "mentally retarded" (Gorril 1976; Shamsie 1977; L. Stone 1981). Within such reconfigured terms, an autism mother's gaze was scientifically retrained away from her own disordered psychic and emotional life and toward her participation in her child's behavioural and biological remediation through a new form of intensive labour in the mother-child dyad. Although echoes of the refrigerator mother and her disordered psyche would remain, ascending biological and genetic views meant that autism mothers – an identity still predominately white and middle-class – were relieved of their damaging feminine nature and could now be a potentially therapeutic (healing or corrective), rather than destructive, force in their children's lives (e.g., see Callwood 1976; and Ross 1989). Although the mother-child dyad and relationship would still be central to the governance of autism mothers and to the paradox of care, biological views shifted governance away from maternal treatment and overt mother blame and toward the intensive practice of new scientifically grounded therapeutic techniques to change her child's biology and correct her child's autistic "behaviour." This newly emerging good mother was that of autism's mother therapist, who carried her own forms of covert blame.

New Forms of Knowledge: Cognitive Psychology and Behaviourism

First, let us consider American psychologist Bernard Rimland's (1964) biological argument in *Infantile Autism: The Syndrome and Its Implications for a Neural Theory of Behaviour* and its place within autism advocacy history and cognitive-psychological views more broadly as key within the shifting forms of governance during this time. Like Bruno Bettelheim's (1967) arguments in *The Empty Fortress: Infantile Autism and the Birth of the Self,* many of Rimland's arguments would weave their way through popular media and science as well as through autism mother networks, although other autism experts also helped along the way (e.g., see Frith 1993; and on Ole Ivar Lovaas, see Moser 1965). An autism father himself, Rimland attempted, with the publication of *Infantile Autism,* to refute oppressive understandings and treatments like psychoanalysis that physically removed children from mothers and families. Rimland emerged as both a pseudo-scientific authority and what sociologist Howard Becker (1963, 147–49) called a "moral entrepreneur," using his position of privilege to crusade with near religious fervour to change the rules around autism and parenting. For Rimland and other parent advocates, this work included, among other things (see below), debunking the psychoanalytic view of autism and replacing it with the biological. In 1965, Rimland started the Autism Society (later renamed the Autism Society of America) and widely disseminated behavioural and other pseudo-scientific treatments for autism, such as vitamin therapy, that were grounded in his biological theories (Rimland 1993, xiv–xv).

Rimland's advocacy and research were part of a larger shift in scientific understandings of the human during these years. Cognitive psychology and the newly emerging neurosciences rose to dominance (Nadesan 2005, 80–137). Discussed in the Introduction, one common theory of autism that emerged during this time is Theory of Mind (ToM), a cognitive structure thought to be lacking or disordered in so-called autistic minds. (ToM remains a popular approach today.) ToM is understood as an innate, evolutionary structure that is the precondition for joint attention and normative empathy, the presumed bedrock of human sociality (Baron-Cohen 1995; Baron-Cohen, Leslie, and Frith 1985; Frith 1993; McGuire and Michalko 2011; Yergeau 2013, 2018). According to psychology researchers Simon Baron-Cohen, Alan Leslie, and Utah Frith (1985, 38) in their pivotal article on ToM, autistic people do not comprehend "that other people know, want, feel, or believe things." In his later publication *Mindblindness: An Essay on Autism and Theory of Mind,* Baron-Cohen (1995, 3) elaborates, "A theory of mind remains one of the quintessential abilities that makes us human … The theory of mind difficulties seem to be universal among such [autistic] individuals." As autistic rhetorician M. Remi Yergeau (2013, para. 9) points out, within this biological logic, one that has now become an "empirical fact" supporting "whole academic enterprises," autism is the inhuman and involuntary effect of a disordered neurology that grants those *with* ToM their humanity (see also Yergeau 2018).

The empirical fact of Theory of Mind and its dehumanization of autistic people was echoed by everyday text such as journalist Geoffrey Cowley's (1995, 67) article in *Newsweek:* "[Autistic people's] worlds are peopled not by fellow beings with thoughts, feelings and agendas but by skin-covered bags that approach and withdraw unpredictably" (see also Adler 1994, 248). During the years 1970–99, new technologies such as positron emission tomography (PET) and magnetic resonance imaging (MRI) mapped cognitive structures such as ToM onto physical brains themselves, producing ever-deepening, penetrating images of a troubled autistic interiority, images that were now a biological and tangible empirical fact instead of psychical and emotional (e.g., see Bower 1986; Nadesan 2005, 156–57; and Rose 1999a). These newly emerging forms of knowledge brought the autistic population and autism mothers into view in radically new and discontinuous ways from that of psychoanalysis and the refrigerator mother.

In *Infantile Autism,* Rimland (1964) conducted an in-depth "review of the evidence" for and against the "psychogenesis of autism." Evidence in support of the psychogenesis of autism, according to Rimland, means both the absence of "organic" causes and the presence of possible psychological origins of autism, including emotionally deficient parenting (the prevailing psychoanalytic view), maternal deprivation, or damaging psychological events in a child's life (42).[2] Rimland concluded that there is "no support for the psychogenic point of view. The evidence is instead highly consistent with expectation based on organic pathology" (61). In fact, wrote Rimland, the evidence suggests that autism is the result of brain impairment, one that he thought might be in the "reticular formation of the brain stem" (93). He believed that this sort of impairment led to the cognitive impairments seen in autism, making it impossible for autistic children to link incoming perceptual stimuli to memory, the primary disability associated with autism, he theorized. Like Leo Kanner's (1943) earlier assertion that autism is present from birth, Rimland speculated that disordered behaviour in children, including autism, is likely affected by prenatal factors – injury to fetal brain development during pregnancy through, for example, stress or birth injury. In addition, Rimland (1964, 120) postulated a genetic vulnerability to autism due to "an inborn capacity for high intelligence." He concluded with a neurological theory of behaviour, positing that impairments to the reticular formation inhibit autistic children from making normal associations between positive rewards (e.g., food, love, and comfort) and social behaviours (e.g., communication and affection). In these ways, Rimland rethought autism as a neurocognitive impairment, one linked to fetal brain development, prenatal maternal factors, impairment of the physical brain, genetics, intelligence, and a biological – rather than relational (i.e., mother-child relationships) – view of so-called disordered behaviour and disruptions to normal development. This understanding of the biological origin of autism also opened scientific ground for intensive behaviourist research experiments on shaping normative (non-autistic) social behaviours.

Other popular texts about autism and mothers circulating during the years 1970–99 also refuted the refrigerator mother theory in favour of biological views. In "Living with an Autistic Child," an article in *Parents* magazine, psychologists Julius Segal and Zelda Segal (1992, 90–91) state, for example, "Cold, remote, and unfeeling, the so-called refrigerator mother was long viewed as the chief architect of her child's miserable existence ... Today we know better. In fact, it is clear the disorder's origins are the result of biological problems." Rimland's (1964) popular *Infantile Autism* was perhaps the most comprehensive, scientific, and polemical of these refutations. He began to appear in newspaper articles in Toronto as an authority on the biological view of autism, particularly as linked to the new landscape of autism advocacy. As one *Globe and Mail* (1976, 14) article, for example, reported about the founding of the Canadian Society for Autistic Children, "Dr. Bernard Rimland of the Institute of Child Behavior Research in San Diego said too many psychiatrists have blamed parental treatment for the child's condition." The article also described Rimland's research on elevated brain chemical levels in autistic children, as well as his recommendations for educational/behavioural treatment and "megavitamins." Indeed, Rimland's neurological theory of autism and behaviour would lend great weight to popularizing early and intensive behavioural treatment of autistic children and to reconfiguring the refrigerator mother as mother therapist. Recall Anna's experience during these years with this newly emerged mother therapist identity and its failure to totalize her more affirming understanding of autism and practice as a (m)other, described in Chapter 1. Anna encountered newly emerged autism "experts" grounded in biological views of autism and was instructed in intensive home-based educational/behavioural therapies aimed at "recovering" her nonspeaking son, David.

Unlike the psychoanalytic emphasis on the relationship between mother and infant, one that directed a mother's gaze inward upon her own psychic life and disordered love as the initiating factor in autistic withdrawal, biological and neurocognitive understandings meant that mothers and families might now positively contribute to their child's (normal) development, a compelling, if medicalized, view for beleaguered parents and especially mothers. Consider the following excerpt from a lecture that Rimland delivered to several chapters of the National Society for Autistic Children throughout the United States between 1967 and 1970:

> The psychogenic theory has cast blame on the parents, and thus immobilized the child's strongest ally in what should be his struggle to recover. It has caused stagnation in research – what biochemist wants to analyze

a "fractured oedipus complex"? It has caused educators to shrug their shoulders and leave the problem in the hands of the psychiatrists, psychologists and social workers. It has cost families untold fortunes in money, time, convenience and human dignity. And worst of all it has cost far too many children's lives. Such children are not medically dead – just psychologically dead, existing like human vegetables in institution after institution. (Quoted in Silverman 2012, 87)

There are several key features to notice in Rimland's speech to parents. First, he advocates with fervour. Rimland is Becker's (1963) "moral entrepreneur" of the emerging neuropsychological, behaviourist regime. He at once challenges Bettelheim's theories, calls for a bioscientific research agenda in autism, invokes a "recovery" discourse for autism incipient in earlier decades, and calls to parents and professionals alike to take up the new role of "their child's strongest ally" in recovery. Here, Rimland conflates being an "ally" with advocacy for the biological remediation and psychological recuperation – the recovery – of autistic children, who otherwise are "psychologically dead, existing like human vegetables" within institutions.

The neurodiversity movement that emerged in the 1980s would eventually challenge Rimland's view of what it means to be an ally. Autistic self-advocate Jim Sinclair (1993, paras. 3–4; emphasis in original) states, "Autism is a way of being. It is *pervasive;* it colors every experience, every sensation, perception, thought, emotion, and encounter, every aspect of existence. It is not possible to separate the autism from the person – and if it were possible, the person you'd have left would not be the same person you started with." Being an ally, then, means recognizing that autism is a different, viable way of being in the world with its own embodiment and language, or for the neurodiversity movement, a being in neurodiversity. In solidarity with autistic self-advocates' understanding of autism as valuable and viable, an ethic of disruption and attention to knowledge production through affirming care employs the understanding that the choice for parents is not that of recovery versus abandoning a "psychologically dead" child. Creative possibilities for different ways to care about autism, (m)othering, and autistic offspring beyond individual biomedical interventions and the normal-abnormal binary are its promise.

Rimland also, and importantly, linked the neuropsychological agenda of the recovery of autistic children to deinstitutionalization, a movement that was emerging in North America at the same time that he undertook his advocacy campaigns. Deinstitutionalization refers both to the political movement and to the social policy that fought to close large-scale custodial institutions and to establish community living, supports, and services for disabled people and their families, although such supports were inadequate from the beginning (e.g., see Enright 1989; Galt 1995; Levinson 2010, 9–36; Panitch 2008; and Wright 1995). In Ontario, deinstitutionalization began, in part, with the work of mother activists in the 1950s. And although the movement of people out of institutions peaked between 1975 and 2005 in Ontario, this movement continues to play out in the present day in some respects (Panitch 2008). Thistletown Regional Centre in Toronto, for example, where the most "extreme" autistic children had been incarcerated under custodial care since the 1950s (*Toronto Daily Star* 1958), has only recently been closed.[3] Professionals, policy makers, and parents have been a key part of the deinstitutionalization movement (Dolmage 2011; Levinson 2010). Influential, too, was the work of sociologists such as Erving Goffman (1961) and Howard Becker (1963) as well as the work of Michel Foucault ([1965] 1988a) and others who began to expose professional authority and categories of so-called mental retardation and mental illness as social and historical processes rather than as objective or measurable attributes of individuals (Levinson 2010, 30–36). Popular media and science also influenced governments' closure of institutions by exposing their often violent, neglectful, and dehumanizing conditions (20–21). A *Toronto Star* (1973, 21) article, for example, describes a reporter's chilling visit with an emaciated autistic girl who, having been institutionalized at eighteen months, now screamed as she was taken away by staff for therapy, "Not shocks! Not shocks! Please!"

Mothers' roles in deinstitutionalization have been contradictory and complex and have often been a missing part of scholarly histories (Dolmage 2011; Panitch 2008). In the 1950s and '60s, pressure from medical professionals to institutionalize so-called medically hopeless children understood to be damaging to siblings was intense and often traumatic (Freeman 2019; Levinson 2010; Manning 2011). Whereas some mothers abandoned their child to institutional care during this time, many others engaged in activist pursuits to improve the quality of life within institutions (Dolmage 2011; Levinson 2010; Manning 2011; Panitch 2008). (M)others also innovated and pressed for ways to keep their children at home and fought for educational and community inclusion (Dolmage 2011; Hopper 1976; Manning 2011; Panitch 2008; L. Stone 1981). With the closing of institutions like Thistletown in Toronto, Ontario, some (m)others also publicly fought against deinstitutionalization, arguing that community supports were inadequate (Enright 1989; Freed and Gombu 1995; Galt 1995; Panitch 2008; Wright 1995). Rimland's conflation of the autism parent "ally" with "recovery" and the deinstitutionalization movement is troubling. It glosses over complex, layered, and locally inflected histories showing that many autism mothers and parents were often already working strategically and collectively as their child's "best ally." Rimland's advocacy also occurred in a historical moment when care was beginning to be pushed back into the private realm, home, and community as women's (and often women of colour's) responsibility. It would be the rise of the mother therapist and of reconfigured intensive mothering (rather than, for example, the public investment in living well in difference) and the possibility of recovery opened by neurocognitive understandings of autism that would inflect the identity autism mother and the paradox of care in new ways during this time.

New Forms of Visibility: Mother Therapists

Whereas the disordered refrigerator mother of the 1950s and '60s was included in her child's healing through maternal treatment that often also meant the physical separation from and institutionalization of her child, emerging biological understandings of autism opened a different ground of possibilities. Within everyday text, the mother therapist emerged as a new, and key, form of visibility and impulse toward what Zygmunt Bauman (2004a, 20) calls Western culture's heightening "duty and ... urge to act" in order to achieve a self-same identity for all (see also Stiker 1999). Through detailed descriptions of systematic, intensive, and even violent methods of training and through the strategic use of before and after photographs of autistic children as new diagrams of power in popular media and science, an autism mother's gaze within the mother-child dyad was retrained away from her so-called disordered inner life and toward the scientific reshaping of her everyday, embodied practices of mothering.

Clara Claiborne Park's (1967, 195) subversion of psychoanalytic views of natural mothering through her argument that love melds both emotion *and* technique, what she terms "intelligent love" (see also Vicedo 2021), would ironically find its full embodiment in this mother therapist figure, with scientific backing. Parents, particularly mothers, were now to be trained in behavioural techniques as rehabilitators of disordered autistic biology through intensive labour (which for some middle- and upper-class mothers meant the labour of a paid carer, who was often a woman of colour), as midwives to normal development, and as curers of autism. This new, and newly intensive, role was ironic. Mothers – particularly white, bourgeois mothers since working-class, Black, and other (m)others of colour had always participated in paid labour – were entering the workforce in record numbers. At the same time, the care of disabled or ill family and kin was being pushed back into the private market, home, and community, and public support of social programs was being cut (Brodie 1995; Ehrenreich and English 2005, 351–54; Vandenbeld Giles 2014). The autism mother therapist, vis-à-vis new biological understandings of autism, emerged in paradoxical terms as an intensification of an already contradictory and intensive maternal femininity. This mother could – indeed *must* – work heroically within the mother-child dyad and patriarchal, heteronormative nuclear family to both love and "recover" her autistic child through instrumental behaviourist techniques, all within the heightening demands of a gendered political economy of care and paid labour force (Douglas et al., "Mad Mothering," 2021; Hays 1996; Vandenbeld Giles 2014; on the intensification of contradictory neoliberal femininity, see also Ringrose and Walkerdine 2008). As Sharon Hays (1996, 165) elucidates, not only does the dominant Global North's social construction of intensive mothering conceal unequal gender relations in the imperative that women work in paid employment and take primary responsibility for parenting, but it also pathologizes and individualizes any failure to care intensively. In our case, this care configuration blames mothers of autistic offspring – particularly mothers of colour, immigrant mothers, and other marginalized mothers – rather than unjust systems and ideologies, for failing to achieve normalcy for their child. In one of our focus group discussions, Jennifer, a social worker and immigrant (m)other of colour of a seven-year-old autistic son, illuminated the debility and precarity of this care configuration for women of colour (see also Puar 2017). She shared about organizing a parent information and support network where she offered unpaid work (over and above her paid employment and primary caregiving and advocacy on behalf of her son), acting as a hub for her community, whose members, she stated, were merely "surviving" and "struggling" to help their children because of "language barriers" to mainstream autism and other services. Below, I consider how the autism mother therapist operated as a new form of visibility, bringing intensive bourgeois, white, Global North mothering practices and behaviourist modes of scientific governance into dramatic view for all (m)others, redrawing the lines between "good" (or white, middle-class) and "bad" (m)others.

Among other popular autism researchers during these years, Rimland felt that a "structured, purposeful education program" using behaviour modification was key to reshaping disordered autistic biology and should replace psychoanalytic therapies (quoted in *Globe and Mail* 1976, 14; see also Rimland 1978). Rimland publicly supported, with some reserve, psychologist Ole Ivar Lovaas's behaviourist experiments on autistic children using positive reinforcers for normal behaviours: food, play, and hugs for attending to lessons or for using spoken language; and violent aversives like slaps, electric shocks, and reprimands for autistic behaviours such as flapping, rocking, or averting one's gaze (101).[4] During the mid-1960s, the role of "moral entrepreneur" and "expert" (Becker 1963, 147–63) commingled in the figures of Rimland and Lovaas, both of whom lent scientific expertise as well as moral conviction to the emerging behavioural treatment regime and retraining of autism mothers. In May 1965, *Life* magazine published a much-read article by journalist Don Moser (1965, 94), "Screams, Slaps and Love," which describes Lovaas's experimental study at the University of California, Los Angeles. Lovaas was hopeful that his experiments would provide a scientifically grounded behavioural method for all parents and professionals to use with children who had "broken minds" (94; see also Lovaas 1987). Unlike psychoanalysis, behaviourist views of human learning and sociality are not interested in causes or in the psychic interiority of human behaviour and cognition, although they typically accept biological views of the human. Instead, changes in the external environment – rewards/reinforcers and aversives/punishments – result in changes in human cognition and behaviour, as well as, according to Rimland, possibly even in biology (Lovaas 1977, 1981; Rimland 1964, 1978; B. Skinner 1963).

In "Screams, Slaps and Love," autism mother and child are brought into view in graphic before and after photographs and behavioural descriptions. As beholders of these images, we witness the wild and intense disruption of untreated autistic biology in "before" photographs of writhing, raging, contorting, rocking, and flapping youngsters and read about it in descriptions of life with an autistic child. Moser (1965, 101) writes that one mother confided, "It was like living with the devil." These are, states Moser, "utterly withdrawn children whose minds are sealed against all human contact and whose uncontrolled madness had turned their homes into hells" (90A). Reason and science in the form of therapeutic behavioural techniques are offered by Lovaas as what might bring control and certainty to the "madness" of an uncivilized/wild and dangerous/hellish autistic nature in the domestic realm. Therapists working with rewards and aversives are pictured and described in the article until finally the reader ostensibly sees normalcy in after photographs and reads normalcy in their accompanying descriptions: two children hugging and being rewarded with food, affection shown for a therapist, attention during a lesson, and a mother with hands clasped over her heart and head thrown backward with joy at her son's progress toward normal behaviour. Here, the mother figure becomes a joyful observer and participant in the normative correction of her child by any means. Moser reports that Lovaas had "broken through" to the most unreachable of humans through behaviour modification, namely "by alternating methods of shocking roughness with persistent loyal attention," and that he had succeeded, at least in part, in normalizing them (90A).

Some years later, Lovaas would extend his crusade for behavioural treatment and the moral framework already apparent above – autism as bad (even evil) and normalcy as good – articulating violence as the link through which parents, especially mothers, must fight for their child's humanity in love: "Nobody punishes a child who doesn't also love that child ... Once you lay your hands on a child, it morally obligates you to work with that child" (quoted in Chance 1974, 80). This behaviourist approach is, first, a mechanistic view of the human and mother-child relationship that leaves little room for agency, ambivalence, reciprocal influence, or learning from or in a relationship with this different child.

Moreover, the behaviourist approach conceals the unarticulated background of the prestige of science in the lifeworld for having already accomplished the meaning of autism as "bad" and "wrong," such that the disruption of autistic bodies is rendered intelligible and remedied through these same interpretive schemes (Husserl 1970, 110; Natanson 1970, 63; Schutz 1967, 82–83). In other words, to borrow M. Remi Yergeau's (2018, 4) phrase, the "critical exigence" to stop autism and the idea of normal human development as non-autistic make sense of this everyday appearance of violent corrective treatment as not only shocking but also ordinary, acceptable, and even humane acts of love, care, and moral enterprise; these therapies were, after all, for the benefit of disordered children, their families, and wider society (see also Becker 1963, 147–63). As we shall see, through training in behaviourist techniques, the mother therapist would, ironically, again come to embody coldness, only now she was rejecting "autism" and embodied difference rather than her child (recall Bettelheim's understanding of autism as the withdrawal of a normal child). Although she no longer causes autism through rejection, she now cures it (Sousa 2005) through scientifically defined and measured techniques that include not only rejection in the form of slaps, punishments, and other aversives but also love in the form of reinforcers and rewards in a newly shaped paradox of care. The duty to achieve the embodiment of normalcy in her child would soon be the clarion call of the mother therapist.

It would be a short distance to travel from mother as joyful observer of expert behaviourist intervention to mother therapist – the rehabilitator of her autistic child's so-called disordered biology through the paternalistic guidance of science. In 1974, less than a decade later, Lovaas would state, "The parents become the principal therapists and we become consultants to the parents" (quoted in Chance 1974, 76). Of course, earlier ties to psychoanalytic approaches did not entirely disappear during these years. As reported by journalist June Callwood (1976, 7) in the *Globe and Mail*, the Crèche Institute in Toronto, for example, continued to involve mothers in their child's therapy through maternal treatment: "West End Crèche works on developing parental skills by bringing parents together in group discussions of their problems and by meeting with them individually to help them sort out their own childhood misadventures." Here, it was mothers who still needed therapy. Overwhelmingly, however, beginning in the 1970s, everyday text brought autism mothers into view as therapists and behavioural interveners in their child's disrupted development.

In 1972, for example, the *Globe and Mail* described a talk given by Dr. Eric Schopler at the newly formed Toronto Society for Autistic Children (Kirkwood 1972, 12). Founder of the North Carolina–based TEACCH program for autism, which uses a combination of approaches, including behaviour modification, "Dr. Schopler ... trains the parents to be co-therapists for their autistic children." Later that same year, the *Toronto Star* reported one family's long journey to find treatment for their autistic child (Cornell 1972, 87). The article describes their advocacy with the Toronto Society for Autistic Children to secure more programs like the new "rewards program" at the Clarke Institute, which continued into the home each night for this mother: "Within 18 months of day long therapy sessions he could make vowel sounds and say simple words ... Each night I went over the vowel sounds, holding Graham's chin and sometimes even shaping his mouth." As journalist Linda Stone (1981, n.p.) reported in the *Globe and Mail,* parents also worked to initiate in-home behaviour modification programs with staff in the autism program at Thistletown – the institutional setting for the most "severe" autistic children in Ontario: "Why, they asked, couldn't they pay a worker to come to their home and work with their son. The parents would see how the treatment worked and continue it when the worker wasn't there" (see also Hopper 1976).[5] Here again, "parents" – particularly mothers – were understood, as Stone (1981, n.p.) reported, to be "co-therapists who help design and implement programs to treat their own kids." Not only did this mother therapist bring mothers' domestic practices into view as a reconfigured space of scientific governance for all – a shift that was only just emerging when Park (1967) confessed to her made up "games" at home with Elly – but it also helped to retrain mothers' maternal gaze away from ordering their disordered inner life and toward the ordering of their embodied practice within the mother-child dyad.

In *Let Me Hear Your Voice: A Family's Triumph over Autism,* for example, Catherine Maurice (1993), autism mother of two, details her journey to recover her autistic children through a behavioural treatment regime. After the "devastating" diagnoses, she frantically researches and tries all the available therapies that she can find, from psychogenic (or holding therapy) to biomedical (or megavitamins). Eventually, Maurice learns of the work of Rimland and Lovaas. After a long consultation with Rimland, she describes her decision to invest her hope for the recovery of her children in the "rigorous" scientific methodology of psychology, "verifiable data, accountability, controlled research, openness to peer scrutiny" (168). She debunks approaches that she calls "anti-behaviourist" as anti-scientific, antiquated, and still committed to psychogenic views of autism as a normal child trapped inside a shell (271–85). Maurice urges parents to keep an "open mind" about behaviour modification, telling her reader that behavioural principles are based on "discrete trials, breaking down tasks, the systematic use of reinforcement and praise ... and an extensive curriculum developed over the past twenty-five years by Ivar Lovaas and other researchers in the professional community" (331). Maurice both learns and adapts this curriculum from Lovaas himself at his clinic at the University of California, Los Angeles, as well as from Lovaas's (1981) *Teaching Developmentally Disabled Children: The Me Book,* where he coaches parents in behavioural techniques. She offers an example from that book: "Select two behaviors, one that your child definitely prefers and one that he does not prefer. For example, you may ask a question such as, 'Do you want candy?,' as contrasted to the question 'Do you want a spanking?' Ask one of these questions, and then prompt the correct response" (quoted in Maurice 1993, 208).

Although Lovaas coaches parents to "let the child experience the consequences of his using the terms yes and no correctly" (quoted in Maurice 1993, 208) – in other words, slap them if they say yes to spanking – Maurice resists his authority and adapts the method. She includes less "harsh" aversive choices such as ice cream versus spinach rather than candy versus violence. Maurice thus brings autism mothers into view both as moral entrepreneurs of the scientific production of normal embodiment in their child and potential – albeit subtle – subverters of scientific authority (Becker 1963; Jack 2014, 60; Sousa 2005, 225). This mother therapist is, ironically, now scientifically governed at a distance. Far from the clinic of Leo Kanner's and Bruno Bettelheim's time, she is governed through her own "freedom" (Rose 1999a) to shape her mothering practices, albeit in a normalizing way for Maurice, on the ground of her own maternal authority.[6]

As a brief aside, in our focus group discussions of "evidence-based" approaches like Applied Behaviour Analysis (ABA), (m)others offered perspectives that went further in subverting scientific authority. Julie, (m)other of a twenty-one-year-old autistic son, observed that in her experience, many mothers reject "evidence-based ABA," perhaps because it is "not the mother's thing." She continued, "Even in the most liberated families," gender ideologies continue to code the "mother domain" as nurturing rather than "scientific and systematic." She offered the example of diet modifications and relational therapies (see Chapter 1) as a closer fit with conventional gendered domains in the nuclear family and wondered whether dominant gender ideologies might have fuelled the appeal of such pseudo-scientific treatments also taken up by autism's mother therapists during these years, including megavitamin therapy (Rimland 1964, 1978). Jennifer, (m)other of seven-year-old Eric, also questioned the authority of Western science: "I think as a parent you need to know a little bit of everything." Jennifer included in this "everything" not only advocacy work (as noted, she had started an autism information-sharing network) but also discernment based on her own academic study and experience as a (m)other of what was needed for her son. Whether or not we agree that the "mother domain" excludes science or that "you need to know a little bit of everything," Julie and Jennifer raised a key point within their descriptions of intimate moments in their own governed lives during this time when resistance became a possibility, at least occasionally, within powerful regimes that compel mothers, through the gendered authority of science, to work exhaustively to achieve normalcy in their child. The fact that such power fails to govern us completely (Rose 1999a) is ground for hope, one that is alive in these (m)others' lives.

To return to Maurice and the emerging mother therapist identity, by linking the paternalistic authority of science through her work with Rimland and Lovaas to her self-claimed intuition and maternal knowledge of her children, Maurice creates and implements her own behavioural curriculum. As she moves from trial to trial, the skills that she teaches become increasingly complex. Maurice (1993, 334–52) begins with the skill of "attending" and over time moves, for example, to "following one-step instructions," "play," "making choices," "toilet training," "asking 'when' questions," and "elicit[ing] spontaneous questioning." Teaching her child how to "be" human is broken into skills and mechanized, seen most ironically here in the scientific control of human spontaneity and creativity itself (as presumably autistic spontaneity and creative stimming are not considered valid). Skill number eighteen from Maurice's diary for the period from September 1 to November 15, 1990, includes the following:

> 18. *Monitor Tuning Out, Tantrums, Whining, Aggression, Self-stimulatory Behavior*
>
> Increase pace of material to counteract tuning-out behaviour. Spend no more than five minutes at a time in chair. Use DRA [differential reinforcement of alternative behaviour] for "Good sitting," "Good listening," "You're not whining," etc. Increase reinforcement schedule. Experiment with different motivators. "Time out" for aggression (hair pulling). Note: One way to unpry little fingers from your hair is to press firmly down on the knuckles: his fingers will open naturally. For hand-flapping, body-tensing, and toe-dancing, state "Quiet hands," at each occurrence, and hold his hands by his side for three seconds. Praise for being still. (343)

In this excerpt, the language of behaviourism delivers the autistic body as an object available for the scientific expert and mother therapist to "work on" (McGuire 2016, 37). This breakdown of human relationality and difference into the mechanized teaching of normal embodiment and "skills" thus links the social construction of mothering and its paradox of care to larger processes of modernization, including the ableist, capitalist production, industrialization, and scientific management of social life (see Braverman 1998).

Recuperated from her infantilized psychoanalytic subject position as natural mother, the mother therapist becomes a "skilled worker," a natural fit for her biologically disordered child (McGuire 2016, 37). Her primary goal is to work for the achievement of normalcy, the shape of which she knows in advance. Her methods are predetermined, scientifically guided, normalizing techniques learned from experts and adapted through her maternal love and her practice, which includes reinforcing and increasing so-called normal behaviour like "Good sitting," reprimanding with words like "Quiet hands," and restraining autistic embodiment, such as by "hold[ing] his hands by his side for three seconds." In other words, although tempered by her adaptations of the "harsh" methods of experts, the mother therapist must nevertheless conform to the ideal of the good, white, bourgeois mother who shapes productive citizens through her labour – in this case, by caring for normalcy and extinguishing autistic embodiment, including tuning out, hand-flapping, body-tensing, and toe-walking. Tracing how the coupling of mother therapist and scientific expert emerged in practice as a new form of visibility and site of intensively lived governance and care for autism mother and child extends Anne McGuire's point that normalcy emerged during this time as an "embodied *practice*" rather than as a natural attribute of some bodies but not others (50; emphasis in original). Normalcy, McGuire continues, becomes something that can be practically "achieved, or perhaps more accurately approximated," by an intensive good mother therapist who is self-governing, simultaneously shaping her embodied practices through both scientific expertise and her own authority (50). As we have seen, power is also resisted by (m)others who live with and love their child in everyday life, the topic of the next chapter.

The mother therapist as she emerged and appeared in popular media and science came to embody and bring into everyday view a newly shaped paradox of care for all mothers. She is guided both by "natural" love for her child and by the reason of Western Cartesian science, where, to borrow from philosopher Susan Bordo (1986, 451), "the key term is detachment: from emotional life, from the particularities of time and place, from personal quirks and prejudices, and most centrally from the object itself." This contradictory mother therapist must both care (as good mothers do) and reject the particularities of her unique child (or the "object") in front of her as she mothers from the cold remove of science. For Maurice, this undertaking meant softening the approach of experts while also complying by scientifically observing, containing (literally, through physical restraint), therapeutically correcting (or making identical), and caring for (or rewarding) the production of normalcy. For (m)others Jennifer and Julie from my focus groups, this approach meant questioning science and gender roles while also, at times, taking up conventional roles and practices. Understanding the "particularities of time and place" or cultural ground of a world that produces an autistic child as a problem object to be "worked on," at times violently, by mothers within the mother-child dyad is not a task that is included in the mother therapist role. The mother therapist's irremediable ethical paradox – to care and eliminate, govern and naturally love – is brokered through the scientific ordering of her intimate bodily practices as ones that must also include the rejection of and even violence toward difference. These violent tactics of unfreedom that "stop" alternative forms of embodiment, including autism as well as brown and Black bodies (labelled, for example, as emotionally disturbed rather than autistic during this time) make up part of the powerful Western scientific care regime that governs us through our "freedom," as incomplete in its reach as this regime may be (Dean 2002; Dehli 2008; Foucault 1982, 1991a, 2003).

Detailed descriptions in everyday text popularized the mother therapist as a figure aligned with paradoxical terms to which all mothers were to adhere during this time. The autism mother was no longer a destructive force but a healer and skilled worker – one who, ironically, used both love and rejection, nurturance and violence to humanize her child. And she held lessons for all mothers. For example, a 1975 article in *Psychology Today* titled "Autism: A Defeatable Horror," written by psychologists Laura Schreibman and Robert L. Koegel (1975, 61), draws from experiments with autistic children to prescribe "five essential steps" to successful behaviour modification for *all* parents struggling to "civilize their children, autistic or normal." Before photographs show frustrated parents and broken household items, whereas after photographs depict affectionate, attentive autistic children engaged in therapy sessions and play. Such depictions of autism and autism's mother therapist invited all (m)others to retrain their gaze, this time on intensively ordering and governing their own (m)othering practices in systematic and scientific ways. Psychologists Julius Segal and Zelda Segal (1992, 92) write, "You cannot depend on experts alone to straighten out your child. You have to get involved too" (see also Bower 1981, 1989; Chance 1974, 1987; and Schreibman and Koegel 1975). Indeed, say Segal and Segal (1992, 89) in their description of behaviour modification and life with an autistic child, "the courage and dedication of these mothers and fathers can be a source of inspiration to all." The contradictory figure of the mother therapist, the paradoxical meaning of care, and biological understandings of autism and normal human development had now come to regulate the good/bad mother in new ways for all (m)others, redirecting a (m)other's gaze toward the intensive and scientific self-governance of her own mothering practices, time, and emotional investment in the achievement of normalcy. This achievement was the product of a new seductive coupling of the scientific expert and the skilled, bourgeois, white mother therapist, both of whom also lent their power and privilege to the moral enterprise to scientifically order the disorder of autistic children.

A New Technology of Affect: Covert Blame

No longer the overt cause of autism, autism mothers had now become responsible for their child's recovery – or at least for training their child to behaviourally approximate normal development. This shift would involve a new and subtle form of blame, or technology of affect, for autism mothers, one that would take place through their own scientifically shaped self-governance. Indeed, part of what seems new in everyday text by and about autism mothers after the late 1960s is the retraining of a mother's gaze onto the scientifically informed and systematic reordering of her mothering practices not as that which causes autism through disordered love but as that which must now remedy, heal, treat, and cure autism (Sousa 2005).

Interestingly, emerging neurocognitive understandings of autism offered several different ways that mothers might have been enticed to care about their child's treatment over and above dominant behavioural approaches. As we have seen above with megavitamins, these alternatives included biomedical interventions such as vitamin therapy and serotonin studies (e.g., see Maurice 1993; *Globe and Mail* 1976; and Segal and Segal 1992), twin studies and other genetic research looking for the cause of autism and establishing banks of family genetic information (e.g., see *Globe and Mail* 1982, 9; Singh 2016; and *Toronto Star* 1985), and research on prenatal factors such as a mother-to-be's anxiety, maternal measles, fetal brain injury, brains that grew "too big," and folic acid (*Globe and Mail* 1971; *Science News* 1977; *Scientific American* 1972, 42; Wu 1995, 116). This research reflected the growing understanding of autism as a developmental disorder, as reported by journalist Bruce Bower (1986, n.p.) in a *Science News* article: "There are several indications that changes in the autistic brain occurred before birth."

However, the rise of alternative biomedical interventions and of preventative and genetic mothering would wait for the turn of the twenty-first century. These alternate interpretations of autism, mothering, and care, here in their incipient beginnings, would vie for power with behaviourist views and with the mother therapist owing to the rise of genomic views of the human and to the rise of the warrior mother (see Chapter 6). For the years following Rimland's and Lovaas's work, it would be the success or failure of the mother therapist and her use of intensive, systematic, and scientifically guided interventions into her child's disordered biology – behaviour modification or the more "loving" educational approach advanced by Maurice – through which a technology of covert blame would come to operate anew. We can again grasp this moment in Foucault's (1982; 1984, 86) genealogical sense of the human subject as the emergence of different interpretations of human life through histories of struggle and forces of domination and subordination. In this case, as we shall see, this process occurred not only through the newly emerging neoliberal instrumentalities of intensive mothering and the Global North's patriarchal, middle-class nuclear family but also through autism science within the heightening marketization of care and human social life (Brodie 1995; Hays 1996; Vandenbeld Giles 2014).

The first noteworthy point in the operation of this new form of covert blame is that despite new neuropsychological understandings of autism, it was still the scene of the mother-child dyad and relationship where normal development was to unfold or fail. The difference, however, is that it was now through a mother's scientifically guided self-conduct and proximity to her child as mother therapist (a kind of distant/loving figure) that development was to unfold and be corrected. For example, in a behaviour modification training program for parents (read, mothers) of autistic children, the experimenters note that the successful parent therapist "cared a great deal about succeeding, showing happiness when the children improved, and anger when the children interrupted the sessions ... Instead of pitying and excusing bizarre behaviour, they concentrated on increasing normal behaviour. They showed a willingness to commit a major personal effort to helping their child, instead of relying on professional help" (Schreibman and Koegel 1975, 66). Here, a mother's disordered natural love is no longer considered a factor in autism, which is now squarely located within individual biology rather than between (disordered) mother and child. Instead, the parent (read, mother) is now a skilled worker and healer responsible for externally shaping her autistic child's biology. She must learn to read her child's behaviour through the vocabularies of neuropsychology as "normal" versus "bizarre" and provide corrective, therapeutic responses – happiness or anger, rewards or punishment. Autistic behaviour meets aversive, extinguishing responses, whereas normal behaviour meets loving, encouraging ones, all with the goal of reshaping behaviour to appear more normal, meaning appearing as close to middle-class, economically productive, autonomous subjectivity as possible. Although the mother-child relationship remains the scene of this mechanistic developmental drama, a mother's role and responsibility have changed. She is now a mother therapist, shaped by behaviourist science. Changed, too, is the Westernizing psychological scientific view of human development underpinning this new therapeutic mother's work. Development is now a vulnerable yet universal unfolding that is *biological* (as opposed to psychic) and that is marked by predictable stages of normal development known in advance (Ehrenreich and English 2005, 237, 240). Normal development, however, is also susceptible to various threats (both environmental and genetic) along the way, thus a mother's constant attention and scientifically guided, corrective intervention are needed in addition to her natural love (McGuire 2016). It is worthwhile to pause momentarily to recall that it is an individual *mother's* (most often, a biological mother's) attention and natural love within the mother-child dyad that this drama requires. Alternative, collective modes of (m)othering and the disability commons that we might glimpse in the words of (m)others in my focus groups or in a few brief pages of memoirs remain illegible based on this behaviourist view. No excusing – explanation, defence, justification, or tolerance – of autistic behaviour is allowed for by the successful mother therapist. Autism appears as an already accomplished fact of biological deviation and mothers as the therapeutic solution, leaving the cultural ground and interpretive work of the accomplishment of normal development "concealed," to borrow a word from phenomenologist Edmund Husserl (1970, 104). In a sense, too, this new technology of blame adds a new layer of contradiction to the paradox of care and social construction of mothering: left on her own, without the paternalistic guidance of science and professional help, a mother's unconditional love or affirming care is not adequate. She must also, and simultaneously, be intensely self-governing through science and, increasingly, capitalist consumption (to learn the therapies), and she must demonstrate, in Schreibman's and Koegel's (1975, 66) words, a "willingness to commit a major personal effort to helping their child, instead of relying on professional help."

The ideology of intensive mothering that arose during this time meant that the attention of a mother – or her hand-picked alternate, preferably another woman caregiver, who was often a woman of colour, but also perhaps a father, never a lesbian partner – to this kind of scientific care for normalcy in her child had to be self-directed, intense, individual, and constant (Ladd-Taylor 1998, 14; Hays 1996, 8). As Sharon Hays writes on intensive mothering, "A mother must acquire detailed knowledge of what the experts consider proper child development, and then spend a good deal of time and money attempting to foster it" (8). One article in the magazine *Commentary,* for example, describes an autism mother's journey to treat her autistic child as the "dogged, powerful, single-minded commitment of a mother ... providing every day a kind of attention unimaginable in any treatment center" (Rudikoff 1972, 65–66). Autism father Barry Kaufman (1976, 38), too, founder of the Son-Rise Program, a more "loving" educational approach than the autism mother therapist, explains that his wife Suzy's intensive at-home program (which he oversees as patriarch) to draw their son Raun out of his autistic world "would take many hours of constant work." In *Parents* magazine, twenty years later, autism researcher Laura Schreibman is quoted by Segal and Segal (1992, 92) as describing this mother in similar terms: "Since parents are with their children more than anyone else ... they can create an around-the-clock treatment environment." And again, in an article in *Today's Parent,* we are told that "Matthew has a team of people ... When they leave, mom takes over ... It's a round-the-clock job rewarded by Matthew's progress" (F. Stone 1999, 110). This account again shows the shift to locate autism squarely in individual yet-to-be-developed bodies – autistic futures are never imagined as possible, valid, or viable (see also Yergeau 2018) – understood as objects constantly available for mother therapists to work on. In contrast, the feelings, experiences, desires, and preferences of autistic children within intensive therapeutic regimes were not depicted in popular media or science during this time. Within intensive mothering and biological logics, the mother therapist and her objectified child are tied to the Western clock of normal development and its orderly stages. Armed with therapeutic techniques, a scientifically trained gaze, and natural love for her child, the mother therapist must constantly strive against the relentless threat of autistic biology gone wrong and, as McGuire (2016, 105) puts it, against "too slow" or not quite right development. An autism mother's and child's time together has become factory time in the service of "progress" – an endless production toward normalcy and the achievement of the productive worker for her child through an unending consumption of autism therapies (Broderick and Roscigno 2021). Historian Tithi Bhattacharya (2017, 1), in theorizing social reproduction, puts the matter this way: "If workers' labor produces all the wealth in society, who then produces the worker?" (see also S. Ferguson 2019). Indeed, this mother's clock and productivity never stop. Autism's mother therapist is not only intensely governed through her own practices, which are shaped by the dominant scientific sense of autism as a bodymind gone wrong, but also privileged to be available to mother her child in this way (see below). She is producing future workers, and it is urgent. Philosopher and social theorist Karl Marx said about factory production, "It is not the workman that employs the instruments of labour, but the instruments of labour that employ the workman" (quoted in Braverman 1998, 157). Here, domestic spaces and the intimate bodily practices of mothering an autistic child are on the clock of capitalist production and ordered through its instruments – therapies, remedial care, and paternalistic science – which are tuned toward the interests of capital and neoliberal markets and are played out upon the objectified bodies of autistic children.

Given these new scientific and intensive neoliberal capitalist logics, the mother-child relationship was reconfigured as a space of governance that operated at a distance, ironically, through a mother's own self-conduct – a covert form of blame. Although she was no longer responsible for initiating autistic withdrawal in her child, the autism mother therapist was now responsible for correcting – treating, reshaping, and ameliorating – her child's disordered biology, brain, and behaviour. The implication was that in her failure to treat her child successfully, this mother continued to cause autism. Amy C. Sousa (2011, 221) writes, "Whereas seemingly cold mothers ... were once considered responsible for causing their children's intellectual disabilities ... mothers are now responsible for curing the disability, or at least accessing the intervention that will mitigate the disability's impact on their children." Reconfigured neoliberal family-market-state relations and heightening ideologies of intensive mothering that pushed care back into the private market and home as the primary responsibility of families and mothers from the 1970s to the 1990s, even as middle-class, white mothers newly entered the workforce (see Brodie 1995; and Vandenbeld Giles 2014), meant that not all (m)others could work (or wanted to work) on capitalist time to provide such intensive, expensive, time-consuming interventions (Hays 1996). It took a particular kind of mother – one with the courage, determination, and commitment to love her child to normalcy and with the capacity (often white and middle-class) to shore up the necessary resources, time, and desire – to practise this kind of mothering. As described by mother advocate Annabel Stehil (1991, 215; emphasis in original) in her memoir *The Sound of a Miracle: A Child's Triumph over Autism,* one of her doctors declared at the end of her journey to ostensibly recover her autistic daughter, "You are *relentless. That* is why she got well." Judy Barron, co-author of *There's a Boy in Here* with her autistic son, Sean, said, "We used everything we had – our love, our rage, our frustration, patience, inventiveness, violence, ignorance and humor" – to set Sean "free" (Barron and Barron 1992, vii–viii). This newly configured technology of blame was not only gendered but also raced, classed, and abled, linking the accomplishment of normal development and the normal human to intensifying Western, individualizing, white, bourgeois mothering practices within the mother-child dyad for all (m)others (Douglas et al., "Mad Mothering," 2021; Runswick-Cole and Goodley 2018; Walkerdine and Lucy 1989). This technology also inserts autism into continuing Western scientific histories and hierarchies of developmentalism that pathologize and devalue alternative ways of being and caring – Black, Indigenous, working-class, Global South, queer, and so on – and that link disorder to femininity, this time through covert mother blame (e.g., see Paré 1982; Bailey and Mobley 2018; Garland-Thomson 1996, 1997, 2001; and Rice 2015).

Given this new technology of blame, little room is left within public discourse for caring about autism differently as anything other than a tragic, biological problem to be solved (Abberley 1998, 93; D. Mitchell 2002, 15; Titchkosky and Michalko 2009, 2) in large part by individual mother therapists. One autism mother articulated the problem of autism in a *Toronto Star* (1972, 61) article this way: "This thing [autism] has its ups and downs and is a terrible strain." The article goes on to clarify that "more research and intensive therapy aimed at changing behaviour through the reward system will change this for many" (61). In other words, when a mother and family inevitably falter in what *Parents Today* columnist Janet Enright (1989, n.p.) calls a "round the clock" treatment regime, parent advocacy for relief programs, scientific research, and more services are put forward as crucial to the solution: "This family is so burnt out they are hanging onto their life by a thread ... Parent relief means time off ... from the never-ending responsibility." A little bit of rest would free mothers to continue in their intensive mothering. More services, continues Enright, would give families "emotional resources ... strength and courage" to "educate and advocate" for their child. Although services and relief are crucial (indeed, for all parents and families), it is the meaning of care and its link to covert blame and normalizing regimes that I want to note here. For example, rather than advocating for more understanding of autistic difference as a viable way of being in the world or for the creation of shared knowledge and supports to live well in autistic difference within families, advocacy for more behavioural services, research, and rest breaks from the intensity of these regimes bolster covert mother blame and its requirement of constant therapeutic mothering in the service of normalcy and future productive workers.

Within everyday text, then, the failure of a mother to achieve normalcy, or at least progress, in her child was understood not only as her individual failure but also as the failure of governments to provide enough behavioural services, relief programs, and support for scientific research, as well as the inevitable result of autism and an irremediably disordered child. At best, failure meant a grief-filled, frustrating, isolated, and anguished journey to accept that you could not recover your disordered, "brain-damaged" child in a world that values – and expects – progress, productivity, normalcy, and sameness. For example, although involvement in Lovaas's experiments yielded some hope and minimal skills for their son Noah, father and author Josh Greenfeld (1972, 175) and his wife, Foumi, who had trained at Lovaas's California institute to be a "therapist" to her son, lived the failure to normalize him: "Yesterday I told Foumi I have little faith in any therapy – vitamins or operant conditioning or anything. She said, 'Then why don't we just put him in an institution?'" Throughout *A Child Called Noah: A Family Journey*, the Greenfelds' battle with the idea of the institution (which remained one of the only alternatives to home care in 1972 when the book was published) operates as a placeholder for the anguish of the ultimate failure of autism mothers within the Western scientific, capitalist scheme of recovery: failure to normalize their/our children so that they might live a normal life (see also Greenfeld 1978a, 1978b, 1986). At worst, failure appeared in everyday text as the abandonment or murder of an autistic child by a parent, the tragic yet inevitable defeat of some mothers and fathers as fallen "heroes" in the face of the constant proximity to autism and failed behavioural services. For example, describing the murder of six-year-old Charles-Antoine by his mother in 1996, one article in the *Toronto Star* (1996, A8) quotes the president of the Quebec Society for Autistic Children, Peter Zwack, speaking about Charles-Antoine's mother: "Her life was a nightmare. She was all alone and that would have made things even more impossible" (see also Corelli 1998; *Macleans* 1996, 23; Unland 1997; and White 1997). Rather than questioning the cultural ground that values sameness and scientific conceptions of the normal human so completely that mothers, parents, and families must work constantly, intensively, and even violently to systematically treat and normalize (or eliminate) their autistic child and rather than fostering the creation of collective supports and knowledge for families to live well in disability, this newly configured technology of blame conceals this cultural ground through the spectre of failure. When behavioural therapies and autism mothers fail, life with an autistic child can be nothing more than a "nightmare." Outside of the hope of treatment and some measure of normalcy, it can be no life at all.

The new covert technology of blame compelled autism mothers – and perhaps all (m)others – to retrain their gaze and scientifically reorder their mothering practices toward the achievement of normalcy in their child. For example, the article "Living with an Autistic Child," by Segal and Segal (1992, 92), in a section entitled "Lessons All Parents Can Learn," instructs parents, "To change behavior, use positive reinforcements instead of painful punishments, and be sure to reward brave efforts even if they fail." A 1975 article in *Psychology Today* by Schreibman and Koegel (1975, 62), entitled "Autism: A Defeatable Horror," coaches parents (read, mothers) on the "five general procedures" in becoming a parent therapist based on the authors' behaviourist research with autistic children. These procedures include "presenting proper instructions" to their child: "The [parent] therapist must first wait until any inattentive or disruptive behavior has stopped, then establish eye contact with the child. Then the [parent] teacher should present a simple instruction such as 'touch red.'" As a behaviour expert, Lovaas, too, in his forward to Catherine Maurice's (1993, 208) book, popularized tips to the mother therapist: "You can help the child formulate the correct answer [to your question] by grossly exaggerating your gestures when you ask." Through this subtle and invitational technology of blame – being invited to be a co-therapist and held responsible for her child's recovery – biological ways of knowing our life together invaded conceptions of care and tied a (m)other's practices to her child's disorder (and its elimination) anew through her own self-governance rather than maternal treatment. At stake in such bourgeois mothering, state Valerie Walkerdine and Helen Lucy (1989, 63), is nothing less than the "future of civilization" itself. The authors continue, "Mothers, many studies concluded, were so good at all of this that they were inimitable and irreplaceable. It was them that would ensure their children's mental health" (62). Like the refrigerator mother before her, autism's mother therapist emerged as a cautionary tale, only this time she was covertly blamed for the stubborn persistence of autism through her failure to succeed as a skilled worker. This more covert technology of blame compelled a new kind of self-governance for (m)others, one that was at once bodily intimate and attuned to her child while scientifically distant and even violent and rejecting (recall Lovaas's slaps, screams, and planned ignoring). The identity autism mother and the paradox of care – to love your child and to eliminate autistic difference by working intensively within the mother-child dyad – had emerged in newly layered ways as a lived site of contradiction through which new biological versions of autism came to regulate the good/bad mother in new ways for all (m)others. This mother was now scientific and intimate, loving and rejecting, violent and therapeutic, intense and ordered, self-governing and intensively governed.

New Forms of Identity: Autism's Mother Therapists as Cultural Heroes

I briefly address what became of autism and autism mother as new forms of identity made possible by the rise of biological views of the human and by neoliberal shifts in the political economy of care. Throughout this section, I also gather the threads of the chapter before considering in Chapter 5 new forms of resistance that emerged during these years. Although neurocognitive views would come to eclipse the psychoanalytic, threads of the latter still glimmered within everyday text during these years. In her diary about the recovery of her autistic son, Sean, for example, autism mother Judy Barron weaves the cognitive and psychogenic together: "Sean and I have written the story of his release from the terrifying imprisonment of his own mind" (Barron and Barron 1992, viii). Here, Bettelheim's "terrifying imprisonment" meets cognitive psychology's disordered mind in the identity of autism. Other depictions within popular media and science were less equivocal about the meaning of autism. In an article in *Scientific American,* for example, Uta Frith (1993, 108), a leader in Theory of Mind (ToM) and cognitive neuroscience, offered an understanding of autism that erased any trace of the psychoanalytic view. Autism is not a "beautiful child imprisoned in a glass shell." Autistic people "are not living in rich inner worlds but instead are victims of a biological defect that makes their minds very different from those of normal individuals."

This "different mind" – one understood as mapped onto defective brains and rooted in neurobiology – packed quite a wallop. Associations with the uncivilized and amoral abound in everyday text about autism during this time, as well as in popular expert works. For example, one mother quoted in a magazine article outlining a behaviour modification study describes her son as crushingly "unresponsive," "violent," a "wild animal, a living terror" (Schreibman and Koegel 1975, 61). Here, autism is an untamed animalistic nature that is "violent" and therefore "unresponsive" and unpredictable, making it terrifying and even dangerous. Autistic difference means brains and bodies understood as nonhuman objects outside of civilization, implicitly identifying the rational, certain, scientific, and controlled, to come back to Bordo (1987, 5), with the good human subject (see also Yergeau 2013, 2018). The use of these racist metaphors in everyday depictions of autism – savage, animalistic, uncivilized, wild – prop up the urgency of behaviourist campaigns to eliminate autism (McGuire and Michalko 2011). Frith (1989, 16–35) also draws on metaphors of the uncivilized as she describes histories of educating "feral children" in the late 1700s and early 1800s in her popular book *Autism: Explaining the Enigma* as likely instances of autism. Also, as we saw above, in his essay *Mindblindness: An Essay on Autism and Theory of Mind,* which was much cited in popular media as well as scholarly sources, developmental psychopathologist Simon Baron-Cohen (1995), a student of

Frith, suggests that autistic children lack Theory of Mind as what most makes us human (according to evolutionary psychology). To reiterate, for Baron-Cohen, ToM is an evolutionary cognitive structure that bridges the gap between animal and human and allows us to read the contents (e.g., desires and intentions) of others' minds through empathy (on ToM, see also Douglas and Klar 2019; McGuire and Michalko 2011; and Yergeau 2013, 2018). Not only is the depiction of autism as nonhuman and feral in popular media and science reminiscent of Goffman's (1963, 5) "not quite human" characterization of stigmatized individuals, but it is also a destructive biological force that victimizes children, particularly white, male children (those historically disproportionately diagnosed with autism), who are then understood to be in need of remedy. Within this universalizing biological "gaze" (Haraway 1991, 188), the possibility of understanding autistic embodiment as an alternative way of being human within disabled-nondisabled relationships disappears.

If autistic children were victims of destructive neurobiological defects, mothers and families were too. For example, Maurice (1993, 25) uses victimizing language in depicting her shock upon learning about her child's diagnosis: "A fist was crashing into my chest ... I felt no grief, only shock. And numbing fear." Similarly, Greenfeld (1972, 5) states, "Not the least victims of this common but rarely foreseen malady will be the child's parents and family." Autism, according to journalist Bonnie Cornell (1972, 87) in the *Toronto Star,* meant "endless days and sleepless nights of frustration and confusion," as well as a life for mothers, says journalist Helen Kohl (1979, n.p.), that was "a burden." This framing raises the possibility for a disability studies and disability justice critique of feminist political economy and care research that conceives of caring for and about a disabled child as a burden for mothers, a point that I return to below (see Hughes et al. 2005; Kelly 2013; Kröger 2009; Nishida 2022; and F. Williams 2001). Here, autism's destructive force victimizes mothers and families physically, emotionally, and presumably, financially, too, as families cope with this burden. And although life together in disability and with an autistic family member under austere neoliberal, ableist care regimes can indeed be difficult and costly, care for mothers and families appears as little more, in Don Moser's (1965, 96) words, than the "taming and teaching" of autism as an individualized, terrifying, burdensome problem of defective biology in need of a solution. It is interesting to note that although disordered autistic brains and bodies appear as stubbornly "wild," the notion that they might be tamed and taught relies on the emerging concept of "neuroplasticity," a neuroscientific tenet that holds brains/minds to be malleable, changeable over time, and remediable (Nadesan 2005; McGuire 2016, 50). Nevertheless, other possible ways to approach the disruptive, novel, and surprising aspects of autism's so-called wildness – for example, as something to "think with" (Michalko 2002, 168; see also Re•Storying Autism Writing Collective 2022; Rodas 2018; Snyder and Mitchell 2006b, 192; and Yergeau 2018) – as well as other possible understandings of alterity, caring (m)other-child relationships, or the constraints of our late-modern life together, are lost within the neurocognitive understanding of autism and autism mother that animates everyday text during this time.

As we have seen, autism mother as skilled therapist/worker was the natural fit for biological understandings of autism. By the 1990s, autism mothers had come to embody the intensive mother par excellence, as Amy C. Sousa (2011, 227) puts it: "Mothers became the primary advocates, spokespeople, service providers, researchers, and first responders for their children." However, as the above suggests, more than biology "gone wrong" (Michalko 2002, 22) was at stake for autism mother identity. Autism was also a biological force that victimized mothers, families, and children. Autism mothers, then, were also tasked with taming and civilizing this unruly, violent, disruptive biological force and with bringing it "in line" with white, bourgeois, heteronormative, economically productive subjectivity (Ahmed 2006a, 2006b, 2007). This was the task of a hero. This heroic mother appears, for example, in a *Publisher's Weekly* book review of a popular guide to autism written by autism mother Karyn Seroussi:

> When her son was diagnosed with autism at 19 months, Seroussi, a small-business owner and wife of a research chemist, determined to do everything in her power to help her child achieve normal functioning. In addition to pursuing recommended speech and behavior modification therapies for her son, Seroussi devoted her considerable energies – often against medical advice – to researching alternative approaches ... Now a crusader for dietary intervention, Seroussi has written a book that will give hope to many families. (Zaleski et al. 1999, 71)

Not only does Seroussi pursue conventional behavioural therapies, but she also confronts medical authority, develops expertise out of her maternal experience and scientific research, writes books, innovates her own approach, crusades for alternative approaches, and starts a dietary intervention organization. During this time, autism mother's therapist identity had become an intensification of the intensive mother and cultural hero crusading against the force of defective biology in her autistic child as well as advocating for the public services, research, and supports needed for her journey (Sousa 2005). Unlike many of Western culture's heroes, autism mothers were driven by their love, understood as natural. As Kaufman (1976, 19) put it with regard to his wife Suzy's intensive treatment of her son Raun, "in our love for our son and for his beauty we had found a determination to persist." Autism mother Beth Kephart (1998, 235), too, narrates "love as the only possible solution" and a "fierceness of heart" for this hero's task. Researchers Segal and Segal (1992, 89) also describe this mother's "courage and dedication" within the exhausting battle for normalcy.

Autism's mother therapist emerged as a cultural hero who must fight to normalize her child or suffer defeat by autism (recall the "wildness" of autism, this mother figure's exhaustion, and even her murder of her child). The mother therapist was now regulated through a newly inflected paradox of care: she must be both heroic and nurturing, expert-driven and practice-oriented, loving and rejecting, proximate in her intensive at-home treatment of her child and distant in her paid work roles. Using an ethic of disruption and affirming care to rethink this mother's narrative suggests that feminist disability scholars might "bridge" (Kelly 2013) the tensions of ableism and patriarchy (Douglas, Rice, and Kelly 2017; Hughes et al. 2005; Kröger 2009; F. Williams 2001) to reveal the ways that intensive mothering and Western scientific conceptions of the normal human constrain and do violence to the humanity and freedom of us all.

5

Retraining Behaviourism

Both the constraints and possibilities opened by biological views of autism and autism's mother therapist, alongside the failure of power to reduce autistic children and (m)others to the same, would create space for new forms of collective resistance against earlier psychoanalytic forms of mother blame. Chapter 4 described how parents began to organize against overt forms of blame. In this chapter, I reread autism mother memoirs – what literary scholar Brenda Clews calls "maternal texts" (quoted in T. Thomas 2003, 186) – which gained popularity from the late 1960s onward, as both an often unconsidered site of social action (for a notable exception, see Vicedo 2021) and a form of resistance that begins to "unmother" autism (E. Kim 2017; Runswick-Cole and Ryan 2019), even if fleetingly. I also weave insights from focus groups throughout the chapter. To do this work, I first tease out how the new identity of autism's mother therapist invited constraining practices of mothering and care as intensive normalizing labour within the mother-child dyad. I then describe how this new autism mother identity, in its failure to eclipse alterity, also opened moments of ethical narration as a form of resistance and engagement with a "disability commons" (Runswick-Cole and Goodley 2018) in memoirs – glimmers of something other than more of the same that began to collectively challenge scientific expertise, forward expertise emerging from (m)others' experiences, and affirm autistic difference. This content forms a largely untold part of the "disability story of parents" (Dona M. Avery, quoted in Ryan and Runswick-Cole 2009, 43; see also Panitch 2008) within the history of disability movements in Canada and the United States and reclaims it as part of the challenge by disability activists and critical allies to regimes of normalizing care – including practices of violence – that continue to appear as sensible and ordinary within dominant Western, neoliberal, capitalist, scientific care regimes (Broderick 2022; Titchkosky 2011, 3–6).

To reread everyday text in this way is to engage what feminist philosopher Megan Boler (1999, 166) calls testimonial reading: "What is at stake is not only the ability to empathize with the very distant other, but to recognize oneself as implicated in the social forces that create the climate of obstacles the other must confront." Testimonial reading moves beyond "passive empathy" (166) with, in our case, autism as a tragic biological disorder and autism mother as a devastating fate. Instead, testimonial reading engages a form of empathy that retains something of the irreducible difference of the "very distant other" and thus redirects the reader's gaze onto our own complicity within normalizing regimes. M. Remi Yergeau's (2018, 31) provocation also helps here: "How can we – in the classroom, in the clinic, in the pages of our scholarly annals – how can we transform social spaces in ways that enable those distant Others to speak back?"

The activity of rereading returns me to an ethic of disruption and the space of rupture – that "liminal space between subject and ground" (Titchkosky 2007, 21) where autism and autism mothers might be made anew. Through testimonial reading, I work the edges of disruptive knowledge – interpretive, critical, and feminist approaches in disability and critical autism studies – to reveal moments of ethical narration that might open possibilities about human difference and care in a manner that is a little different from that of autism advocacy, behavioural therapies, and biological regimes. Rereading and retelling the "disability story of parents" (Avery, quoted in Ryan and Runswick-Cole 2009, 43) in this way also means grappling with the limits of language to disrupt narrow Western biomedical conceptions of the human while avoiding the pitfalls of essentializing autistic difference. I inevitably slip in this ethical task. As we shall see, within everyday accounts of loving a different child and the Western cultural imperative for parents, particularly mothers, to participate in normalizing, individualizing intensive care, something of the excess of autism is revealed, an excess that also gestures to the fundamental alterity of us all and that contains the ethical call to respond to alterity without the violence of reducing others to the same (Boler 1999; Levinas 1969).

Ethically navigating relationships across and between difference continues to be one of the most vexing issues of our time; rereading memoirs written by mothers and attending to the experiences of (m)others in my focus groups advances this conversation in helpful ways.

Rereading Autism Mother Memoirs

In many ways, Chapter 4 catalogued how everyday text forms part of oppressive scientific and neoliberal, white, Western, bourgeois regimes of care and mothering as intensive normalizing labour within the mother-child dyad. In autism mother memoirs, mothers are complicit. As we have seen in Chapter 4, autism mother therapist Catherine Maurice (1993), for example, wrote a highly influential memoir and how-to chronicle telling a heroic tale of "recovering" her autistic children through her own intensive scientific self-governance and practice. Maurice's intellectual, financial, affective, and practical investment in the scientific method of behaviourism was intensive, alongside her understanding of autism as a tragic, biological disorder and her view of normalcy as an unquestioned good. Working with her daughter's first behavioural therapist, Maurice describes, "I just wanted her [daughter's] autism to go away and a normal personality to blossom" (71). Intensive behavioural therapy became the vehicle for this blossoming, "a radical but necessary means in assisting her to form a self" (131). The possibility of affirming her daughter's autistic self was unthinkable. Compared to emotion-based, psychogenic treatments, the behaviourist approach represented to Maurice "voices of reason within the wilderness" of autism treatment (117). Any "moral scruples" about the "authoritarianism" of behavioural therapies were justified by the controlled scientific delivery of the normal, autonomous, reasoned, and so-called civilized (read, white and bourgeois) self (130).

The behaviourist approach compelled parents – particularly white, middle-class mothers searching for alternatives to oppressive psychoanalytic blame and treatment – to take up the approach as "one of the most rigorous long-term evaluations of a therapy program ever conducted ... It indicates that many autistic children can not only be helped but can go on to lead normal lives" (Chance 1987, 44). Disability and critical autism studies education scholar Alicia Broderick (2011, n.p.) calls Maurice's best-selling *Let Me Hear Your Voice: A Family's Triumph over Autism* a "watershed moment" in public autism discourse, one when behavioural therapy was widely disseminated as the only scientifically proven method and hope that ostensible recovery from autism may be possible (see also Yergeau 2018, 119–20). Maurice's memoir is one beginning point, as both M. Remi Yergeau (2018) and autistic researcher Michelle Dawson (2004) point out, of the rhetoric of hopelessness that surrounds parent advocacy today – a rhetoric where cancer and death are uncomfortably equated with autism and where chemotherapy and hope are equated with behaviourist treatment. Without behaviourist treatment and early intervention, autism is a "fate worse than death" (Yergeau 2018, 119). Treatment is therefore urgent. On the blog *Emma's Hope Book,* Ariane Zurcher (2012) – (m)other of Emma Zurcher, who types to communicate and now directs her blog – has posted about the experience of reading Maurice's book, the first book on autism that she read, describing the seduction and promise of Applied Behaviour Analysis (ABA): "When Emma, then two years old, was given her diagnosis we were told, if we employed 40 hours of ABA a week she would undoubtedly be mainstreamed by Kindergarten. This was what we were told. This is what we hoped for. This is what we chose to believe."

Autistic self-advocates and critical autism scholars have articulated a critique of the behaviourist approach as a form of violence toward autistic people, and empirical studies showing the harm of intensive behaviourist regimes are emerging (Anderson 2022; Bascom 2012; Broderick 2011; Dawson 2004; Gibson and Douglas 2018; Gruson-Wood 2016; Pyne 2020; Sequenzia 2016).[1] It was in the writings and advocacy work of the founders of the neurodiversity movement during the years 1965–99 where challenges to the dominant view of autism as a biological disorder and tragedy were first made. Self-advocates called on parents: "For their own sake and for the sake of their children, I urge parents to make radical changes in their perceptions of what autism means" (Sinclair 1993, paras. 3–4). Glimmers of autism as a valuable and valid way of being also began to emerge in autism mother memoirs even as the genre remained entrenched in biological understandings of autism as a disorder and in the sense of a mother's care as the solution. As early as Clara Claiborne Park's (1967) *The Siege: A Family's Journey into the World of an Autistic Child,* mothers began to challenge medical doctors, psychiatrists, psychologists, and other professionals (Fisher and Goodley 2007, 72–74; Jack 2014, 60; Silverman 2012; Sousa 2005, 225;

Waltz 2013). The move to wrest authority and expertise away from the scientific and biomedical and to push back against individualizing, neoliberal, patriarchal mothering within the mother-child dyad also began to pry open space where glimpses of something different – a way of being together that valued and affirmed the humanity of autistic people and (m)others simultaneously – might emerge. Judy Barron, for example, writes,

> For better or worse, we were going to depend on ourselves from now on. We'd fight for Sean our way ... We couldn't bear to raise our hopes again by taking him to one more professional and encountering yet another dead end ... And Sean did not need to be the object of another experiment. "*I'm not sick!!!*" he had screamed one day as he sat facing twenty-seven vitamins and minerals he was supposed to swallow. (Barron and Barron 1992, 171–72; emphasis in original)

Despite intensive governance that invited this autism mother's "conduct of conduct" in normalizing ways (Foucault 1982, 1994), she also dwelled within an intimate space and relationship with her autistic child, Sean – "*I'm not sick!!!*" – beyond the grasp of science, professionals, and normative Western narratives of progress and development (Fisher and Goodley 2007). Indeed, as Michel Foucault (1980a, 94) tells us, governance is never total: "Where there is power, there is resistance." In this mother's case, the rejection of scientific authority was a moment of resistance. A compelling example of resistance also occurred during one of my focus group discussions with (m)others about their experiences of living autism's mother therapist. Anna, in contemplating how she might support her adult autistic son who did not achieve so-called recovery through intensive therapies, put it this way: "I started to kind of ... think, first, you know, we need to give up at a certain time." What Anna was "giving up" was the intensive labour to recover her son and the seduction of achieving normalcy. Zurcher (2012), too, came to question and critique ABA and to advocate for affirming care as the intensive therapies that they were doing with Emma failed, an outcome for which she, her husband, and Emma were blamed by doctors and therapists:

> I don't agree with the basic tenets of ABA because it is a methodology based in looking at those it treats as deficient and inferior. This is not a

model I believe will help Autistics or any of us in the long run. We, who are not autistic are in a position of power, we are the majority, we are the ones making the rules. That does not mean the rules we make are correct or even right.

Thus, through the very ground of defeat – the failure of power to eradicate difference or to govern (m)others and autistic children and adults completely – spaces for affirming understandings of autism, (m)othering, and care emerged within maternal texts and everyday lives, even if just for a moment.

Within such intimate spaces, ironically opened by the push of care back into the home, by the emergence of intensive mothering, and by neoliberal, capitalist regimes of self-governance, (m)others experimented with alternatives, adapted conventional approaches, and narrated a different kind of care and understanding of autism. For example, as noted, Barron responds to her son's alarm at and resistance to being an object of intensive curative therapies (behavioural or otherwise) with a resolve not to erase his agency and his desire and not to defer to scientific or biomedical authority: "We were going to depend on ourselves from now on" (Barron and Barron 1992, 171). Many parents, including Catherine Maurice (1993) and Josh Greenfeld (1972), both of whom worked directly with Ole Ivar Lovaas, described modifications that they made to the violence and harshness of his treatment, learning "how to take what worked, how to learn from those who could teach us, and how, finally, to trust our own instincts and reason" (Maurice 1993, 209). These modifications were grounded, at least in part, in (m)others' experience of their relationship with their different child as well as in qualities associated with the alternate and the maternal rather than with the scientific – such as empathy, intimacy, and instinct – even as autism's mother therapist (and these memoirs) remained troublingly tied to and often championed (as in the case of Maurice) dominant recovery narratives. These barely discernible spaces of resistance dispersed across maternal texts – in which, at least some of the time, some (m)others resisted individualizing, neoliberal, ableist, patriarchal care configurations and deficit understandings of autistic difference – represent the disruptive and often occluded sites of a dispersed disability commons from which to recuperate knowledge production and care differently. These are disruptive spaces in the everyday movements of life where the paradox of care begins to unravel, where ways of being together beyond the achievement of a neurotypical self with our autistic child(ren)/offspring might be glimpsed, and where everyday text and research about autism and care might attune to autistic people and revalue knowledge production as an interpretive, political, and ethical endeavour toward autistic and disability justice (Haraway 1991, 187; Scott 1991; D. Smith 1992, 91).

Other examples within everyday text that grappled with what it means to care and become human together in difference also began to circulate during this time (e.g., see Dineen 1991; Enright 1989, 3; and McDonnell 1993). In her memoir *News from the Border: A Mother's Memoir of Her Autistic Son,* academic mother Jane T. McDonnell (1993, 324), for example, narrates her own self-transformation toward accepting and affirming her son Paul's autistic personhood: "At first I thought of Paul as a changeling, a shadow of his real self which had been taken away ... Only later did I begin to see Paul as complete and whole, an entirely wonderful person in his own right, exactly and precisely the way he was." Another mother, talking of her autistic adult son, expressed hope during an interview with the *Toronto Star:* "I'd like to know he's somewhere where he'll be cared for ... and not in an institution" (Yaffe 1977, 4). Such moments in everyday text, albeit constrained ones, granted (m)others and ways of being identified as autistic at least a hint of a viable sitpoint in the world and opened space to imagine new possibilities for a good life together in what is identified as autistic difference, a life beyond that of intensive remedial care within the mother-child dyad, painful normalizing therapies, ideas of victimizing biology, and practices of institutionalization versus autism advocacy.

Descriptions through which alterity shimmers also appeared in moments within everyday text when autism mothers grappled with what it means to care in relationship with their different child. McDonnell (1993, 51), for example, describes the uniqueness of her son's way of being, and their way of being together, on a car trip to a friend's cottage:

> Paul had recently discovered flashlights and preferred them to any toy we could give him. So, the weekend before we were to leave for Devon, I went to a local hardware store and bought five flashlights, beginning with the tiniest penlight size, on up to one that was about ten inches long. On the

trip to Devon sitting in his car seat in the back, Paul could take the flashlights apart. I knew this would keep him happy for hours as he unscrewed
the bottom, took out the batteries, and removed the light bulb and the
spring behind the batteries. Then he could put them back together again.

Although McDonnell offers this to readers as her way of managing her
autistic son during a car trip (he did, after all, prefer flashlights to toys and
people), there is something of the stubborn uniqueness of Paul in this
description, as well as McDonnell's acceptance and even affirmation of
him – his love of repetition, sameness, order, and "adult" objects rather
than toys. Similarly, many autism mothers writing during these years
attempted to include the voice of their autistic child/offspring within their
narratives through co-writing (e.g., see Barron and Barron 1992; and
McDonnell 1993), subtly disrupting otherwise easily consumed and seductive narratives. For example, despite traces of a psychoanalytic understanding of autism and recovery narratives, *There's a Boy in Here* features Judy
Barron's son and co-author, Sean, who described his experience of spending
hours flipping light switches on and off: "I loved repetition. Every time I
turned on a light, I knew what would happen" (Barron and Barron 1992,
20–21). Another such moment in which alterity flashes is when Barron
loses her ability to make sense of her autistic child. "I couldn't understand,"
Barron writes of her son's inconsistent memory for tasks that he had previously learned (61). Here, in Barron's failure to contain the difference of
her son's memory in her description or to reduce it to the same cultural
ground by making it a disorder to be remedied, Sean's irreducible alterity
appears, pointing to other possible ways of being human together that
affirm the difference of autism (on alterity, see Levinas 1969, 79–81; 1989).

Paying attention to the simultaneous complicity in and resistance to
the intensely patriarchal and ableist paradox of care by autism mothers in
maternal texts offers a critical "bridge" (Kelly 2013) across and between
feminist and disability studies approaches to care. Care is fraught with
ambiguity, power, and paradox for autism mother and autistic child alike.
As disability studies and care scholar Christine Kelly writes, "It represents
the failure of medical cure and neoliberal progress; it is a deep compassion
and empathy; a highly intimate relationship; an institutionalized approach
to disability; a transnational supply and demand of feminized labour; a

dependency on state funded programs" (790; see also Douglas, Rice, and Kelly 2017). (M)othering a disabled child can be understood as a site of both oppressive patriarchal, ableist governance and a potentially liberatory and subversive practice within powerful regimes (Douglas et al., "Mad Mothering," 2021; Douglas et al., "Making Memories," 2022; O'Reilly 2007, 2016; Rich 1986) that "carries a jolting, perhaps irresolvable paradox – that of transgressive possibility and coercive constraint, intimate inter-dependence and constraining power, love and violence. In this, care seeks to normalize or cure while also holding possibilities for individual and collective transgression and freedom" (Douglas, Rice, and Kelly 2017, 4–5). Attending to ethical moments of the narration of difference within everyday maternal texts between 1965 and 1999, the years when autism's mother therapist emerged, disrupts the paradox of care and neoliberal, patriarchal, ableist ways of caring and being together as well as tensions between feminist and disability studies approaches to (m)othering, disability, and care.

The paradox for (m)others of caring for and about a unique and different autistic child and the cultural imperative to therapeutically – and often violently – intervene (the earlier the better) to achieve identity with normal development played out within everyday text during this time. As we have seen, manifold maternal-hero narratives with the goal of normalization and recovery emerged (Barron and Barron 1992; Kaufman 1976; Maurice 1993; Stehli 1991). Yet moments of alterity and resistance glimmer and reach across nondisabled-disabled difference to touch us, as readers, to humanize the difference of what is identified, reified, and othered as autistic difference, and to recuperate (m)othering and care. My rereading of autism mother memoirs in this chapter through an ethic of disruption reveals how care might also be ethical and affirming, disrupting dominant understandings of autism as pathology and of autism mother as governed by science as solution, even if just for a moment (Michalko 2002; Van Manen 1990, 23). Affirming care means a relationship with difference "replete with lessons about the self, other and world including histories of power and marginal-ization, resistance and reclamation, normalcy and deviance, affect and violence, fleshy sensuality and dehumanizing systems" (Douglas, Rice, and Kelly 2017, 4). Here, conventional understandings of autistic difference give way, and space is opened, even if just for a moment, where we might, as readers, encounter difference, (m)othering, and care as ethical, relational, and affirming, revelatory of the fundamental alterity of us all (Levinas 1998). This chapter shows that moments of resistance and alterity within everyday text are one site that begins to unmother autism, delinking (m)othering from intensive, individual remedial care and claiming alternative, affirming practices of care through a disability commons – in this case, as I have documented it across maternal texts that emerged in these years.

6

Autism's Warrior Mothers
The Genomic Gaze

This chapter traces the emergence of autism's "warrior mother," a powerful cultural figure that emerged in everyday text starting approximately in 2000 and that remains with us to the present. The warrior mother is a fierce advocate who must not only fight against autism in her child but also fight against the genetic and environmental risk of transmitting autism for generations to come. Biological understandings of autism still prevailed during this time, and although the predominant neurocognitive approaches (e.g., Theory of Mind) and behavioural therapies have been overlaid with a genomic approach in autism research and potential therapies (Singh 2016; Nadesan 2005), these earlier approaches continue to have considerable influence (e.g., see Baron-Cohen 1995; Blacher and Howell 2007; and Renzetti 2011). The incipient "discursive explosion" (Foucault 1980a, 17–18) of autism – the bringing of autism and autism mothers into everyday text and scientific discourse – and the Western cultural fascination with autism noted for previous years also intensified after 2000 (Grinker 2007; Hacking 2010; Mallett and Runswick-Cole 2012; Murray 2008). Manifold magazines, newspapers, blogs, and memoirs depicting the good and the bad of life with autistic children and documenting autism mothers' heroic tales of recovering their child have flourished (Hacking 2010; see also Barnett 2013; Cooper 2016; and McCarthy 2007). Television shows such as *Parenthood* and *Atypical,* documentaries such as *The Autism Enigma* (Gruner and Sumpton 2011) and *A Mother's Courage: Talking Back to Autism* (Fridriksson 2010), as well as motion pictures like *Mozart and the Whale* feature autistic as well as autism mother characters. Autism mothers begin to appear, too, in fictional accounts during these years such as *Love Anthony* by Lisa Genova (2012), a novel that tells its story, in part, and jarringly, through a mother's imagined conversations with her son in her own and her autistic son's voice.

Rates of autism spectrum disorder (ASD) diagnosis as compiled by countries of the Global North have also increased sharply since 2000. In 2018, the National Autism Spectrum Disorder Surveillance System, "a collaboration of territorial, provincial and federal governments, working to build a comprehensive picture of ASD in Canada," reported that 1 in 66 children and youth are currently diagnosed with autism in Canada (Public Health Agency of Canada 2018, 3). The following year, this figure was reported to be 1 in 50 (Public Health Agency of Canada 2019, 4). Recall that between 1970 and 1999, rates of diagnosis were 1 or 2 in 1,000. Calls for a national autism strategy from advocacy groups such as the Canadian Autism Spectrum Disorder Alliance (2019, 4; now known as Autism Alliance Canada) identify autism as "the most common and fastest-growing neurodevelopmental disorder in Canada" and urge policy makers that "the time to act is now."[1] Extensive stakeholder consultations were also recently held about social inclusion, autism, diversity, and public policy by the arm's-length body the Canadian Academy of Health Sciences (2022). The summary report includes the language of intersectionality, neurodiversity, and autism acceptance; these terms have entered public discourse in Canada. It remains to be seen whether the policy making that follows will be crafted in affirming ways inclusive of autistic people, (m)others, and families and kin.

Rebirthing Autism Mothers: Watch Out for ... Everything!

Urgent public health concerns call for urgent action. Within everyday text, this action has included the retraining of a mother's gaze toward her own genes, the environment around her, and her own choices: Do I vaccinate my child, or will this cause autism? What diet do I follow? What supplements do I take during pregnancy? Do I live in a polluted area? Is climate change influencing autism rates? Do I carry the "autism gene"? Am I educated enough about the warning signs of autism? Is my doctor? (e.g., see Belli 2010; Jack 2014, 64–104; McCarthy 2008; *Mothering* 1998; Nadesan 2005, 194–96; A. Park 2017; Rutter 2000, 5; and Seroussi 1999). It was striking how (m)others in my focus groups asked similar questions and shared how the identity warrior mother and the notion of risk occupied them bodily and affectively. (M)others posed questions and shared worries about vaccines, diet, nursing, the transmission of "autism genes," genetic testing, sleep, and more as they took up the work of (m)othering and care in the fraught space between lived experience and everyday text. However, within (m)others' lives, power was never totalizing, an important point that the next two chapters illustrate. For example, Julie, (m)other to nineteen-year-old Kyle, was not convinced by conventional autism experts and treatments and found herself questioning "the rise" of alternative approaches. She shared, "You wonder if the rise of things ... the RDIs [Relationship Development Interventions] and the Son-Rise's [program] and the diet and things is a way to take back ... some control over the situation."

In all the questioning, there is also a slippage between diagnosis and incidence of autism, one that betrays the Western scientific impulse both to describe the presumably natural (and therefore universal) nondisabled body governed by discoverable laws and to explain disability – such as struggles with gluten – as a deviation from it (Michalko 2002, 30). As disability and critical autism studies scholars have shown, autism and the rising diagnosis of autism is a cultural, historical, and interpretive production linked to twentieth- and twenty-first-century Western scientific, neoliberal, capitalist understandings of the normal and natural human (Grinker 2007; McGuire 2016; Nadesan 2005; Yergeau 2018). And, as poet and disability activist Eli Clare (2017, 14; emphasis in original) invokes, biomedicine's cure is not far behind the mythical natural body: "As an ideology seeped into every corner of Western thought and culture, cure rides on the back of *normal* and *natural.*" Indeed, as we shall see, fighting ever more intensively for a cure against what appears as an alarming rising incidence of autism – or at least for the approximation of normalcy (cure through care) – is the mark of the postmillennial good mother within popular media and science (see also Blum 2007; Douglas et al., "Mad Mothering," 2021; and Sousa 2005). The work of the chapters to come show that (m)others who resist this ideal and who affirm difference and alternative ways to care are often met with labels of "madness" and are dismissed and gaslighted by systems (Douglas et al., "Mad Mothering," 2021; Runswick-Cole, Fogg, and Douglas, forthcoming).

Autism mothers' everyday implication in the search for the cause and cure of autism since 2000 has co-occurred with the rise of autism epidemic language (e.g., see Scherer 2012). Although contested by autistic activists, scientists, and (m)others alike (Gernsbacher, Dawson, and Goldsmith 2005; McGuire 2016; Ne'eman 2018), the language of epidemic introduced a new and somewhat pernicious layer of meaning to the cultural scene of everyday text after 2000, including allusions to autism as an uncontained, unpredictable global spread of a contagious disease that is akin to the plague and, as anthropologist and father Roy R. Grinker (2007, 3) points out, "threatening the ones you love." Epidemic rhetoric is frightening and lends even more urgency to the maternal "duty and … urge to act" (Bauman 2004a, 20) in order to circumvent autism and respond quickly, earlier, and with maximum resources, in the language of Autism Speaks Canada (n.d.), to any "early indications of autism" in one's child. Indeed, over the past twenty years, autism's mother therapist has intensified into today's cultural figure of the warrior mother. The warrior mother is a superhero and mother expert who fights through love and in a warring register *against* the enemy autism and its environmental and genetic causes. Autism's warrior mother is also up against so-called incompetent medical practitioners and government systems that block her crusade to forward genomic research and to secure genetic and other therapies that will normalize her child and family (Darling 2003; Jack 2014, 64–65; Sousa 2005). She is Howard Becker's (1963) "moral entrepreneur" and more, enlisting the expertise of scientists, policy makers, health care providers, lawyers, popular and social media, and international health networks (Autism Speaks n.d.a), as well as her own maternal expertise, in her crusade against autism and its threat to normalcy (Douglas 2013; Jack 2014, 64–104; Silverman 2012; Titchkosky and Michalko 2012). As the work of this chapter will show, this newly contradictory and intensive warrior mother figure, situated within a now-dominant biogenetic understanding of autism, has come to regulate what it means to care and be a good mother during the post-2000 years.

The language of war that skirted public media and science about autism and autism mothers before 2000 – fortress, imprison, fight, siege, courage – has also become a central feature since 2000. This is one site within what disability studies scholar Anne McGuire (2016, 25) calls "a culture at war with autism," one that, in its hostility to difference, "structures and supports possibilities for violence against those noticed as embodying autistic difference" (58). This "culture at war" includes intensifying and powerful globalizing parent advocacy (at times softened by using the language of autism acceptance and affirmation forwarded by autistic self-advocates and the neurodiversity movement) for curative genomic research and behavioural and biomedical treatment, as well as representations of autism and policy responses infused with the scientific and moral understanding that autistic life is a nonviable, nonvaluable, and tragic life posing a significant threat to the health of individuals, families, nations, and indeed, the world. This "war" also includes, tragically, the murder and neglect of autistic individuals at the hands of caregivers and police (Ryan 2021; see also below).

The only possible response to the problem of autism framed as such is to scientifically elevate and coordinate a "fight" to "defeat it" (McGuire 2016, 58). For example, white parent advocates and scientists of the Global North are exporting the war on autism nationally and internationally through Internet campaigns, websites, and international health initiatives (Douglas 2013; McGuire 2016, 56–58), simultaneously exporting Western culture's enduring commitment to a very particular yet universalizing version of the human – one that is rational, autonomous, self-enterprising, productive, bourgeois, and white. This signals the importance of proceeding with an ethic of disruption that is attentive to the complicity of the lived identities of "autistic" and "autism mother" within ongoing Western, neoliberal, capitalist (Broderick 2022), and settler-colonialist projects (Bevan-Brown 2013; Douglas et al., "Beyond 'Inclusionism,'" forthcoming; Roy and Balaratnasingam 2010). These projects enlist scientific hierarchies of race, gender, and disability in the colonization of bodies and minds. I do not invoke, as Eve Tuck and Wayne K. Wang (2012, 20) caution, "'colonization' as a metaphor" here. Instead, as a white-settler scholar, I learn about allyship and decolonizing from, among others, Michi Saagiig Nishnaabeg scholar, writer, and artist Leanne Betasamosake Simpson (2017, 15), who writes about a white-settler mentor who "created the space to put Nishnaabeg intelligence at the centre and use its energy to drive the project" of decolonizing research and about the importance of "holding space" in the academy for this approach (see also D. Mitchell and Snyder 2003, 2015). In this book, to borrow a phrase from cultural theorist Stuart Hall (1997, 290), I spotlight the "deadly political" nature of the undertaking to export universalizing Western scientific and biomedical understandings, and to thereby normalize therapeutic practices, health policies, and the autism industry (Broderick 2022), as a force within colonizing projects (McGuire 2016; Titchkosky and Aubrecht 2015). The larger context of the cultural war on autism operates on and profits from making the same of alternate bodies through the intensive labour of autism mothers within the mother-child dyad. This cultural war emanates, at least in part, from everyday text by and about autism mothers in the Global North. It is now autism's warrior mother who must watch out for autism and who faces the paradox of care as she wages war against autism (and her autistic child) at every turn.

An Example from Ontario

The documentary *The Autism Enigma* (Gruner and Sumpton 2011), which aired on the popular science show *The Nature of Things*, is one such every-day example. Narrated by Canadian environmentalist David Suzuki, it tells the story of three Canadian autism mothers – two white-settler, Western mothers and one Black, Westernizing, Third World immigrant mother – as they grapple with the meaning of autism in their lives vis-à-vis their children and the current state of genetic and other scientific research. The beholder of the documentary is presented with the facts of autism, mothering, and care as they observe these moms move through their daily lives while engaging intensively in autism therapies, advocacy, medical appointments, autism conferences, specialty food preparation, research, and more. Autism, Suzuki tells us, is a neurodevelopmental disorder, a biological enigma located in individual brains and behaviour that must be remedied. It is caused by an unknown combination of genetic and environmental factors. It is on the rise. And it is a tragedy immediately caught up with the intensive labour, love, grief, and care of mothers. I note that the expected mother in this documentary as well as other popular media and science described in this chapter is still gendered; it is most often biological mothers who are expected to labour intensively to remedy autism in their child. If, as ethnomethodologist Harold Garfinkel (1967, vii) suggests, such facts of social life are a practical "accomplishment" of social interaction within the everyday occasions through which they come into being and are given meaning, then *The Autism Enigma* engages viewers in such an occasion. I describe two of the mothers' stories depicted in the documentary to highlight the new meaning that it makes of autism, the social construction of mothering, and care.

Despite her young adult son's "delightful" presence in her life, expert mother Ellen Bolte tells viewers, "I cling to the hope that research is going to be done in time and that he'll be able to receive treatment and that he will be able to still respond." She narrates the years of intensive research, based on her intuitions regarding what had triggered her son's autism, that she undertook in her attempt to fight against autism in her child. Her fierce advocacy with scientists based on her efforts resulted in a new research project in Canada investigating the gut-brain connection in autism and antibiotic use. Echoing the case studies that we encountered in previous chapters, Ellen shares home videos and detailed records with viewers of her young son's "behaviour" before and after the biomedical treatments that resulted from this research. In the before videos, viewers watch Ellen's son running back and forth, ignoring her attempts to get his attention, and at times, curled up in a ball, rocking. In after videos, we see her young son talking to the camera, smiling, and cuddling playfully with his mom. Despite Ellen's "delight" with her adult son (who is depicted in the film talking, smiling at, and hugging his mother), she speaks openly of her grief after the biomedical treatments failed to permanently eliminate autistic behaviour (see also Gordon 2013). For Ellen, a kind of warrior mother who fights against autism by accruing expertise as well as intensive advocacy for better science, a life together with her son in the difference of autistic embodiment seems inconceivable (Titchkosky and Michalko 2012; Yergeau 2018). Autism, as it is made to appear in her son's rocking, moving, and seemingly non-attentive body in the documentary, signals disorder, failure, and grief for Ellen, despite her apparent delight. Through Ellen's narration, autism is accomplished as a nonviable sitpoint (Garland-Thomson 2002), an unnatural, disruptive, noncongruent, and undesired form of life that disrupts the ground of normal development and sociality (Schutz 1962). After her failed attempts as a warrior mother to produce a cure for her son, Ellen's only "hope" is that scientific research will yield more effective future treatments for him. There is no recuperation of (m)othering, autism, and care through affirming care and a disability commons here. The only justice and care on the horizon are to be attained through intensive individual advocacy for better science.

Viewers also meet Adar Hassan, introduced as a Somali immigrant in Toronto with two autistic sons she cares for full-time. Unlike her privileged, white-settler, Western counterparts in the documentary, who have extensive advocacy experience and are fierce movers of scientific agendas, Adar is learning what to make of autism. The beholder of the film watches, listens, and learns along with her as she seeks Western medical help, engages autism services, and searches for answers about autism and its treatment. There is no word for autism in Somalia, Suzuki tells us, but it is being identified in the Toronto Somali community by Western psychologists and doctors to such an extent that Adar and other families have been asked to participate in genetic research at the University of Guelph and the University of Western Ontario (see also Kediye, Valeo, and Berman 2009). Both she and Suzuki name the shift to an industrialized country and the loss of "simple foods" as a possible cause for the apparent rising incidence in the Somali community. Adar is depicted as a developing Global South subject alongside her Black autistic sons. Along with Suzuki's narration, viewers are shown images of the so-called simple autism-free life that Adar left behind in Somalia and are in this way directed to a romanticized picture of a more pure, natural, preindustrial, autism-free world from which Adar came and to which we must all return, but this time on the ground of Western scientific, capitalist production and intensive mothering within the mother-child dyad. In a sense, Adar is depicted as the good Westernizing subject by virtue of bearing, and learning how to bear, the pathologizing effects of late modernity – autism diagnoses for her sons, intensive scientifically informed expert warrior mothering, advocacy, the impulse toward cure, and the engagement of normalizing treatments. *The Autism Enigma* ties a mother's love in the domestic realm to the return to a healthier and more pure state, where we see Adar, for example, preparing raw foods. However, a mother's fight to find a cure for her autistic child is also tied to the consumption of products and expertise in the private market (Broderick 2022; Broderick and Roscigno 2021). We watch as Adar, for instance, attends the annual AutismOne Conference held in Chicago, where parents, scientists, celebrities, and capital collide in the search for and promotion of treatments and cures. Indeed, the very "duty and ... urge to act" that Zygmunt Bauman (2004a, 20) ties to the accomplishment of modern forms of identity composes Adar's new

Westernizing selfhood, as she learns to consummate both herself and her sons into being through Western, neoliberal, scientific versions of the human and through Western discourses of development delivered by the autism industry. Adar's story demonstrates a key shift in the governance of autistic populations between 2000 and 2020. Autism's expert mother warrior identity, as exemplified by Ellen Bolte, has become a Westernizing cultural phenomenon, one that is now encircling and governing the good/ bad mother far beyond Leo Kanner's (1943) and Bruno Bettelheim's (1967) chilly white, bourgeois, North American or western European mother who works (see Jimenez 2009; and H. Kim 2012).

The Neurodiversity Movement

Against the backdrop of rising rates of autism diagnosis and the push of Western, white, nondisabled versions of the human into the autism industrial complex and new global-capitalist markets (Broderick 2022; Broderick and Roscigno 2021), autistic self-advocates and the neurodiversity movement have brought autism into view in new ways and have challenged the language of epidemic and war (Ne'eman 2010, 2018). The term "neurodiversity"[2] was coined collectively in the 1990s by autistic activists (Botha et al. 2024) and introduced widely in 2008 in a *New York Magazine* article, where autistic sociologist Judy Singer describes her activist aspirations with the term neurodiversity: "I was interested in the liberatory activist aspects of it – to do for the neurologically different people what feminism and gay rights had done for their constituencies" (A. Solomon 2008, n.p.; see also Singer 2017). Neurodiversity has been a formative concept within the establishment of autistic self-advocacy organizations in Canada. For example, groups such as Autistics for Autistics (A4A) and Autistics United Canada have an active online presence and advocate for autism acceptance and affirmation, take a public stance against Applied Behaviour Analysis and other treatments grounded in deficit understandings of autism, organize affirming public events such as Day of the Stim, offer educational resources, collaborate with critical allies in the disability community, and forward broad legislative and cultural change. Predating these Canadian organizations are many autistic bloggers who have forwarded autistic acceptance and affirmation,[3] as well as organizations like the Autistic Self Advocacy Network in the United States, which forwards autism as a viable way of being and argues that autism (parent) advocacy should not advance a world without autism as its goal (Baggs 2010; McGuire 2016, 58–66; Sequenzia 2016). More recently, autistic self-advocates and scholars have forwarded the identity of neurodivergence to mean any divergence (including, for example, autism, attention deficit hyperactivity disorder, dyslexia, and others) from what is considered (through Western science) to be neuro-normative (Walker 2021). Autistic blogger Amy Sequenzia (2016), who coined the term "neurodivergence," and autistic scholars like Nick Walker (2021) and M. Remi Yergeau (2018) bend the concept further through the concept of "neuroqueering." This latter concept implies, at least for this author, that any neuro-norm from which we might diverge is also itself socio-culturally constituted in the space where body and world meld. These are important challenges to dominant biomedical understandings of autism and care. They forward a generative understanding of autism that opens space to (m)other and to care in a way that is different from that of autism's warrior mother. For example, a number of (m)others of autistic children/offspring and autistic (m)others (categories that are not mutually exclusive) who are also scholars, artists, and activists have recently forwarded this more affirming and collectivized understanding of autism, care, and support in their work to challenge the ableist, neoliberal, patriarchal, capitalist association of autism and care with individual, intensive, remedial, maternal labour (e.g., see Ashburn and Edwards 2023; Hammond 2023; Klar and Wolfond n.d.; and Re•Storying Autism Writing Collective 2022).

I work in solidarity, hold the meaning of autism open, and proceed with an ethic of disruption to intervene in the paradox of care – love for and war against your autistic child simultaneously – that relies on damaging the binaries between normal and abnormal, between us and them (i.e., autism mother and autistic child or adult) (Runswick-Cole 2014). This is to say that I continue to work in this chapter to unmother autism (E. Kim 2017; Runswick-Cole and Ryan 2019), uncoupling (m)others from oppressive, misogynistic, curative care regimes and from the "natural" imperative that mothers must labour ceaselessly to remedy autism. This work opens space for affirming, collective ways to (m)other and care in solidarity with disability justice and autistic self-advocacy (Runswick-Cole and Goodley 2018). The remainder of this chapter examines the shifts and intensifications within everyday text by and about autism mothers during the postmillennial years. I maintain my focus on Canadian newspapers readily available to a Toronto audience, consistent with my previous chapters, in order to manage the sheer number of texts now available and to continue tracing local genealogies. Again, my aim is not to catalogue or survey every magazine, blog, memoir, or newspaper article available but to trace the many tangled threads of the identities autism and autism mother as they emerged during the post-2000 years. I document new forms of identity, knowledge, visibility, and technology for these years and include moments from my focus groups that bring this everyday text alive in all its complexity.

New Forms of Knowledge: From Genetics to Genomics

The new the millennium marked a turning point in terms of the forms of knowledge that would come to dominate Western culture's understanding of autism and of the human. Everything from obesity to diabetes was now understood to have a genetic basis (e.g., see Abraham 2011). In 2000, psychiatrist Michael Rutter, a research scientist in developmental psychopathology in the United Kingdom, published a pivotal review article on genetic studies of autism since the 1970s. In this article, Rutter (2000, 5) asserts that twin and family studies show that "the heritability of an underlying liability to autism was above 90%." Rutter states that genetic studies will successfully uncover the causes of autism, along with "effective means of intervention or prevention" (11). Although the confidence of such early genetic research to locate a heritable "autism gene" (or genes) has more recently waned due to the failure of research to yield results (Singh 2016, 47, 97), similar stories began to appear around autism, such as the article "The Early Origins of Autism," published in the same year in *Scientific American*. This article describes genetic research into mutations of the gene HOXA1, located on chromosome 7, a gene thought to be a trigger in some cases of autism (Rodier 2000; see also De Rubeis and Buxbaum 2014; and Rosen-Sheidley, Wolpert, and Folstein 2004). I concur with Majia Holmer Nadesan (2005, 141), who argues that for autism, as for other genetic disorders, "observable and measurable expressions of 'mental illness' are directly caused in degree and form by the underlying organic disorder such that the observed expressions of the disorder are seen as mere epiphenomena of the 'underlying' condition." In other words, ways of being identified as autistic such as a preference for solitude, limited social interaction, or an averted eye gaze are reduced to mere biology and become nothing more than involuntary symptoms of biology gone wrong (see also Yergeau 2018, 12).

In different ways, (m)others in my focus groups both took up and challenged this reductive biogenetic understanding of autism. Rosa, for example, whose nonspeaking autistic daughter Elizabeth is now an adult, countered reductive scientific views when she recommended books by autistic authors to (m)others in the group whose children were younger, such as *The Reason I Jump: The Inner Voice of a Thirteen-Year-Old Boy with Autism,* authored by Naoki Higashida (2016), who offers an alternative and more affirming understanding of so-called autistic behaviour from his own lived experience. Another (m)other, Esther, whose ten-year-old son, Ryan, had more recently been diagnosed, described how she grappled with the power of the genetic paradigm in her interactions with her doctor. He invited her and her family to be tested for the so-called autism gene. Esther both took up the dominant genetic understanding of autism in accepting her doctor's invitation and resisted it when she asked, "What do I do with that information?" The possibility of documenting family inheritance seems to have compelled this doctor's desire to include Esther and her family in a genetic study. In Esther's question, we can glimpse resistance against the power of medical authority and expertise – for example, to shape a decision about whether to have a child or not – as well as the reductive understanding of autism as a genetic problem. To push this example a little further, within encounters like Esther's experience with her doctor, the Western scientific "god-trick" is at play, what Donna Haraway (1991, 188) calls a "conquering gaze from nowhere" that erases socio-cultural and interpretive processes and histories (like the doctor's interpretive move to reduce autism to inherited genes) through which bodies come to have meaning. This reductive understanding of autism elides the constitutive nature of the so-called normal human through the marking of autistic and alternate bodies/minds as object and Other – in this case, as mere inherited genes – to the exclusion of considering Esther's loving relationships with her autistic son and kin. This scientific search for certainty, control, and a way to make the same of autistic difference through genetic research aimed at eliminating autism is arguably a twenty-first-century version of eugenics, what Claudia Malacrida (2019) calls "newgenics," harkening back to scientific studies of measurable traits, such as craniometry and its measurement of bumps on skulls, in the late 1800s and early 1900s. These studies, much like the early biological psychiatry of the 1900s and today's genetic research, attempted to link so-called social deviance, based on race, class, and mental difference, with heredity (Nadesan 2005, 140; see also D. Mitchell and Snyder 2003). It is autism's warrior mother who is now invited, in encounters like Esther's experience with her doctor, to carry this new version of eugenics forward.

Yet genetic research has failed to identify any major heritable autism gene or genes. However, rather than shifting the emphasis of research to supporting autistic individuals and their families and kin within their everyday lives, this failure has resulted in a shift to genomic thinking and research about autism and, as Nikolas Rose (2007) articulates, about "life itself." This orientation means that autism research, which shapes the landscape of care for autism mothers, now involves taking part in large-scale scientific efforts to map the full genomic sequence of autistic individuals and their families, resulting in a new understanding of autism (and other conditions) as multiple diseases stemming from spontaneous chromosomal mutations at the molecular level and involving hundreds of interacting genes. Esther shared her discovery in one of our focus group conversations that both she and her son have a marker for autism on chromosome 16. "We don't have the bigger deletion. It's the smaller deletion." Sociologist Jennifer Singh (2016, 84) has called this shift to "multiple autisms" a new "thought style" emerging out of our contemporary socio-political moment and genetic understanding of the human. For Esther, this discovery of a partial deletion on chromosome 16 for her and her son also invited new questions and "views" of the struggles that her two sons are encountering (autism and "obesity," respectively) in ways that align with genetic causality.

The scientific shift in thinking about what autism (or the human) is has galvanized parent advocates, autism researchers, and both public and private funders to initiate large-scale, international, public and private genomic-sequencing initiatives and mass data-sharing efforts. Projects of this ilk include Autism Speaks Canada's (2019, para. 1) MSSNG project, which brings fifty-eight academic and research institutions in sixteen countries together with Toronto's Hospital for Sick Children (SickKids),

Autism Speaks (which has donated $16 million), Google (where the database is hosted), and the genomic-engineering giants Verily and DNAStack (para. 5). As stated by Dr. Stephen Scherer, director of the Centre for Applied Genomics at SickKids, "We know there are many subtypes of autism. The more data we include related to different types of autism in each research study, the more inclusive the results will be, fueling a flow of discoveries" (para. 4). This "flow of discoveries" includes progress toward the development of a DNA test for autism, one that might be given prenatally, raising complex bioethical issues for medical practitioners, (m)others, families, and kin (see also Abraham 2007, 2008, 2010; and Talaga 2013).

Arguably, such projects can be understood as investing in a particular kind of progress: a version of the human that excludes autism and locates it in individual disordered bodies and brains that become the objects of scientific study (along with their families) within an academic research market where autism is a hot commodity and booming industry (Broderick 2022; Mallett and Runswick-Cole 2012). After all, the purpose of these international efforts is to reduce, prevent, or even eliminate the expression of autism in the human population by finding autism's cause, as well as by offering genetic counselling to at-risk families and DNA tests more broadly (versions of which are already on the market) that screen for autism susceptibility in family members and fetuses (Singh 2016; see also McGuire 2016, 52–53; Nadesan 2005; and Rosen-Sheidley, Wolpert, and Folstein 2004). The effect of such international efforts, too, has been the public and private investment in and generation of, to borrow from Anne McGuire (2016, 53), "multi-million-dollar biomedical autism research industries." What was formerly the crusade of "moral entrepreneurs" such as Bernard Rimland (1964) and Catherine Maurice (1993) to establish autism on biological research agendas is now professionalized and institutionalized "big business" (Mallett and Runswick-Cole 2012, 40; see also Broderick 2022). This crusade is self-perpetuating and proliferating in its search for new problems to be solved (e.g., more genes to discover, different subtypes of autism, and DNA tests for the general market) and for new solutions to the unsolved problem of autism (e.g., prenatal screening, new technologies, pharmaceutical interventions, and more intensive labour by mothers) (see Bumiller 2009).

Because so many genes and gene interactions are understood to be involved in a complex relationship to the expression of autism and other genetic disorders in individuals, many autism researchers also believe that environmental influences must play a role. The field of epigenetics, in lay terms, studies how environmental factors, such as prenatal stress, diet, exposure to toxins, viruses, pesticides, antibiotics, and drugs, can chemically alter gene function and expression in the developing fetus or child, leading to turn-on or turn-off conditions like autism (e.g., see Abraham 2011; Jimenez 2009; and Parsell 2004, 311–12). According to pediatric neurologist Andrew Zimmerman, environmental influences include "anything that affects pregnancy" (quoted in Parsell 2004, 311). These influences are, along with our DNA, beginning to be understood as heritable. As explained by Rosanna Weksberg, epigenetics researcher at Toronto's Hospital for Sick Children, "there's an epigenetic memory" for environmental influences such as maternal stress or malnutrition (quoted in Abraham 2011). Epigenetic memory affects not only cell regeneration but also transmission across generations through sperm and egg cells, finding expression in generations to come beyond mother and child (M. Skinner, Manikkan, and Guerrero-Bosagna 2011). If this is indeed the case, it would seem reasonable to invest in broad public programs that support equity and health for all groups. However, individual mothers continue to be held responsible for not labouring intensively enough against epigenetic influences within the mother-child dyad, as we shall see below. This development raises the spectre of a new kind of epigenetic mother blame as autism diagnoses begin to extend to previously excluded marginalized groups such as Indigenous, Black, and other people of colour.

Rimland's (1978) earlier suggestion not only for a behaviourist approach to understanding autism and autism treatment but also for an alternative biomedical approach has also thrived in the genomic age. Alternative biomedical approaches fault the toxic environment for triggering autism, including childhood vaccinations, prenatal exposure to toxic chemicals, and oral antibiotic use in young children. Autism, in this view, is an environmental illness from which recovery is possible through biomedical interventions (many of which are dangerous and unsubstantiated) such as vitamin therapy, chelation therapy, and more (e.g., see Belli 2010; Jack 2014, 64–104; McCarthy 2009; Nadesan 2005,

194–96; and Seroussi 1999). The risk of autism, to borrow from McGuire (2016, 56; emphasis in original), can now *"come from anywhere,"* including the very practices that mothers engage to protect their/our child, adding new layers to the paradox of care and regulation of the good mother in the postmillennial years, such that a mother is now both risky and protective as well as a hot new commodity within ever-expanding research markets searching for autism's cause.

Dominant genomic science is a proliferating research market that animates popular renderings of autism and autism mothers with a yet to be satisfied demand for a solution to the problem of autism (Mallett and Runswick-Cole 2012). Given this context, and following philosopher Rosalyn Diprose (2005, 537), an ethic of disruption must "make sense" of such knowledge production in another sense, one that moves beyond the location of identity and difference in our genes and the environmental influences that turn genes on or off:

> It is as bodies that our finitude and uniqueness are signified to others; hence it is as bodies that we are both social and moral beings. This uniqueness is expressed through and is inseparable from being open to others within a context of social discourses (scientific, ethical, sociological). As such, identity, and therefore difference, is never self-present; the body makes sense, but never completely, or in and of itself.

Through our openness as embodied beings irretrievably caught up with and in social, material, and discursive relations with others, the meaning that we make of bodies comes to make sense. Diprose suggests that there is a remainder in the openness between us, in our embodied uniqueness and finitude. She directs us not only to recognize the ways that genomic discourse makes sense of alternate bodies in deficit terms as problem objects in and of themselves, with any epigenetic excess assigned to the labour of autism's mother warrior, but also to pry open space where ethical knowledge production might proceed, a task premised on remaining "open to the openness by which bodies make sense" (238). I proceed below to pry open the openness of how the good warrior mother and autistic child emerged and now appear in everyday text.

New Forms of Visibility: Mothers as Risky Genes

With the rise of genomics and the multiplication of potential causes of autism, autism mothers have appeared in new ways since 2000 – as simultaneously risky and potentially protective. Everything from a mother's genes to epigenetic influences (e.g., what she eats during and before pregnancy) and parenting choices (e.g., whether to vaccinate or not and how sensitive she is) are now potential factors initiating or curing autism in her child. Autism Speaks (n.d.c), for example, lists "increased parental age" and "prenatal vitamins" as environmental risk factors that "increase – or reduce – autism risk in people who are genetically predisposed to the disorder." In this shift within everyday text, it becomes a family's – grandparents and others now count! – particularly a mother's, self-governance of choices and "movements of life" (Foucault 1980a, 25; Titchkosky 2007, 158) that have become new sites of visibility, governance, and control. Mothers and families are now invited to watch out for everything that might pose a risk. In the popular magazine *babytalk*, for example, an article entitled "Is It Something I Did?" by freelance writer Kelly K. Heyworth (2013), reviews genetic research, rehearses the "red flags" of autism (or signs for mothers to watch for in their growing child),[4] advocates for preventative (m)othering (e.g., "take extra care to point at and label objects") (32), and supports early intervention (starting as early as six months) as protective practices against autism that individual women can engage to "alter the course of brain development" (30). The article also cautions women and "expectant mothers" about potential epigenetic factors:

> You can take steps before and during pregnancy that may reduce the risk ... Environmental factors may turn many autism genes "on" or "off" ... For instance, women who take a folic acid supplement before and during pregnancy are 40 percent less likely to have a child that develops autism ... Expectant mothers who have a fever for longer than a week also pass along a higher autism risk (33 percent) as do those who contract the flu (25 percent). Other increased risk factors: living near a freeway (50 percent) or being overweight or diabetic (60 percent). (30–33)

Here, individual women and "expectant mothers" are doubly implicated. First, they must watch every movement they make – from where they live (by a freeway) to the supplements that they take (or don't take), the viruses that they come into contact with (i.e., the flu), their food intake (i.e., no fat mothers allowed!), and the health conditions that they manage (i.e., diabetes). A (m)other's own self-governance of her intimate bodily movements of life – her health and consumer choices – is now part of a larger calculus of risk around autism, invoking care and mothering as intensive labour within the mother-child dyad, but this time, the risk is only yet a thought. (M)others who do not choose to or who cannot watch and regulate themselves in this way are implicitly riskier. But more, (m)others also bear risk factors themselves and can "pass along a higher autism risk" to their child. Autism risk (rather than the expression of autism in her child) may bodily inhabit a biological mother and her child, a risk passed along to that child, that child's child, and so on, one turned on or off along the way depending on environment. Recall Esther from my focus group who discovered that she and her son Ryan both had a "deletion" on chromosome 16, thought to be a marker for autism that Esther or her husband may have passed down. This double whammy of blame and risk – both blame for bearing an autistic child and the risk of passing autism down the generations – is bodily installed in conceptions of today's risky autism mother who must watch herself through a new calculus of visibility. It is a mother's self-governance of her potentially risky intimate bodily movements and choices as calculated epi/genetically and mathematically – rather than her skilled technique as a therapist or her disordered love – that now, at least in part, regulates mothering, care, and the good/bad mother, who still must labour individually to prevent autism (and must labour even before her child arrives).

Biomedical approaches such as vitamin therapy also intensify new modes of risk visibility and self-governance for autism mothers. These nonconventional approaches include links to organizations such as Autism Path in North York, Ontario, and the Autism Research Institute in the United States (founded by Bernard Rimland), and according to Brita Belli (2010, 28), editor of *Environmental Magazine,* they "tend to be anti-drug and pro-supplement, and they insist that autism is, indeed, a treatable condition." Added to the list of things to watch out for by biomedical advocates are childhood vaccines, antibiotics, environmental toxins, poisoned food sources, corrupt governments, and more. For example, in a *Huffington Post* blog post about vaccines that has now been retracted by the editors, author, blogger, autism mother, and biomedical advocate Kim Stagliano (2010b, paras. 5–6) says, "Clobbering parents with the concept of 'herd immunity' rings hollow when your baby calf is the one who falls. Bludgeoning parents of autistic children has failed to connect with parents in its utter transparency to protect corporate and governmental interests" (see also Stagliano 2010a).[5] Here, the good autism mother makes choices about autism risk (i.e., not to vaccinate), rejecting conventional science based on her maternal authority and love for her child, conveyed in the notion that this mother's "baby calf" has fallen (Jack 2014, 88–95). Biomedical approaches also insert new "expensive" and "intensive" (Hays 1996, 8) treatments into a market aimed at recovery for autism mothers to choose from, including "chelation therapy, gluten and casein-free (wheat- and dairy-free) diets and even hyperbaric oxygen therapy" (Belli 2010, 28).[6] The (m)other who makes different choices (i.e., to value and affirm her child's way of being and support them differently) is brought into view as risky.

To gather up what has become of new forms of visibility and autism mother identity since 2000, both alternative biomedical and genomic approaches bring mothers into view as bodily linked to risky environments, whether through a mother's genes, epigenetic influence, or consumer and maternal choices (i.e., whether to vaccinate, serve wheat and dairy, try chelation, or live by a freeway). The mother-child dyad and relationship remain the scene where normal development unfolds; however, today's autism mother is ever more intensive, proximate, and governed, as her risky influence begins before her child is born and is sustained into future generations through her epigenetic influences and consumption of food, supplements, expertise, and so on (see Bumiller 2009). Autism mother as risky environment proliferates spaces of neoliberal governance where (m)others are governed within what sociologist Nikolas Rose (1996, 41) calls "advanced liberal rule," a neoliberal form of rule that "does not seek to govern through 'society,' but through the regulated choices of individual citizens, now construed as subjects of choices and aspirations ... Individuals are to be governed through their freedom" and within communities based on identities like that of autism mother. It is the "choices" of autism mothers that now bear the responsibility for an autism-free future. As Rose further describes, within advanced liberal rule and the dismantling of the welfare state, expertise is relocated in "a market governed by the rationalities of competition, accountability and consumer demand" (41). Within such new neoliberal instrumentalities, autism mother as risky environment introduces new contradictions and meanings that regulate mothering and care in new and paradoxical ways: this mother is both risky and needed in the war against autism, consuming and protective, expert and motivated by love, free to choose and intensely governed. This mother is also implicitly privileged and governed through a consumerist-capitalist market: this mother is industrious! Her differential access to resources such as food of high quality, housing, safe working conditions, expensive treatments, and even the diagnosis of autism (versus, for example, emotional disorder), unlinked from the reality of structural and material inequity through this individualizing form of visibility, is erased through the scientific and neoliberal language of individual risk and choice. Not only are privilege and inequity now (epi)genetically heritable through an autism mother's choices and labour in new ways, but they prevent or cause autism too.

A New Technology of Blame: Freedom, Choice, and Mother Experts

New forms of visibility for autism mothers as risky environments mean that since 2000, more has been required than becoming her child's therapist, although she must continue to fill this role too. In an age when the prevention of autism and disability – or at least their control – via new genetic technologies and treatments is expected of (m)others (Landsman 2009; see also Sousa 2005, 223), the autism mother expert emerged prominently on the scene of popular media and science. Communication through the Internet is a particularly intensive sight of such maternal expertise. Florida autism mother blogger Leigh Merryday (2012, n.p.; emphasis in original), for example, describes at least ten signs of autism in a young child to the wondering and worrying parents who follow her blog, including "doesn't seem to know how to play with toys correctly," "may not show affection," "does not point to what he wants (a *big red flag*)," and "hand flapping." Through such maternal expertise, as depicted in popular media and science, the bodily retraining of autism mothers' – and perhaps all (m)others' – way of seeing her child, drawn from a genetic version of the human that flags embodiments as problematic, is installed in (m)others' watchful and caring practices (McGuire 2016, 54).

This new mother expert must also acquire knowledge about how to respond to the signs of autism in her child. Becoming expert now includes learning how to navigate an ever-expanding capitalist market of treatments aimed at remedying autism, bolstering the "duty and ... urge to act" that Zygmunt Bauman (2004a, 20) describes in the achievement of modern forms of identity and that M. Remi Yergeau (2018, 4) describes as the "critical exigence" to stop autism. In an article in the popular women's magazine *Redbook,* one mother's journey to become autism's mother expert included, for example, hiring behavioural consultants, working with occupational therapists and homeopaths, learning about the science of the brain-gut connection, practising Floortime therapy, consulting a DAN! (Defeat Autism Now) doctor, studying nutritional supplements, and mastering a gluten-free, casein-free diet. As the article concludes, "There's no magic bullet for treating autism spectrum disorders ... But given the many treatment options there are to explore, there is plenty of hope. Using a combination of methods is usually most effective" (Rones 2008, 179). Expertise that was once situated within interactions with professionals is now resituated within a market of expanding choice (Rose 1996, 41) that is at (m)others' fingertips (literally, through the Internet) and that includes both conventional and biomedical approaches (Silverman 2012). A mother's hope for the child she loves has come to mean the freedom to choose, as Jordyn Jack (2014, 68) puts it, from "the many treatment options" to achieve normalcy, and this process of choosing constitutes a new technology of blame, one that invites and impels all (m)others in this normalizing quest. So-called bad mothers who move outside of this problem-solution dialectic or care paradox are often dismissed as deluded about their child's problems (Blum 2007, 203; Douglas et al., "Mad Mothering," 2021; Douglas et al., "Making Memories," 2022).

Love and self-sacrifice are what drive today's good autism mother expert in her choices to accumulate scientific expertise about autism and act to achieve normalcy in her child (Jack 2014, 88–89). This motivation is depicted with salience in specialty magazines, autism mother memoirs, and parenting guides that emerged after 2000.[7] For example, the documentary *A Mother's Courage: Talking Back to Autism* (Fridriksson 2010) follows autism mother Margret, compelled by love to leave her Icelandic home and travel throughout the United States and United Kingdom to search for the expertise that might "unlock her autistic son's mind." In a paradoxical twist that faintly echoes the instinctual mother of psychoanalysis, whose coldness and so-called disordered love manifested autism in her child, today's good mother expert is also grounded in natural love for her child, only this time, signs of autism in her child become measures of her success or failure to intensively accumulate scientific expertise and to make the right choices.

Sociologist Linda M. Blum (2007, 221–22) argues that today's "good" mother of disabled children is held to a "standard of relentless action" as her child's "proximate" rather than direct cause, which "reinforces normative femininity and women's 'natural' devotion." For example, a recent autism mother memoir by Kristine Barnett (2013), *The Spark: A Mother's Story of Nurturing Genius,* powerfully depicts these new paradoxical layers of mother blame and intensive care within the mother-child dyad as installed through a mother's freedom and choice. *The Spark* is the story of how Barnett reclaims expertise from professional therapists and merges it with her love and intuition about the "spark" that she sees in her son to "reach" him. He emerges from autism as a "genius." Barnett states, "I wasn't formally trained to administer the kind of therapy Jake needed ... But like every other parent of an autistic child, I'd been in the trenches with Jake's therapists since day one. Plus I knew my child better than any expert could. And I saw a spark in Jake" (58). Barnett went on to start Little Light Daycare, where she "recovered" her son and helped other autistic children by beginning from their strengths. Although Barnett draws on familiar autism tropes – a trapped, intelligent child, a commitment to recovery, and the language of war – what is new with this autism mother is how intensively she now reclaims authority from scientific experts and professionals, both on the ground of the maternal – her love, experience, and intuition – and through her freedom and choice.[8]

In some ways, like the mother therapist before her, today's autism mother expert "wrests authority" away from paternalistic science and professionals, revaluing maternal authority and expertise, albeit still contained within the constraints of the social construction of mothering as intensive, individual remedial labour (Jack 2014, 60). Gail Landsman (2009, 3) also identifies this revaluing of the maternal in her study of the meaning that mothers make of caring for and about an "imperfect" disabled child in an age when "perfect" babies are both a choice and a commodity promised by the control of science and technology. In Landsman's study, "mothers repeatedly describe coming to recognize and value their own expertise" (99). Mothers have an intimate knowledge of their child as well as commitment and passion to gather biomedical knowledge that opens a different ground of knowing, one that merges the maternal with the scientific on a (m)other's terms. (M)others with whom I spoke in focus groups (and my own experience) mirrored this depiction of autism's mother expert; (m)others pursued conventional and/or alternative autism treatments aimed at ameliorating autism in their child early in their (m)othering journeys. (M)others in my focus groups also extended their "expertise" far beyond that of remedy. Some of us (Jennifer and myself) pursued graduate degrees focused not on remedy but on critical and anti-oppressive studies of autism, (m)othering, care, and social work. Others undertook their own self-sustained study, drawing on popular science, nonfiction, medical lectures, and research studies to develop expertise. Esther, for example, pursued a deeper understanding of genetic research by attending lectures, including by Dr. Stephen Scherer, director of the Centre for Applied Genomics at SickKids, whom we met above. Julie and Rosa mined popular science and nonfiction by autistic authors and parents, including books like *The Reason I Jump: The Inner Voice of a Thirteen-Year-Old Boy with Autism* (Higashida 2016) and *Far from the Tree: Parents, Children and the Search for Identity* (A. Solomon 2012), for more affirming approaches. In other words, neoliberal, ableist, patriarchal, scientific power failed to govern (m)others completely and, in this failure, opened room for resistance in the form of affirming care across a disability commons – including the writing of this book – and across the formal and informal networks that (m)others forged both through their discussions together and in their own communities. This resistance is an important challenge to the scientific governance of (m)others.

At the same time, it is now this very same freedom to fashion herself as expert and "citizen scientist" (Solovitch 2001)[9] – one whose level of commitment to achieving normalcy has been intensified to that of a warrior – that frames the ways that autism mothers are governed and implicitly blamed. This autism mother's freedom and choice are paralleled by the heightening constraints of neoliberal, patriarchal, ableist capitalism that continue to push care back into the home and private market while expecting – perhaps more than ever – the performance of the natural, intensive mother and the achievement (in herself and her child) of a scientific and Western version of the normal human as autonomous, economically productive, self-governing, rational (Rose 1996, 40–41), and non-autistic. Gender, class, and race inequities and the neoliberal marketization of human life are elided within this newly intensified version of autism's warrior mother (Douglas and Klar 2019; Hays 1996, 157, 165; see also Blum 2007; and Sousa 2005, 221). A new layer is added to the paradox of care: a (m)other's freedom, choice, and expertise are also a new site of intensive self-governance. Through autism's warrior mother, a restrictive, neoliberal, capitalist political economy and Western scientific version of the normal human have come to regulate the good/ bad mother and to orchestrate cultural understandings of what it means to mother and to care.

7

Resisting Genomics and War

I work a little differently in this chapter and more centrally include my own embodied experience of reading everyday text from within our contemporary moment's living archive. I pursue the cultural ground of autism's warrior mother, an identity that holds autism mothers – indeed, all (m)others – to a "standard of relentless action" (Blum 2007, 221). As in previous chapters, this disruptive method of rereading acknowledges reading and writing as fully social activities that might also, even if only slightly, remake the world (Boler 1999; D. Smith 1999, 145; Titchkosky 2007). I proceed with an ethic of disruption and enter, through rereading, the "liminal space" where power, discourse, and embodied subject enfold (Lewiecki-Wilson and Cellio 2011; Merleau-Ponty 1968; Titchkosky 2007, 21). I return to insights from my focus groups in Chapter 8, where I offer a sustained analysis. To get close to autism's warrior mother in this chapter, I perform a phenomenological description of one version of her – the feminine warrior – within one Internet campaign to recruit autism mothers. Images of the online campaign continue to circulate. Phenomenology as informed by sociological, feminist, and disability studies approaches offers an entry point that reveals new aspects of autism's warrior mother and new possibilities for being together beyond the constraints of intensifying neoliberal, capitalist, biogenomic regimes. I conclude the chapter hopefully, with the interventions of (m)others in everyday text who push back against today's paradox of care of love and war. In identifying everyday sites of resistance, I document a disability commons (Runswick-Cole and Goodley 2018) dispersed across everyday text and work to unmother autism.

Autism Mothers Global Recruitment Campaign: Part One

I sit with laptop on my knees and revisit the Autism Mothers Facebook page, now the first hit when I search for "autism mothers" on Facebook. One of the photos strikes me. In it, six women who appear brown, Black, and white stand with crossed arms, holding hands. Those who appear white are dressed in black and those who appear brown or Black are dressed in bright colours. They are holding hands through crossed arms and smiling at each other.[1] I wonder what this image has to do with autism. I browse the page and quickly come across a series of photographs of predominantly white mothers posing together and dressed in a uniform of black, although other versions of the pose appear: white mothers in black T-shirts on motorcycles and white mothers in white shirts on a beach, both reproduced from the *Autism File Magazine* (2009b). Apart from the *Autism File Magazine* (formerly with its own media channel), the site is linked to the Autism Trust, a UK advocacy organization founded by anti-vaccine activist and autism mother Polly Tommey.

A recurring image in the archive on the Autism Mothers Facebook page features six autism mothers, who appear white with long brown or blonde hair, standing posed in a line, their bodies angled in and toward one another. Each wears the same uniform of black evening gown with a low neckline and high heels. Their stance is wide, as though they are ready for action. They appear slim and fit and stand tall, their necks long, with their bare shoulders thrown back. Hands on hips, no one smiles.[2] The image appears along with other images of autism mothers from England and the United States, as well as groups from South Africa, Dubai, and New Zealand. I search for this autism mother campaign on Google and come across the same image of the same mothers in a UK newspaper article in *Mail Online* (O'Brien 2009). The photo shoot was organized by Polly Tommey as part of United Nations World Autism Day in 2009. Something stirs in me. Grief? Guilt? Recognition?

Autism Mothers Global Recruitment Campaign: Part Two

Images from the World Autism Day photo shoot also appear in an *Autism File Magazine* (2009a) video on YouTube linked to the same newspaper article (O'Brien 2009). The article calls the campaign a "global phenomenon." I am beginning to get the picture of a far-reaching, multimedia campaign "to bring mothers of autism together across the world," as the description on YouTube states (*Autism File Magazine* 2009a). I find similar videos made in other Western countries and images used in other campaigns. A photo of the 2014 "Advocacy Edition" of *Autism File Magazine,* for example, archived on Facebook, features autism mothers in black gowns with red boxing gloves on, ready to fight.[3] Returning to the *Autism File Magazine* (2009a) video, I am mesmerized by the dozens of images of autism mothers in some version of the black gown who appear ready to run and ready to fight too: some have boxing gloves on, or they hold racing flags; others pose as if pointing a gun, or they stand with motorcycles, ready to race. A forceful statement follows, "Autism mothers, a powerful alliance. Standing together, fighting for our children. We will win. We will win."[4]

The images are set to Leona Lewis's cover of the pop band Snow Patrol's (2004) song "Run." The song starts slowly. Its haunting progression builds to inspirational peaks, with lyrics that might very well have been written from this warrior mother to her autistic child: "To think I might not see those eyes, makes it so hard not to cry ...." I watch the video over and over again, absorbed by its drama. The words, images, and music haunt me and return to me at unexpected times – while driving in my car, walking up the stairs in my house, shopping for groceries. I search these images, looking for something, scanning the poses and determined expressions. These mothers know something, I think, and part of me knows it too – the secret of a shared, violent, and irremediable ethical paradox that compels mothers to fight against autism even while loving their/our unique and different child. This paradox is the secret that these autism mothers seem to keep that binds them together and to me. I struggle with grief at this figure and with outrage. I find the campaign exhausting.

I now have two descriptions of my experience with two different iterations of a global campaign to recruit autism mothers. One appears on the popular Autism Mothers Facebook page, and the other takes the form of a YouTube video produced by a related autism advocacy organization. Both use language and images. Both continue to be available and searchable through virtual worlds. The campaign is global in reach as it makes the now-familiar, almost taken-for-granted call to mothers to join the fight against autism. The call emanates from autism mothers of the United States and the United Kingdom who are summoning others "across the world" to join the fight (*Autism File Magazine* 2009a). Like other campaigns put forward by Autism Speaks and the World Health Organization (e.g., see Autism Speaks Canada 2019; and World Health Organization 2013a, 2013b), the recruitment campaign globally exports Western scientific understandings of autism as a problem of the body/brain and more – a threat to the well-being of children, families, nations, and indeed, the world.

Within the Western scientific frame of autism as a disorder, the recruitment campaign issues a call to mothers that is also a "duty" (Bauman 2004a, 20) to join the war against autism. After all, according to Western frames, a mother's nature – her calling – is to bear, love, and protect her child in line with a particular shape of care (Douglas et al., "Mad Mothering," 2021). This mother's "because-of" and "in-order-to" motives are clear (Schutz 1967, 86–96). That is, given the Western scientific cultural ground of sameness and certainty that yields autism as disorder, a nonstandpoint, unnatural, a withdrawal, a threat to normalcy, and more, it makes sense that a mother would grieve the loss of her normal child *because of* autism and fight against autism *in order to* secure her child's future well-being. This mother's child has been taken by autism. Telling a different story about autism, care, and (m)othering requires a reorientation away from depictions of autism as a problem and toward unravelling the normal human and its Others as a *cultural scene* – a background – upon which the troubling paradox of care and autism's warrior mother has emerged in the postmillennial years.

Autism as a Cultural Scene

The *Merriam-Webster Dictionary* (n.d.) defines a campaign as "a connected series of operations designed to bring about a particular result." The global campaign to recruit autism mothers started in 2009 as a series of images and a video widely distributed on Facebook and Twitter as well as in issues of the *Autism File Magazine*. It is like other global campaigns to recruit autism mothers, such as those undertaken by Generation Rescue, a parent advocacy organization committed to the biomedical recovery of autism and spearheaded until recently by Jenny McCarthy.[5] Images from the global recruitment campaign continue to circulate online, suggesting that autism recovery is an ongoing fight, one with duration, one *in progress,* one that needs particular types of mothers to make a particular kind of progress toward an autism-free future that will allow for individual and collective well-being and economic flourishing. Mothers are the campaign's operatives, both its subjects and its actors. Indeed, the campaign needs mothers to act in this new warrior-like way in order to succeed. I note here that the mothers sought out by the campaign are often individual biological mothers who labour intensively for normalcy within the mother-child dyad. The campaign is not part of the disability commons described by Katherine Runswick-Cole and Daniel Goodley (2018, 232) as a "collective and affirmative alternative approach to individualising models of parenting that oppress both mothers and disabled children." Instead, the sought-after result of the campaign, albeit a type of collective, is clear: "to bring mothers of autism together across the world" in "a powerful alliance. Standing together, fighting for our children. We will win" (*Autism File Magazine* 2009a). With the massing of warring mothers "across the world" who are called to uniformly orient to autism as a deficit, this most powerful force "will win" the fight. We are "fighting for our children," the campaign declares. The alternative, it suggests, is the tragic loss of our children and the failure to make the right kind of progress toward a future free of autism.

Moved through Affect

The campaign orients its viewer – autism mothers and allies – through affect and the play of powerful and now-familiar Western cultural narratives: a terrifying threat to a child's well-being, the loss or withdrawal of a child, a mother's love and grief, and the courage of a warrior. Despite myself, I was captivated, mesmerized, and even exhausted by the video. The words, images, and music occupied me. I searched the images for something. Remembering my own struggles, I feel uncomfortably bound to these autism mothers. The campaign is personal, and it betrays urgency: "Even if you cannot hear my voice ... we'll run for our lives" (Snow Patrol 2004), sings Lewis. Hundreds of autism mothers abandon their so-called natural place as proximate to their own child so that they might promote the campaign and be proximate to normal development and an autism-free future. We know that they will return home, alone in the face of the "threat" of autism. How do these narratives operate on and with viewers here?

    Within the campaign, an orientation of affect – love, grief, fear, and blame – moves and implicates viewers (autism mothers and allies) in the fight against autism, shifting them toward Western scientific versions of the human. Indeed, the campaign makes its impression through affect, reshaping the very shape and direction that our embodied subjectivity and relationships of care might take (Ahmed 2004). In other words, affect operates in the campaign by making us subject to and the subjects of this new paradox of care as feminine subjectivity at war against autism. "There are two meanings of the word 'subject,'" states Michel Foucault (1982, 781): "subject to someone else by control and dependence; and tied to his own identity by a conscience or self-knowledge." Let us leave Foucault's first meaning aside for the moment and instead concentrate on his second meaning (perhaps in a way that he may not have intended). The second meaning – "tied to his own identity by a conscience or self-knowledge" – implies that we come to know ourselves through identity (such as autism's warrior mother) as subjects who embody a particular historical possibility. In our case, then, like the tie that binds us to the autistic life we care for and about, mothers are paradoxically tied to this historical identity by a so-called nature-given duty to protect our child from threats like autism. In the global campaign to recruit autism mothers, this duty is to be fulfilled through autism mothers' heightened fight for recovery and more as part of a coordinated worldwide effort. This duty is understood to be outside of time even as it shapes time through actions toward the achievement of normalcy in our child, such as withholding vaccines or subjecting children to chelation, all for their purported well-being. Who decides what shape these practices and well-being take? How do autism mothers turn away from the unique autistic child and toward working at any cost (including financial loss and harmful therapies) to make this child the same?

To press the point about coming to know ourselves as subjects, I suggest that the orientation of affect within the campaign invites and even compels its beholders, especially (m)others, parents, and kin, to take their own "backward glance" (Ahmed 2006b, 507) of perception. It turns us toward memory and the familiar, taken-for-granted cultural ground of the everyday lifeworld, which includes understandings of a mother's care, autism, and the human. We are called to know again a particular type of mother and a particular type of threat – a mother warrior (in the shape of the feminine warrior) fighting intensively against autism and the threat of a child lost to autism, environmental illness, or disordered biology. In reference to French philosopher Louis Althusser's (2001) notion of the ideological recruitment of subjects, Sara Ahmed (2007, 157) describes this interpretive move of perception in this way: "The subject is recruited by turning around." What's more, Ahmed says, such "recruitment functions as a technology for the reproduction of whiteness" (157) and, in my case, both for whiteness (this autism mother is predominately white or Westernizing) and for the reproduction of neuro-normativity. Recruitment, through powerful narratives and compelling affect, operates (now globally) within the campaign to reorient autism mothers toward a Western, white, neuro-normative, and patriarchal scientific understanding of autism, mothering, care, and the normal human that necessarily works for the elimination of autism and for the installation of Western, white, bourgeois ways of being.

In her work on gender constitution, feminist philosopher Judith Butler (1997, 403) suggests that it is through repetition – knowing/doing ourselves and knowing/doing ourselves again – that identity becomes a historical, embodied possibility. Through the campaign's various iterations (alongside the discursive explosion surrounding autism), autism mother, this time as feminine warrior, becomes a familiar embodied identity. Ironically, it is through Foucault's first meaning of subject as a historical situation of constraint – "subject to someone else by control and dependence" – that we might become a particular type of autism mother who knows herself, recognizes herself, and turns to act in the world. My freedom to act – my subjectivity – is paradoxically formed in this situation of discursive constraint and authority. Alternative ways to care and (m)other outside intensive labour in the mother-child dyad, ways that this book advances – affirming, collectivized care – are elided. To loosen the grip of the warrior mother and the natural attitude a little further and to open possibilities for other historical iterations of (m)othering, autism, and care, I turn next to Butler's work and examine the role of language in world making, both within my own description and within the campaign (402–4).

The Role of Language

Fleshy words saturate my description and discussion of the campaign thus far – words like *mesmerize, secret, stir, haunt, touch,* and *outrage.* What might these words disclose about subjectivity and my activity of rereading my own living archive? How might this undertaking help me to tell a new story? First, my activity of rereading and description is much more than mental image making alone. An object cannot be *familiar, grieved, stirring, outrageous,* or *mesmerizing* without ties to a cultural ground – some kind of proximity to or touch of bodies, histories, and language. These words elicit a living, touching, feeling experiencing body/subject. They betray an intimate relationship of body/subject and word/world. As Butler (1998, x; emphasis in original) phrases it, noting that our relation to and knowledge of the world is one of "kinship" steeped in language, "Consciousness is always consciousness *of* its object, it is nothing without its preposition, and its preposition marks its kinship with the world that it interrogates." My activity of description, and subject making, involves embodied, felt, interpretive acts of consciousness that build up a knowable world through the language of the campaign. I know this world intimately as one that can only ever be done through the instability and openness of language. Embodied subjects do not "stand alone" but *become,* "gearing" into the world (Schutz 1970) as well as being moved by it in a relation of touch and proximity to and with their inseparable object – in this case, that of autism's mother warrior.

Furthering my point and moving now more directly toward the "feminine" and "warrior" language of the campaign, I want to think about how the viewer is presented with campaign language that appears in direct correspondence with the so-called real of the world. For example, body and world are separated in the campaign's images: autism is a threat external to history, and autism mother is its natural warrior. The interpretive schemes surrounding autism and mothering (i.e., Western, patriarchal mothering, genetic personhood, and biomedicine) that tie us to particular, and embodied, understandings of "types" of people (here, of problem types) simply become part of the scenery. They fade away into the background. But objects – campaigns and identities – cannot be recognized or oriented to without these already constituted, and constituting, interpretive schemes. There is nothing natural about the natural attitude. As Alfred Schutz (1970, 96) tells us, language is "a treasure house of ready-made preconstituted types and characteristics, all socially derived and carrying along an open horizon of unexplored content" (and here I include image as a kind of visual language). Language is integrally implicated in world making, in the making and undoing of selves, identities, and lives, and in the recognition of others. We are all caught by a language that renders invisible the processes that make the real (here, autism and mother warriors) appear as an empirical given. It is the threat of autism and its corollary, the feminine warrior mother figure, that is real here rather than the loss or exclusion of different forms of care – collective forms that, in aligning with disability justice calls for a disability commons, might orient us to the difference of our autistic child differently (Michalko 2002). Taken-for-granted interpretive schemes keep well hidden this autism mother's secrets – the irremediable ethical paradox to care through gendered, raced, curative labour, the fundamental alterity of us all, the human and its Others as culturally and materially produced rather than essential biological facts – tucking them away in a background that easily fades from view. Through its language, we are oriented to the campaign's meaning as a closed matter and to consciousness as separate and internal, a disembodied, unremarkable thing in and of itself.

If we stay with the idea that language is a world-making activity, then what might the images and language of the autism mother campaign itself teach us about the feminine warrior? First, this autism mother is no longer Bruno Bettelheim's (1967) refrigerator mother. This mother is hot. Her uniform is not that of the soldier but a feminine, sexualized one. Her feminine curves and flowing hair are accentuated by her black gown and high heels against a white background. She is exposed, vulnerable, even physically compromised in her evening gown and heels. She could not "run for her life" here, as Leona Lewis sings in the background of the autism mother campaign video. What's more, the very strangeness of the formal black gowns and other uniforms suggests that something extraordinary is going on here. By Western standards, this autism mother is very formally, and publicly, grieving. At the same time, she is courageous, strong, and independent. Head held high and shoulders thrown back, she stands not delicately but proudly. She is empowered. Unlike the hesitant feminine corporeality that feminist philosopher Iris Marion Young (1980) has depicted as shrinking in space, the feminine warrior occupies and even extends into space. Hands are on her hips; she has a wide stance. She does not smile or glance away but looks straight at the camera as if she might spring into action. Yet even this gesture of strength and aggression is encased by softer, nonthreatening, sensual qualities. She is made up. Her bare shoulders meet cleavage. Here, characteristics that are feminine-coded mingle with masculine-coded ones. They contradict and more.

The violence of the campaign's language and images is ironic given Western notions of bourgeois, white femininity and of mothers as naturally caring, sensitive, and nurturing (Ringrose and Walkerdine 2008). The campaign seems to contain some contradictory messages not only about gender and care but also about that most sacred, loving, and close of bonds: that of mother and child. A (birth) mother carries and must cut free the infant she births. She is that bodily close to her child. This tie, one that binds mother to child and child to mother, is understood as timeless, situated in biology, and therefore natural. Following this logic, it is only "natural" that mothers are protective and nurturing of the life that they give. This certainly appears to be true of autism's feminine warrior mother figure. Her willingness to protect her child and family from the supposedly hostile threat of autism is unsurpassed. She is willing to go to war and by implication to abandon her child (indeed, no children appear in the campaign) and even to lay down her life or the life of her child. This cultural figure's violent aspect sanctions, at least in part, violence as an inevitable part of caring for and about an autistic child. Without diminishing the severe need for supports for autistic people and their families, we can bear witness not only to the murders and murder-suicides of autistic children by mothers and parents over the past fifteen years (see also Autistic Self Advocacy Network n.d.; and McGuire 2016, 195–201) but also to the rhetoric of hopelessness and war that surrounds the stark intertwining of autism, violence, mothering, and care.[6] Recall that violent practices are an integral part of late-modern forms of power that govern us through our freedom (Dean 2002; Dehli 2008; Foucault 1982, 1991a, 2003) – in this case, through the choice to go to war to protect and recover our child and, in the extreme, to succumb to defeat and commit murder. Below are just a few of the multiple, and tragic, murders of autistic children that occurred in North America during the years 2000–20:

> **Alejandro Ripley**, murdered, May 21, 2020. Nine-year-old Alejandro was murdered by his mother, Patricia Ripley. She is reported to have stated during her police confession, "He's going to be in a better place" (quoted in Carrega 2020).

Robbie Robinson, murdered, April 3, 2014. Twenty-three-year-old Robbie was murdered by his mother, Angie Robinson, who also took her own life. "Angie loved him more than anything on earth," a relative said (quoted in Boesveld 2014, para. 3).

Tony Khor, murdered, October 25, 2009. Fifteen-year-old Tony from Mississauga, Ontario, was murdered by his mother, Seow Cheng Sim, in a hotel room in Niagara Falls, Ontario. His father reported that Tony's mom "loved her son so much" (quoted in B. Mitchell and Wilkes 2009).

Paradoxically, as conceived in relation to the figure of autism's warrior mother, the closeness of the mother-child bond demands violence. An autism mother's aggression and hostility toward autism (she is, after all, fighting a war) – qualities more commonly associated with what is understood as masculine and thus contradictory – remove her from the close and loving bond of the feminine. Although she operates in the feminine and affective (she is loving and nurturing), she also operates in the masculine, coded as instrumental, logical, and hostile. Here, the figure of autism's feminine warrior mother draws on the Global North's neo-liberal, capitalist motherhood, and on limited notions of the human including Western Enlightenment's bourgeois, white, nondisabled "Man" as the standard (Wynter 1992) to wage her war against the problem of autism. Her fight must be waged, at least in part, through a hopelessness and hostility toward autism, one paradoxically and disturbingly born of her care for her child. As stated by mother Xuan Chen, to provide another example, who drowned her autistic daughter in 2004, "I miss my daughter every day. I still love my daughter. I hate autism" (quoted in Friday 2010, n.p.). This autism mother, tragically, is fighting against a threat that is personal, one located in her home and, even closer, in her child's body and her own (recall the discussion of epi/genetics in Chapter 6). Failure to shore up the resources required to eliminate autism in one's child is met, by some mothers and parents, with murder. There is no "backward glance" (Ahmed 2006a, 570), or hesitation, at the intensive care within the mother-child dyad and at the paradoxically violent, unethical duty of eliminating autism. The images and language of the campaign, along with the media reports of murder, justify tragic violence and betray only determination and finality.

The Empowered Feminine

The feminine warrior, as one example of autism's warrior mother, is an intensification of neoliberal and postfeminist discourses of the empowered feminine. Feminist sociologist and critical psychologist (respectively) Jessica Ringrose and Valerie Walkerdine (2008) argue that the empowered feminine is a contradictory neoliberal subjectivity in which qualities coded masculine combine with and contradict qualities coded feminine. Success and independence outside of the home meet success in the achievement of so-called innate feminine qualities: beauty, allure, and nurturance. Notions of beauty adhere to Western, white, bourgeois standards: this warrior is slim, fit, white, and flawless. There are no drug store bleached-blonde dye jobs here, no fatigue from domestic labour, and no shortage of resources, whether financial or temporal. She is liberal feminism all grown up. Like the neoliberal, postfeminist "yummy mummy," the feminine warrior has it all: kids, career, beauty, and health. But moreover, this mother has all the strength of the masculine to fight autism by going to war. She is not only the alluring feminine object but also an exaggeration of the masculine agentive subject. She must be simultaneously both distant and proximate in order to resolve the irresolvable paradox of loving and caring for and about her child while eliminating autism. The feminine warrior autism mother thus not only intensifies the implication of mothers in terms of delivering a future free of autism. She also, through love and proximity, operates as an extreme pole of Ringrose and Walkerdine's (2008) empowered feminine subjectivity.

Neoliberal discourses (whether as ideology, policy, or forms of governance) articulate and incorporate the marketization of every aspect of human life, whether the governance of the market, social institutions, or indeed how we understand and do ourselves (Larner 2000; Vandenbeld Giles 2012). Under neoliberal governance regimes, the ideal self is the self-entrepreneur. In a globalizing consumerist-capitalist society, this ideal means, following Ringrose and Walkerdine (2008, 230), that owning the "means of consumption" to "consume ourselves into being" has become the route to humanness and to our freedom, well-being, and happiness (see also Rose 1999). We have been compelled by markets to become our own experts. What does the feminine warrior figure consume? Beauty, fashion, and fitness products, to be sure. Perhaps websites, parenting books, and therapies too. But there is more. The feminine warrior must not only consume herself into being a sexy object/commodity and agentive mother/career subject. She must also learn to be a successful warrior, and as such, she must consume her autistic child into being as non-autistic. Biomedical interventions, behavioural therapies, gluten-free and casein-free diets, and endless information (genetic, biomedical, environmental, or otherwise) must be on her list too. These are her weapons and her instruments of war. She is the ideal feminine and more, "an intensification of feminine as site (both subject and object) of commodification and consumption" (Ringrose and Walkerdine 2008, 230). This autism mother's task is an impossible one to negotiate: she orients herself through care to eradicate the autistic child who persists in front of her. Failure haunts this mother, as her task is impossible to achieve. Yet when failure inevitably occurs or when progress is slow, these outcomes are cast in the individual, psychological, and pathologizing terms of neoliberal, capitalist discourse (Rose 1999). More therapies are needed! More rallies of empowerment! Reinforcements! Ringrose and Walkerdine (2008, 228) tell us that the ideal feminine "is bourgeois, yet coded universal, normal and attainable for all." In this way, neoliberal discourses masquerade as our freedom, and gender, race, and class inequities deepen and intensify, leaving transgressive bodies to fail in the achievement of the normal human, let alone its exaggeration, as envisioned in an autism mother's responsibility for ushering in a future of individual and global well-being that is autism-free.

Resisting Genomics and War: A More Hopeful Reading

I end this chapter more hopefully and turn to some of the more disruptive "maternal texts" (Brenda Clews, quoted in T. Thomas 2003, 186) that emerged on the scene of everyday text during these years – texts that make room for something other than violence when therapies (inevitably) fail. Rather than rejecting or fighting against autism, these texts reject pathologizing understandings of autism and individualizing forms of care that aim to eliminate autism. These texts, too, reject contemporary forms of mother blame installed through genetic versions of the human (Bumiller 2009) and through the neoliberal empowered feminine. I concur with medical librarian Rachel Walden (2012, 11; emphasis in original) when she writes, "Now, sadly, *explicit* mother-blaming has shifted to *implicit* mother-blaming. The latter is less likely to be challenged as misogynist but continues to identify *women's* actions as potential causes for ASD [autism spectrum disorder]." Health and disease researchers Sarah S. Richardson and colleagues (2014, 131) also identify "the long shadow of the uterine environment" cast for (biological) mothers as the source of ills in their offspring, including autism. They add, "Exaggerations and oversimplifications are making scapegoats of mothers, and could even increase surveillance and regulation of pregnant women" (131). Former self-identified autism mother Cammie McGovern (2006, 2021) goes a little further in challenging Western, neoliberal, capitalist, ableist, patriarchal mothering and its intensive curative labour within the mother-child dyad. Similar to my own journey and that of the (m)others in my focus groups, McGovern – who initially tried all the therapies, conventional and biomedical, to normalize her son – describes laying down her past identity as mother warrior after being defeated in the fight *against* autism and *for* an autism-free future by what philosopher Rosalyn Diprose (2005, 237) calls the "finitude and uniqueness" of McGovern's son in the present. McGovern (2021, 4–5; emphasis in original) says, "At some point it hits you. You look at your child and realize you're not fighting the autism anymore, you're waging a war against the fundamental person your child *is*."

Appearances in everyday text like McGovern's accounts gesture to an alternative way to care both about autistic people and about (m)others, one that is more relational and affirming. It is no tragedy that McGovern has admitted defeat against the problem of autism. Rather, in the space of defeat, McGovern takes a backward glance and breaks the tragedy-heroism binary of disability, mothering, and care, interrupting Western linear narratives of developmental progress toward normalcy through a mother's participation both in therapies and in efforts to control (future) risk factors (Fisher and Goodley 2007). A different kind of risk, that of missing out on the uniqueness and love of your child in the present, is brought into view by McGovern (2006, 140) when discussing her son in moments of ethical narration: "When he laughs at the same intersection whenever you go through it, and says, 'I don't know, I just love that traffic light,' you think. Well, there are worse things to love." Although each of the authors mentioned above also continue to bring autism, mothers, and mothering into view in more conventional and normalizing ways, they also open space to collectively challenge the weight of genetic blame and the dominant scientific sense that the intensive watchful labour of individual mothers is the solution to the problem of autism (Douglas et al., "Mad Mothering," 2021; Fisher and Goodley 2007; Panitch 2008, 12; Runswick-Cole and Goodley 2018; Sousa 2005, 229–30). The ethical risks and harm inherent in waging war against a unique and very present autistic child or adult, as well as the risks of misogynistic scientific mother blame and increased surveillance of all (m)others, are brought into relief by these everyday texts.

Toronto (m)other, artist, activist, and scholar Estée Klar also brings autism, (m)othering, and care into view differently, grounding her approach in a relational sitpoint as well as in autistic affirmation. In 2006, Klar founded the Autism Acceptance project and was one of the first bloggers on the *Joy of Autism* blog (e.g., see Klar 2014). Together with her nonspeaking autistic son, Adam, Klar went on to found and co-direct "dis assembly: a neurodiverse arts collective (formerly The A Collective) ... for neurodiverse, relational-artistic creation and collaboration."[7] As an example of Klar's (2015, last para.) alternative approach, in a blog post entitled "Mental Ability and the Discourse of Disease: Another Comment on the Globe and Mail Article on 'Treating the Brain and the Immune System in Tandem,'" she responds to the article's suggestion that "mental illness" (including autism) is a "disease" with the following reflection:

> Recently, I am interested, as a woman, theorist and mother, in the lovely intimacy I share with my son as caregiving can be a very physical act. Touted as a burden by many charities and the like – including fellow parents who yearn to have an independent child – I have been grateful to be put into a situation where my expectations have been radically altered; where caring has become an important part of my treasured (ever-changing) identity. This has been created by the reality of caring and the mutually negotiated relationship I share with my son. Therefore, reading accounts of genetically ameliorating autism, or relentless and repeated suggestions that disability (often shoved under the "mental illness" umbrella) is biologically caused or wrong, is troubling for my son and I on many fronts.

Two aspects of Klar's response to the pathologization of "mental illness," autism, and disability in the *Globe and Mail* article are particularly striking.

First, in her invocation of the physicality and mutually negotiated reciprocity and relational process of (m)othering and caring for and about her son Adam, which involve practices that continually remake and shape her identity, Klar makes a connection, a "bridge" (Kelly 2013), between this expressed feminist and neurodivergent ethic of care and the call from disability studies and disability justice proponents to reconceive care and disability beyond devalued dependence, rights perspectives, the intensive feminized labour of care (often performed by women of colour), and physical, economic, and emotional "burden." This revaluing of care and disability – and, I argue, of (m)othering amid pathologizing everyday depictions of autistic difference – is vital work toward challenging oppressive notions of the human as white, Western, non-autistic, middle-class, autonomous, and economically productive within an oppressive gendered political economy of care for (m)others, carers, and disabled people (Hughes et al. 2005; Kelly 2013; Kröger 2009). It is worth restating how Runswick-Cole and Goodley (2018, 232) "invoke the 'disability commons' as a collective and affirmative alternative approach to individualising models of parenting that oppress both mothers and disabled children." Klar's work, including the dis assembly collective, is one site that moves us toward the enactment of this alternative (see also Re•Storying Autism, a multimedia storytelling project that reimagines autism as a desired difference, restoryingautism.com).

Second, it is striking how for Klar, as the (m)other of an autistic son, this popular rendering of "mental illness" (including autism) as a problem in need of a solution – something that is "wrong" – means "trouble" for her and Adam (on disability as a problem, see Abberley 1998, 93; D. Mitchell 2002, 15; and Titchkosky and Michalko 2009, 2). From within the biomedical problem-solution dialectic of disability, the only possible way to care for what is wrong – a biological defect – is to objectify autism and to care about its elimination. Yet Klar and other (m)others care about and love children identified as autistic. Klar shares a "lovely intimacy" with her son. In this landscape, caring for what is "wrong" becomes "troubling." It becomes an impossible situation. In this tension between, on the one hand, (m)others who care about and love children identified as autistic in their everyday lives and, on the other hand, conventional mothering and remedial care, conceived as caring for what is "wrong" by making it "right" (or bringing it in line), the problem-solution dialectic of disability begins to break down, along with the naturalness of conventional mothering as intensive remedial care in the mother-child dyad. Autism becomes something more than a problem of defective biology. Autism mother, too, begins to break down, opening space for ways of being together beyond the Western cultural contradiction between natural motherhood and scientific understandings of difference that govern the social construction of mothering.

Tiffany Hammond, a Black autistic (m)other of two Black autistic sons and the creator of the social media profile Fidgets and Fries, adds a race analysis.[8] In her bio on Instagram, Hammond articulates her collective and affirming approach this way: "My activism is rooted in challenging the current perception of Autism as a lifelong burden, cultivating a community that explores the concept of Intersectionality, and inspiring thought leaders through storytelling, education and critical discourse." In addition to her affirming, collective approach, Hammond uses story to ignite dialogue around intersectionality and the marginalization of Black and other autistic people of colour (see also Hammond 2023). In a Facebook post on September 24, 2022, for example, Hammond describes the tensions of ableism and racism that she and her family live, signalling a dire need for intersectional analysis within research and activist spaces:

> I can't mask Blackness. I am what people see. And this skin is considered maladaptive before I even execute a behavior, before I even speak. I sit in Black spaces and they can't even see the Autism in me ... [My son] knows the parts of himself that he cannot hide. Those parts he cannot mask. And it's those parts that have drawn weapons on him. Those parts that threatened him with arrest.

Hammond invokes the paradox of the disjunction between care and the social construction of mothering as one inflected by white supremacy and ableism, including issues such as the absence of access to the autism diagnoses and health care that are taken for granted by middle-class, white people and the carceral logics that normalize the police violence and surveillance that mark and contain autistic Black bodies in public as especially dangerous (see also Bailey and Mobley 2018; Ben-Moshe 2020; Ben-Moshe, Chapman, and Carey 2014; and Schalk and Kim 2018). It is worth quoting Hammond's provocative and much-discussed post on Facebook on August 1, 2022, where she issues a call to the Global North's white, autistic self-advocates and parents for critical reflexivity and a disability commons that includes intersectional analysis:

> Why do so many believe that ABA [Applied Behaviour Analysis] only exists within the walls of therapeutic centers designated as such and not our healthcare system, educational system, carceral system, your job, his job, they [sic] job, all up in your home life, your upbringing, etc? Society has built and maintained systems of order through the creation of social norms we all must abide by to be of any use to the collective and applied them unevenly amongst its people based upon a variety of factors (race, gender, age, disability, etc). Y'all buckle, bend, and break when you cannot behave as they would require you to because deviation from socially established norms makes living that much more challenging for you … You need to live. You need to survive. And to do so, to gain access to all that you require to make it in this world, requires that you bend within yourself … and perform. Y'all learn to exhibit behaviors dominant culture wants you to because you've been conditioned to do so, you needn't set foot in an ABA facility for this. This world will harm you regardless. And this is speaking from my experience as a Black Autistic woman who was in ABA. ABA is a problem, but it isn't THE problem. Expand your scope. I swear it won't hurt you to do so, but I promise you it will hurt others if you don't.

Hammond does not endorse (or dismiss) ABA. Rather, she calls for critical reflexivity and dialogue about the white supremacist, colonialist, patriarchal, bourgeois, ableist, neoliberal, capitalist system that affects all (m)others and autistic people but positions us in vastly different ways. New questions about autism, race, and (m)othering emerge from the provocations of Hammond, Klar, and the work of this chapter: How might (m)others already care for and about their different child outside of the constraints of biogenetic, Western, white understandings of disability and (m)othering, freedom and choice? What else might be possible for being together under late modernity?

Part 3

Reimagining Mothering, Autism, and Care

8

(M)others Speak Back
Affirming Autism and Care

This chapter brings to life my focus group conversations with eight (m)others of autistic children and adults in the Greater Toronto Area about how they have been represented in popular media and science. As a reminder, these conversations are based on collages that I made using texts from my archive, which covers the years 1940–2022. As (m)others arrived at the focus groups, there was a discernible buzz in the air, as though something very special was about to happen, and perhaps it was. In addition to solving practical barriers around care in order to take part, (m)others and I gathered to talk about something quite unique within a landscape still dominated by conventional autism science: our own reflections on and experiences of representations of autism mother identity, autism, and care. In our conversations, (m)others brought the paradox of care and our own archive alive, grappling with dominant representations of autism and intensive remedial care and creatively disrupting their constraints. I have described the doubleness of this lived paradox elsewhere as pedagogic (see Douglas, Rice, and Kelly 2017; and Du Bois [1903] 1994). Here, I adopt an ethic of disruption and affirming care – a stance of perpetual questioning and an ethical quality of attention that together open alternative ways to respond to the disruption of difference, including in knowledge production. I include this chapter as a separate, albeit brief, and final section of the book to show in greater depth how (m)others' insights around lived power and resistance, difference, (m)othering, and care continue to be margin-alized and to spotlight how these insights are also ones that can advance justice by building solidarity across feminist and disability studies and across disability and parent advocacy movements.

I work phenomenologically, influenced by critical autism, feminist, and disability studies and by interpretive and critical sociological thought and modes of inquiry. Education scholar Max Van Manen (1990, 18; emphasis in original) articulates the "complex" nature of such a method: "To *do* hermeneutic phenomenology is to attempt to accomplish the impossible: to construct a full interpretive description of some aspect of the lifeworld, and yet to remain aware that lived life is always more complex than any explication of meaning can reveal." It is with this impossibility in mind that I enter the complexity of conversations with (m)others about lived experiences of autism and autism mother depictions in everyday text. I consider aspects of focus group discussions that reveal the "secrets" that I am after about how autism mother identity is both made and resisted in everyday life, how the "problem" of autism is recognized, and how (m)othering and care might move beyond the Western, developmental (or scientific) sense of autism as the problem and beyond the expert sense that the solution lies in mothers' scientifically guided, normalizing, and oppressive – for both (m)others and autistic people – individualizing care (Runswick-Cole and Goodley 2018). I include some of my own reflections and questions posed to (m)others during focus groups, signalling my feminist and disability justice commitment to challenge researcher-participant hierarchies and to co-constitute knowledge (Rice et al. 2020). Focus groups in this sense were akin to consciousness-raising groups (hooks 2020, 8) and to what Runswick-Cole and Goodley (2018, 240) call the "maternal commons" (a kind of disability commons) – a coming together of (m)others (who may also be disabled) of disabled children/adults to disrupt dominant and oppressive configurations of disability, (m)othering, and care.

Identity and Difference

I begin this chapter with the theme of identity and difference. (M)others and I spoke about contradictory experiences with the identity autism mother as it is depicted in everyday text. For each (m)other who participated, the dominant sense of autism as a problem in need of the solution of individual mothers who labour intensively in the mother-child dyad was bodily and practically experienced within their everyday lives navigating autism mother networks, including schools, domestic spaces, autism service agencies, and medical settings. Summing up a discussion about our experiences of the gendered nature of the expected parent within a large service agency in Greater Toronto, I reflected on how mothers are assumed to be available both to train at the agency and to be home therapists – an observation met with an assenting chorus of "Ya's" and "Mm-hmm's." Parents often cannot access support, even paid support, unless they complete the training offered by the agency, including training in behaviourist approaches and biomedical understandings of autism. And in (m)others' experience of this agency, "parent" predominately means a woman labouring intensively in primary carer roles. Recall sociologist Zygmunt Bauman's (2004a, 20; emphasis in original) idea of identity as a fiction within the emergence of modern Western forms of social life, an "*as-yet-unfulfilled, unfinished task,* a clarion call, a duty and an urge to act." The above example brings vividly into relief the duty and urge that are extended to women through the identity autism mother. At times, (m)others in my focus groups complied with the duty and urge to normalize their/our child, taking up remedial practices such as behavioural consulting through service agencies. However, in the course of our discussions, the disruption and excess of autism and (m)others' relationships with their different child/adult disrupted the expected mother therapist and opened creative possibilities for more ethical understandings and practices of (m)othering and care.

After the participants' initial perusal of the collages and the books on display, as well as the preparation of tea and coffee, the sharing of treats, and a brief welcome, both focus groups began with an anticipatory hush, followed by introductions. We quickly became known to one another as insiders through the ritual of introducing our child's/adult's identification, as well as through recounting our struggles with ableist systems in stories that were remarkably similar for how they closely imitated dominant cultural narratives – including the moment when (m)others knew there was something "wrong," doubts about what they might have done to cause autism, the process of diagnosis and the precarity of navigating and advocating within medical, educational, and governmental systems, and the articulation of a different sense of the meaning of autism and (m)othering. (M)others were rapt as others introduced themselves, interjecting only with brief questions or affirmations – "I know," "Yes," "It's hard" – and they shared their stories generously. However, in the dialogue that emerged from these rounds of introductions and identifications, it was not only the gendered, scientifically ordered, linear narratives of diagnosis and progress (Fisher and Goodley 2007) that became the topics of conversation or that were animated in focus groups. What also began to surface as I probed was a different sense of autism, (m)othering, and care – something more like an ethical attention to disruption and difference, with an orientation toward forging more collective ways to care (Piepzna-Samarasinha 2018; Runswick-Cole and Goodley 2018) and toward affirmative understandings of autism: "Why do we pursue all of this treatment anyways?" "What do *you* think autism means?" "What does it mean to care?" Dialogue within both groups surged at this point and was sustained for over an hour. (M)others often talked over one another, and there was a lot of laughter. There was a sense of excitement in the groups when the shared – and ironically contradictory – aspects of this intensive identity were discovered, and there was a kind of familiar recognition around deeper questions of the meaning of (m)othering and care. As Julie described in her follow-up email to me, "My brain was buzzing by the time I left the focus group, and it wasn't just the coffee! So many questions came to mind." This layered engagement by (m)others typified focus group conversations. I begin below with an exploration of how (m)others articulated their own and their children's identities in relation to dominant renderings of autism and autism mothers and how this self-identification also, ironically, opened them to affirming autistic difference and alternative ways to (m)other and care that gesture to unmothering autism (E. Kim 2017; Runswick-Cole and Ryan 2019).

First, (m)others spoke candidly about the gendered nature of the expected parent in their child's/offspring's lives and about how a mother's "duty" to achieve identity with the "normal" (humanist) human – bourgeois, nondisabled, autonomous, economically productive, self-fashioning, independent, rational – for her different child is part of the often unquestioned ground of their everyday life as an autism mother. After twenty years of workshops and programs, for example, Julie, (m)other of nineteen-year-old Kyle, observed, "Most of the care that is given to our kids is given by women." Julie was the only (m)other who mentioned a father's involvement in a caring role: "My husband is very involved ... but he is almost always, when he goes to a workshop over the years ... in the strong minority." Only one other (m)other, Esther, mentioned her husband or male partner: "Well, my husband's an engineer ... He's convinced that Ryan can access parts of the brain that we can't access. He's smarter than all of us." This account perhaps reflects Jordyn Jack's (2014, 157–58) observation about gender and autism, noted in the Introduction: "Whereas narratives written by mothers tend to take on a quest for recovery, narratives written by fathers tend to take on a quest for understanding – not simply of the child in question but of the father's own character and identity." Julie's observations also reflect the global reality that the bulk of caring labour continues to be done by women, particularly women of colour (Bailey and Mobley 2018), and that care is presumed to be the natural calling of mothers (Douglas et al., "Mad Mothering," 2021; Walkerdine and Lucy 1989).

Indeed, many of the (m)others in focus groups framed their "hunch" that led to their child's diagnosis – despite encountering experts who told them that it was nothing to worry about – as a kind of "mother's intuition" or knowing grounded in their proximity to their autistic child as (m)other. As Helen framed it, "We've always known it's something. Me especially." Esther said, "I'm a first-time mother. I know *nothing* about being a mother, but I know there is something wrong with this kid." Knowing "there is something wrong" did not require expertise or even experience for Esther. Rather, knowing was based on something closer and more immediate, implying that Esther understood how she just knew as a kind of intuition, perhaps even a bodily one, about her child that emerged from within the closeness of a (m)other's ties to and intimate relationship with her child. Already, identity has become not only about identifying autism – many (m)others also spoke about knowing, and watching for, the signs of normal development – but also about bodily knowing the cultural ground governed by the Western scientific sense of normal development that organizes our everyday sense that "there is something wrong."

More was at stake for these (m)others with the "unfinished task" (Bauman 2004a, 20) of identity than hunches. The Western cultural "urge" and "duty" to fashion an approximation of normalcy in their child, particularly when their child was young, had, at least in part, come to bodily inhabit (m)others' identities and everyday practices as guilt and blame. For example, in response to a clipping about refrigerator mothers that I included in one of my collages (a storyline introduced in Chapter 2), (m)others Anna and Rosa spoke about the direct blame that they had experienced for their child's autism through psychoanalytic vocabularies. These (m)others continue to live and resist the legacy of the "bad" mother identity of refrigerator mother. As Rosa, mother of twenty-six-year-old Elizabeth, said of her encounter with a psychiatrist, "I thought she was diagnosing my daughter, but she was really observing me," and the psychiatrist's conclusion was that "the mother's cold"; it was "not about my husband but the mother." Anna, too, experienced overt scientific blame. In addition to the intensive remedial therapy that she had taken up when her son was young to "cure" him (see Chapter 2), Anna spoke about the impact of scientific mother blame: "I never had [or] could have another child ... I mean emotionally ... because I always had [the blame] in mind." Rosa agreed: "Neither could I." Damaging scientific governance and blame of (m)others – often framed by Western narratives of progress that locate overt mother blame as a relic of a less progressive past – continue to be embodied in our contemporary moment, then, in (m)others' intimate embodied and constrained "choices."

To further this point, (m)others in my focus groups also reported experiencing a more implicit form of blame, one reflected in searches for reasons why their child is autistic. Julie, (m)other of nineteen-year-old Kyle, wagered that "every mom ... felt some degree of responsibility for their child's condition, however illogical." Anna, (m)other to twenty-nine-year-old David, reflected on her experience of her decision to vaccinate her son: "I remember he was a little bubbly baby ... I thought that he would be an early talker ... And then after the booster shot, he completely stopped ... He stopped speech." For Esther, (m)other of ten-year-old Ryan, whom we met in previous chapters, it was her struggle with nursing to which she returned as the possible cause of her son's autism: "If I nursed him, the autism would somehow go away." Esther also struggled with the findings of the genetic testing that she underwent while pregnant (which showed that both she and her son have a "deletion" on chromosome 16):

> The smaller deletion is linked to developmental delay and possibly autism, but there are also people in the normal population who have it and don't have any issues at all ... Ryan's a great kid. Would I have not had him knowing that there's a 50 percent chance he was going to have that genetic variation? ... You would erase the population.

Although autism's "genetic" mother, as Esther put it, is a "relief" – as it means that she did not do something to directly cause autism – it also means living an agonizing contradiction between love for her son and the possible scientific elimination of autistic children through a mother's "choice" to undergo genetic testing (Landsman 1998, 2–3). Here, in addition to knowing that something is wrong with your child, confronting autism and autism mother identity in everyday text also becomes about grappling with the ways that (m)others identify with how they are to articulate or live what is wrong: Is it my fault? What did I do wrong? Should I participate in genetic research? These impossible situations – caring about and for your unique child while confronting the intense cultural imperative to remedy autism, a form of mother blame that instrumentalizes human life and erases uniqueness – are moments when space begins to open, at least for some (m)others some of the time, beyond that of the good autism mother who works intensively to achieve normalcy.

The "compelling seduction" of normalcy, as Rod Michalko (2002, 172) phrases it, in (m)others' lives together with their autistic child/adult was also a topic of conversation. Early in their parenting journeys, (m)others intensively pursued both conventional and alternative normalizing treatments, an implicit form of mother blame that balanced on mothers' individual success or failure in achieving the approximation of normalcy in their child (Sousa 2005). It was at least in part through everyday text that the "urge" to treat and find such therapies seemed to enter (m)others' lives: the movie *Son-Rise: A Miracle of Love* (Jordan 1979), online articles about gluten-free and casein-free diets, popular science reviews of Applied Behaviour Analysis (ABA), genetic testing, and more. When I asked, "What are we doing all the interventions for?" Esther replied, "It's for us, to make them be more normal. I don't think it's for them at all." Having a "normal" child was at times compelling, even desirable for Esther, who was pursuing a suite of different therapies. This "making" of normalcy in her son – or at least as close an approximation of it as possible – reveals normalcy's seduction and power, as well as its fabricated nature. What is understood as normal rests on Western culture's natural body. But this mythical natural body is, too, a fabrication, constructed through scientific and socio-political vocabularies that shift over time, as previous chapters have documented (Yergeau 2018; see also Michalko 2002, 170–72). In her statement that we live the constraint and duty of normalizing interventions "for us" rather than for our child, Esther recognized normalcy as a fabrication and instrument of alteration that she wielded in her son's life. In this recognition of her impossible ethical choice, she also opened space for a different kind of (m)othering and care. This space, one where autism just is and requires no explanation or alteration, was lived as a contradiction alongside the urge to treat that (m)others also bodily and affectively inhabited at times, a point to which I return in more detail below.

(M)others described late-modern Western culture's "duty" and "urge" to achieve a self-same identity for their autistic child, as depicted in my collages of everyday text, as an intense and very real paradox of care that they live within their everyday lives. Here, the expected parent in everyday text is not only gendered but also the bourgeois, autonomous, economically productive, healthy, normative, white, neoliberal, Western subject. Against this cultural scene, autism mothers are expected to have access to unlimited resources – financial, temporal, and personal – and to make themselves constantly available to self-educate and train, attend professional appointments, work intensively with their child, closely monitor their child's development, and advocate for their child's needs (Hays 1996; Sousa 2005). Helen, mother to newly diagnosed seven-year-old Hannah, said this about attending an autism service agency for the first time: "It's funny 'cause I went to the orientation evening ... and it's like, 'We're going to simplify it ... Here's 10,000 pages!'" On the same topic, seasoned (m)other Julie shared the following in the midst of laughter and much talking over one another: "It's a wonderful reality that *you* live in ... (*As if speaking to the service agency professionals.*) 'Can I make supper?' I mean, that's gotta be in here somewhere!" Afterward, in my reflection on this exchange, I recalled the many times that I had "failed" as a disabled single (m)other who worked full-time, often arriving late at such autism agency sessions without completing the assigned homework, both because I had no time and because I did not like the way that my "gaze" was being retrained to "see" my son in deficit terms. Service providers threatened to cut off access to supports (available only by completing compulsory training seminars) more than once. (M)others who fall outside the bounds of the expected parent – such as immigrant (m)others, (m)others of colour, single (m)others, and working-class (m)others – encounter multiple barriers and forms of exclusion.

A single immigrant (m)other, Carol, described her experience: "Being a parent is hard. Being a single parent of a special needs child … it's very difficult." Jennifer, (m)other to seven-year-old Eric and founder of a parent support group and information library in her community in Toronto, articulated the exclusions that marked the lived reality for immigrant (m)others and parents: "Because of language barriers, there's lots of other things … We immigrants, we are all busy, struggling, surviving." In the same focus group, (m)others paused during an exchange about challenging expert knowledge to ask about the (m)others who are often absent within service agency spaces:

> JULIE: I am always curious about all the people I don't meet, the parents who … don't have a degree in science … and are they going to say to someone [i.e., are they going to challenge an expert]? I don't think so.
> HELEN: No, they're not! People get mowed over … by the system.

In part, it was the classed, gendered, and raced nature of the identity autism mother and her duty to achieve normalcy in her child that (m)others spoke about and at times poked fun at. Even more, in (m)others' ironic recognition that although identity with autism's warrior mother is impossible to achieve, it must be imitated if she is to be regarded as a good mother who works to achieve normalcy in her child, (m)others' approximations of this identity became a kind of comedic parody and exposed not only the constructed nature of the instrumental, ableist, capitalist aim to remedy autism but also the constructed nature of normalcy. Space for a different way to care about autism and (m)othering beyond oppressive and individualizing configurations was opened through these collective moments of laughter, reflection, and resistance together.

Echoing neoliberal consumer capitalism's empowered feminine (Ringrose and Walkerdine 2008) and citizen scientist (Solovitch 2001), (m)others also articulated how they had become their own "experts" about their child's autism and treatment. For example, Jennifer, (m)other to seven-year-old Eric, explained, "I got all kinds of opinions, like, 'Oh he's fine, he's severely autistic … ' (*Laughter.*) They are all professionals. And oh, my goodness. Now, I just, I'm the expert." Jennifer described how she had gone on to do a social work degree and to read all the articles, books, and treatment options that she could find. As noted, she opened an information and support network in her community to address the limits of conventional Western medical knowledge and autism service agencies. Anna, (m)other of twenty-nine-year-old David, who lives with her, said of these agencies: "They tried to counsel the parents, not help with the behaviour of the children. If you ... do your own research ... it's educating the parent ... They won't even help you to advocate ... They sit in meetings and won't say anything." Although (m)others shifted the ground of expertise away from science and professionals as part of their identity, this undertaking could be read as (m)others embodying the covert blame – the responsibility to recover their child by developing their own expertise – that emerged after 2000, as described in Part 2. That is, according to the conventional narrative about autism, mothering, and care, by drawing on neoliberal rationalities of freedom and choice and on a range of market options, as well as by adhering to genetic and biomedical scientific regimes and ideologies of natural and intensive mothering, a mother is expected to re-educate herself, merge her love with science, and treat her child through her individual labour within the mother-child dyad in order to achieve recovery.

However, unlike in the recovery stories common in everyday text, (m)others in my focus groups did not ultimately articulate recovery as the goal for their child. Rather, (m)others articulated a practice of accepting and affirming their child's difference and, as Anna put it for her son David, a practice of "working *with* him to make his life better." Rosa, too, stated that she "wanted to help" her daughter Elizabeth, not treat her. Even as (m)others governed themselves into autism's mother therapist and expert warrior mother identities and engaged their child in therapies, they simultaneously opened, albeit just a titch, space for a different ground of authority and for more affirming, collective forms of care (Sousa 2005, 229–30). In their challenges to paternalistic experts, initiation of organizations, critical appraisal of therapies, and criticisms of intensive mothering and of the autism industry, (m)others gestured to a different way of being together with their different child or adult, one that also included connecting with other autism (m)others in studies like this one. Helen articulated her challenge to experts this way:

> I started doing my own stuff ... You're telling me this is what it is, and
> that's not what I'm seeing, so maybe you've got a PhD in it, but I'm living

with her every day, and it's not working ... A lot of it comes down to "I'm an expert, this is how it works ... If it's not working, it's because *you're* doing it wrong."

Julie, (m)other of son Kyle, aged nineteen, summed up her view of autism professionals this way: "I mean, they're questioning your ability to parent your child in some ways by telling you [that] you have to parent differently." During a conversation about alternative therapies, Julie also wondered,

> It's interesting though, all the interventions we haven't talked about ...
> So anything to do with food and things ... probably tends to fall more
> on [the mother's] side, and you'll see discussion groups [online] where
> they will say you are harming your child by not doing the diet, or chela-
> tion, or whatever ... Do we [mothers] veer toward things that ... fit within
> how we want to be with our kids ... rather than the more scientific and
> systematic approaches like ABA or other conventional therapies?

Such maternal treatment – only this time, not *on* (m)others but by (m)others on the bodies of autistic children – despite operating in some ways on the same gendered, ableist, and neoliberal terms as intensive mothering and from the same Western cultural urge to treat and normalize, disrupts the ground of scientific and professional authority. Jennifer added, "On the one hand, the parent, you already coped for several years, and there is for sure something you know, but ... you have to be open to learn." This (m)other also criticized costly therapies that offer "big improvement." Here, (m)others articulated an identity forged in relationship with their autistic child that moves away from the impossible identity of autism mother and her intensive, instrumental urges and scientific treatment of her child. Alongside (m)others' critique and parody of the identity autism mother and of their own accumulation of expertise, they also took up practices coded feminine and maternal – love, empathy, listening, relationality, and domestic practices like cooking – and in this way were able to pry open a space of being together where affirmation and love guided their care and relationships. In this respect, (m)othering, autism, and care came to comprise something more than the embodiment of the paradox of care – loving your autistic child while practising intensive curative labour. This something more included intimate, embodied practices that moved with difference and challenged the authority of paternalistic science and professional expertise about the meaning of autism, (m)othering, and care.

For the (m)others in my focus groups, embodied difference identified as autistic included different learning styles, different modes of being social, different ways to love, different modes of communication, and even different forms of what we know as real. As Joy shared about her sixteen-year-old daughter, Anya, "She has a totally different learning style." Playing music by ear, for example, was a way that Anya gathered her focus for more academic tasks. Advocating for this approach to learning within a public school meant the exhaustion of educating others about her daughter's difference. For her part, Anna spoke about an autistic form of love: "I remember when [David] was little, the first time understanding that he really has this deep feeling ... He put this song on about mother ... We don't get [the spoken] ... 'Mom, I love you.'" Esther had a similar experience with her son Ryan, who expressed himself through music on a CD instead of using verbal language. Recounting this experience, Anna was met with lots of "Ya's" and "Mm-hmm's" when she said, "He knew what song was what number when he was two and a half ... We didn't know what he knew." Both (m)others' autistic children had been labelled as having "severe" developmental delays and intellectual disabilities. And although I do not wish to imply that there is an innate and hidden autistic "intelligence," as Leo Kanner (1943) originally suggested, or that (m)others and science should therefore value and prioritize the recovery of this "intelligence," alternative modes of communication and meanings of autism outside of dominant perspectives appeared within (m)others' relationships with their autistic child. Here, autism does not appear as a withdrawn child damaged from disordered mother love or as a defective brain that lacks Theory of Mind and that is materialized in deficient social skills but as an alternative way of being and relating that opens and humanizes non-normative forms of love, sociality, and communication. Anna also said about her son David, "[Autistic people] see life in a different way. They tap us into a different real if you are able to kind of pull down the mask." In other words, if we orient to what is identified as autism not as a pathology but as a different and viable way of being human, the naturalness (or facade) of normative and conventional modes of being human, communicating, and caring for and about one another falls apart. Rosa shared a glimpse of her relationship with her autistic daughter that challenges pathologizing notions of non-normative sociality identified as autistic: "We used to call her a social butterfly, even though she's nonverbal. She liked to interact with people ... [Autistic people are] social. They're really social." Referring to other aspects of her daughter's way of being as "exploring," Rosa explained, "She's going over here; she's going over there. She's too busy to give you attention."

For (m)others in my focus groups, disrupting the paradox of care – to love and eliminate your autistic child through intensive labour in the mother-child dyad while pursuing an autism-free future – featured centrally in their relationships with their autistic offspring as (m)other and autistic child/ adult learned one from each other, embodying a new shape of being together beyond more of the same (Douglas, Rice, and Kelly 2017). In this way, new possibilities emerged for understanding what it means to live a good life together. Anna shared, "My son is my teacher, and no matter how people make fun of that, it is because he shows me ... little ways can sometimes be very big." Here, Anna resisted being labelled a "crazy" mother out of touch with reality (Douglas et al., "Making Memories," 2022), and she refused medical assessments of her son as "severely autistic" and therefore noncommunicative. Anna's son types to communicate. It is precisely the dehumanizing trope "severely autistic" that M. Remi Yergeau (2018, 11) challenges: "Autism is frequently storied as an epic of asociality, of non-intention. It represents the edges and boundaries of humanity, a queerly crip kind of isolationism. We, the autistic, are a peopleless people. We embody not a counter-rhetoric but an anti-rhetoric, a kind of being and moving that exists tragically at the folds of involuntary automation." Resisting this understanding of autism, Anna humanizes her autistic son in ways that resonate with disability and critical autism studies approaches. That is, Anna centres the experiences and knowledge of her son in ways that might also disrupt and transform dominant and exclusionary ways of being, knowing, and caring in the world (e.g., see Fletcher-Watson et al. 2019; Michalko 2022; Re•Storying Autism Writing Collective 2022; Rodas 2018; and Yergeau 2018). As Anna's assertion suggests, to borrow from Tanya Titchkosky (2003, 233), disability becomes a "unique teacher of human alterity within a culture committed to maintaining a singular sense of the ordinary and normal as unexamined values." Alongside moments in their parenting journeys when they sought therapies to remedy autism and occupied the identity of autism's mother therapist and warrior mother, (m)others attended to their child's difference through an ethic of disruption and through the form of attention that I call affirming care (Panitch 2008). (M)others' humour, constant questioning, and resistance to everyday deficit narratives about autism and to ableist, patriarchal mothering collapsed the paradox of care and its tension of loving their autistic child while practising intensive, curative, normalizing labour. (M)others in my focus groups unmothered autism by moving together with their autistic child or adult and with each other toward more collective and affirming forms of (m)othering and care. This shift begins to tell the "disability story of parents" (Dona M. Avery, quoted in Ryan and Runswick-Cole 2009, 43) a little differently, creating potential bridges to forge solidarity between feminist and disability studies, as well as between autistic activists and (m)others.

Affirming Care: Moving beyond the Paradox

Before considering how (m)others' disruptions of dominant depictions of autism and autism mother contain the creative outlines of a different kind of care outside of dominant renderings, I pause for a moment. I do not wish to present the reader with an overly romanticized depiction of (m)others' and autistic people's lives together. Within current configurations of ableist, patriarchal, neoliberal care, which privilege scientific under-standings of the human and the "critical exigence" to remedy autism (Yergeau 2018, 4), (m)others described lives that are difficult. In many ways, some of the experiences articulated by (m)others reflect dominant depictions of autism and mothering as documented in my previous chap-ters, as well as findings reported within medical sociology and other fields. (M)others described experiencing stigma alongside their child, the stress of coping, struggles with depression and grief, as well as a lack of autism supports in Ontario, particularly for immigrants and families of colour and for autistic people after age twenty-one, the cut-off for public school (Goffman 1963; Gray 1993, 2002, 2003; Khanlou et al. 2017; Stoddart 2005, 44). Responding to one of the collages that I made for focus groups, which included an article on murder and depression, Anna, (m)other of twenty-nine-year-old David, was met with a chorus of "Mm-hmm's" from other (m)others when she reflected, "What I'm saying is our path is extremely hard. I think we have these issues with ... being depressed ... and we've all been there." Other (m)others spoke of the stigma and isolation that come with this life when one is up against systemic ableism and a Westernizing cultural ground hostile to embodied difference. Helen commented about stigma, "She does stuff, and people are like, 'Oh, what's she doing that for? Why is that gigantic kid having a tantrum?' And it's like well, we're on the subway, and there's a lot of stuff going on, and then they look at you." Here, Helen shared some of her different child's stigma through a public event infused with blame and reliant on the cultural ground of normal ways of acting (Goffman 1963). Julie spoke about the systemic isolation of (m)others and caregivers: "We're all in silos ... When we go drop our kids at a workshop and I ask the facilitator, 'Could you maybe have a parent group?' and it is 'No, we're not funded for that.'" Julie was expressing how difficult it is within the current system, for example, to find other parents to share driving and the cost of a support worker. You are "on your own," described Jennifer, an immigrant (m)other and social worker who, as mentioned, sought to fill the gaps in services and information for her community by starting an information-sharing library.

Many (m)others also spoke about the exhausting advocacy work required to gain access to very limited problematic services and even to diagnoses. "I would argue that every mom who wakes up every day and faces life with a child with ASD [autism spectrum disorder] is a warrior mom," Julie wrote in a follow-up email to me. Here, the Western biomedical imperative to identify and remedy difference was an urge taken up by some (m)others some of the time (especially around their child's diagnosis). (M)others pursued diagnoses, treatment options, and services, even as they lived the contradiction of a stubbornly autistic child and a desire to affirm autism and to advocate for access. Recall from Chapter 1 the example of Anna, who described her around-the-clock engagement with therapies through the Son-Rise Program – a "gentler" approach akin to behaviourist approaches – as she laboured to "reach" her son when he was young. At no point in these therapies was the experience or desire of Anna's son given consideration, and she soon abandoned these remedial efforts. Given the current landscape of ableist, patriarchal, neoliberal care (Douglas et al., "Mad Mothering," 2021; Runswick-Cole and Goodley 2014), the gendered "duty" to achieve normalcy, particularly for (m)others who fall outside of the expected white, middle-class parent, is real. Yet even amid (m)others' depictions of stress, depression, isolation, and the cultural imperative to conventionally treat their child, (m)others redefined the meaning of autism mother identity, whether autism's refrigerator mother, mother therapist, or warrior mother. As we saw above, (m)others re-envisioned the fight against autism (McGuire 2016) not as one to eliminate autism (or to achieve an imitation of normalcy) but as a collective fight for access to education, work, love, relationships, the arts, and life with and on behalf of their child. Here, through attending to the disruption of autism as one that "makes a difference" (Van Manen 1990, 23), there is a hint – an outline – of the making of a different kind of care that affirms, rather than expelling, embodied difference understood as autistic.

Amid (m)others' descriptions of the constraints of dominant depictions of autism, autism mothers, and care, as well as (m)others' descriptions of the impossibility of achieving them, a very different configuration and meaning of autism, (m)othering, and care appeared through focus group conversations. This new meaning was not only one that critiqued dominant depictions but also one oriented toward learning in relationship with autistic offspring and toward affirming rather than remediating difference. In a phenomenological sense, affirming care describes a quality of attention and a "lived structure of meaning" (Van Manen 1990, 4) in which (m)others attended ethically to the disruption of difference within their relationship with their different autistic child. For (m)others, what makes care affirming is that they meet the call of the alterity, disruption of difference, and uniqueness of the child in front of them with a response that is relational, open, reciprocal, and pedagogically rooted in the give and take of teaching and learning (see Douglas, Rice, and Kelly 2017). The final paragraph of the above section, where I describe how (m)others oriented toward their autistic child's and adult's difference and extended the meaning of the human, begins to describe this affirming orientation to care as one that embraces and learns from, rather than expelling, the difference of autism. The vocation of affirming care, in which (m)others were deeply engaged when listening to, reflecting on, and putting into practice suggestions about what might best support their autistic child's and adult's well-being, can be understood as shaping the lived space where their different child/adult can be at "home," facilitating them and their "safekeeping" in a hostile world, and reshaping the meaning of autism, (m)othering, and care (Van Manen 1990, 59–60, 102–3). This approach involves an ethical orientation to care akin to that evident in the moments of ethical narration described in previous chapters, an orientation that gestures to the irreducibility of difference and to the fundamental alterity of us all. Below, in a more in-depth exploration of affirming care, I consider how (m)others' lived approximations of autism mother identity already contain not only the creative tracings of a more affirming care but also a different meaning of autism beyond Western, neoliberal, capitalist, scientific understandings and beyond the irremediable paradox of care.

Even as (m)others articulated their understanding of autism and care through the language of intensive mothering, Western science, and approaches like the Son-Rise Program, they simultaneously pushed against dominant meanings of autism mother and her role as the "regulator" of normal development (McGuire 2016, 82). "What is normal?" Anna asked. "We keep *missing* it ... We only see it to pull them on our side and make them normal." Anna was speaking about her decision to stop her search for remedial therapies and professionals to "cure" her son and about her shift to working alongside her son in order to "help him out" in ways that affirm his expressed way of being. "I'm getting something out of it. He's getting something too," she shared. For Anna, autism had become "something to think with" (Michalko 2002, 168), both a "mirror" that reflected society's artifice in constructing what is normal out of the disorder of autistic bodies and a valued identity grounded in difference that expanded the meaning of being human. We are all at risk of "missing," in Anna's words, these vital lessons about being human together in difference if we continue to pursue treatment and to turn away from a relationship with our different autistic child. In forging this alternative meaning of autism mother, Anna, too, embodied a different way of negotiating the lived contradiction of the paradox of care in (m)others' lives – the paradox of loving their different child in the face of the irremediable cultural imperative to normalize their child – where what we regard as normal is always already shaped by our Western cultural grounding and by the dominant role of science in governing intensive mothering within the mother-child dyad.

Another interesting exchange between (m)others about the limits of autism mother identity and the meaning of normal occurred while Julie was reflecting on having a child very different from herself. She said, "I honestly don't recall thinking ... I didn't have any grand plans to fall apart." Amid enthusiastic responses to this statement and a lot of talking over one another, Helen sarcastically quipped, "And your dream of a normal life was shattered with a diagnosis of autism," to which Julie replied, prompting the group's laughter, "Who's got one of those normal lives anyways?" Julie and Helen, who did not attend the same focus group as Anna, nevertheless extended Anna's critique of normal to include a critique of dominant narratives about the devastating impact of autism on "normal" family life, so ubiquitous within everyday text. Their quick exchange humorously critiqued the fabricated nature of these dominant narratives and pushed back against their typical tropes, including the grief-stricken mother, the loss of her normal child, her shattered dreams, a family torn apart, and an unimaginable life of stress and self-sacrifice (Douglas et al., "Making Memories," 2022). For the (m)others in my focus group, autism became an occasion to rethink the meaning of care as relational even as, at times, they dwelled within dominant vocabularies. Indeed, Julie also articulated the limits of her understanding of identity and difference: "Maybe a kid who was gurgling and doing [normal things] ... and then the classic, you know, head banging, flapping, rocking. I think I'd think they were withdrawn from the world." Despite these limits of discourse and understanding, the descriptions offered by these (m)others embodied a living critique and alternative to normalizing regimes. Here, we can apprehend that, at least for some (m)others some of the time, there is the possibility of something other than being autism's mother therapist or warrior mother who must act to "stop autism" (Yergeau 2018, 4). For the (m)others with whom I spoke, the possibility that we might care and live otherwise was grounded not in an orientation toward the disruption of autism as a problem but in an orientation toward a disruption that was affirming and attuned, revelatory of rich lessons about difference and power.

At the same time, there was nothing romantic about the affirming care that (m)others articulated; rather, they articulated this care in ways that resonate with what (m)other and disability studies scholar Martina Smith (2021, 112) calls "dispolitical love," which is "not a maternal forgive-all love phenomena but a love-at-work that is fearsome, fearful, intrudes and demands response-ability" from "neoliberal and psy-developmental" systems (113). Here, Smith invokes the materialist concept of response-ability articulated by feminist science and technology philosopher Donna Haraway (2016) and others (see Barad 2007; Tsing 2015) to mark the urgency of practising collective, relational (including across species and ecologies) care within our unprecedented times of social, economic, and ecological disaster. In focus groups, (m)others questioned Western cultural ideas about the meaning of the difference of autism and the response of systems. Many (m)others articulated an understanding of autism that was radically different from the idea that it is a tragic or threatening biological defect that can and should be remedied. One (m)other, Julie, poked fun at the psychoanalytic understanding of autism as a withdrawn or impris-oned self, a view still present today. She quipped sarcastically, "He seems to be in his own world." Amid eruptions of laughter in the group, she added, "Whose world should he be in? I never got that. Wouldn't it be a problem if he was in someone else's world?" And in this quip, she undermined the very notion of autism as an exception or otherworldly phenomenon. Instead of acquiescing to ideas about the withdrawal of an otherwise normal child, an inhuman difference, or a brain gone awry – as articulated within psychoanalytic, cognitive-psychological, and genetic approaches – Julie opened space for affirming her autistic son. Here, not only autism but also (m)other and (m)othering begin to mean something different. (M)othering moves into the realm of attuned and affirming attention, where a carer is learning in difference with their autistic offspring and pressing for a dif-ferent lived shape of care beyond the social construction of mothering as intensive labour to create a home for her child or adult in the world. Carol, mother to ten-year-old Jason, explained it this way: "Not just seeing all the wrong things ... Just accept who they are is the least I can ask." Indeed, most (m)others were unambiguous that autism *just is*. "She will always have it," Helen said in response to questions about a cure for her daughter from curious parents. Autism cannot be fixed or cured. It is part of the human condition. These children were not taken or stolen. Rather, autism is a different and viable way of being human. As Julie again contributed, "The whole issue of the separation of the condition from the child or from the individual ... there is no non-autistic Kyle." And with this observation, Julie undermined Western scientific descriptions of the natural body and the normal human as mythical fabrications that compose the unquestioned ground of our lifeworld. In this way, (m)others' care opened space where we might glimpse how the creative possibility of something new had already appeared within (m)others' relationships with their different child or adult. This revaluing of autism and care also begins to break open the problem-solution dialectic of disability, mothering, and care and to embrace autism as a viable way of being. These are important contributions to a new form of (m)othering and care that affirms difference. Indeed, (m)others in my focus groups told the "disability story of parents" (Avery, quoted in Ryan and Runswick-Cole 2009, 43; see also Panitch 2008) a little differently from how it is told through dominant depictions of autism, mothering, and care within everyday text as well as within feminist and disability studies scholarship. In their conversations together during focus groups as well as in their everyday practices and advocacy within systems, (m)others "invoked a disability commons" (Runswick-Cole and Goodley 2018, 231) that began to unsettle Western, white, individualizing, bourgeois forms of mothering as intensive normalizing labour within the mother-child dyad.

Affirming care also animated (m)others' stories about how the challenges of living in a world that is hostile to autistic difference and disruption opened them to ethical relationships with difference more broadly. Based on their own experience, many (m)others turned toward the world in a stance of compassion, openness to difference, tolerance for ambiguity, protectiveness of others, and humility about their ultimate lack of control over the uncertainties of being human. This stance was a new, affirming, and disruptive place to begin to care about the world differently and to produce knowledge grounded in experience (D. Smith 1999) of caring for and about an autistic child or adult. Esther, for example, spoke about a transformative moment with her husband regarding her son Ryan's repetitive bedtime routine: "We feel like he's being selfish, but he's really not." Esther's statement was met by a chorus of agreement from other (m)others, "no, no they're not, no." He has this routine in his head ... He doesn't know how to do it any other way." Here, a transformative reorientation to the difference of autism as viable and valid rather than "selfish" intimately tied this (m)other and father, through a more critical and conscious intentionality, to an affirming relationship with their autistic son, one that unsettled the ground of dominant scientific depictions of autism and care as remedial.

Rosa also articulated how learning in relation to her daughter's non-normative embodiment opened her both to self-transformation and to the world:
"I'm just more open, more understanding, more protective" of those who
appear different in the world. In response to the depiction of ABA treatment
in one of my collages, Rosa described how she had sought to understand
autistic difference from autistic adults themselves and how she had
expressed her solidarity by visiting autism self-advocate's blogs and publicly
speaking out against normalizing treatments: "This was a fundraiser for
Autism Speaks ... and I quoted [an autistic blogger] that said, 'I don't want
to be doggy trained' because that's what it [ABA, as promoted by Autism
Speaks] is." Attending to the disruption of autistic difference in affirming
ways transformed (m)others and their relationship not only to self and
others but also to a world grounded in Western scientific conceptions of
the normal human. (M)others' critical and creative reorientation to the
disruption of autism – along with their redefinition of autistic difference
as a viable and even valuable way of being human and as a sitpoint – began
to disrupt the meaning of normal sociality as something tied to an assumed
reciprocity of shared perspectives (Goffman 1963, 127) in knowing the
other. These (m)others disrupted the ground of the known about difference
and identity, revealing glimpses of its concealed secrets. In this way, they
began not only to insert a critique of the modernist values of sameness,
certainty, and scientific control over nature and the human body (Stiker
1999) but also to embody and to live new and creative affirming understandings of (m)othering and care that learn from difference identified as
autistic and that reshape the world.

Affirming care also meant that (m)others engaged in caring relationships that aimed to re-fashion the world in more "homey" ways for their
autistic child. Based on their research with families of disabled children,
Rayna Rapp and Faye Ginsburg (2011, 406) suggest that such intimate,
worldly transformations are a "new kinship imaginary": "Parenting with
a difference first reverberates through family life, creating new understandings and orientations of what one author has aptly described as 'life
as we know it' (Berube 1996). Over time, many use the idioms available
to them to reach out beyond the world of kinship to forge a new arena
of public intimacy where atypicality is the norm." For (m)others in my
focus groups, this intimate world-changing activity involved careful

attention to their child's embodied differences in a world that does not reflect their child's way of being – what feminist disability studies scholar Rosemarie Garland-Thomson (2011) calls "misfits" between body and world – and attention to educating others and to changing the world along the way. Helen spoke about seeking out helpful metaphors to use in educating others to accept autistic difference: "I think it helps people, I find, to put it in concrete physical terms." Other (m)others described the persistence required to introduce understandings of autistic difference that might help to shape small corners of the world for their children to live and learn in difference. "I kept pushing and pushing," Joy shared about her journey to get an appropriate school setting for her autistic daughter. She described the same persistence when it came to teaching her autistic daughter and son, now young adults, about how to live in a "misfit" world that does not incorporate their way of being, "I want them to have strategies for dealing ... confidence, self-esteem," she shared. This (m)other explained that such strategies were meant not only to shape the world in more autistic ways but also to let "the world come in." Carol, too, described how she worked to find a daycare and then to educate staff to make space where her son might be at home: "Jason learned a lot from them, but they also learned a lot from him ... They can really see, you know, the inside." Above, I described how Jennifer started an information-sharing library in her community. Julie, Anna, and Rosa also initiated educational and public art events and called upon the maternal and disability commons to join them in advocating for a world that "fits" their child's/adult's difference as a viable way of being human.

In many ways, the vocation that (m)others took up around "safekeep-ing" their autistic child/adult, including attending to their child's unique-ness and making space in the world where "home" is possible, more generally resembles the parental vocation to love and care for one's child (Van Manen 1990, 59–60, 102–3). As parents, we want what's best, including belonging, for our child. Yet (m)others pursued this vocation for their autistic child in a world that is often hostile to difference despite gains made by autistic self-advocates and critical allies. This is a world that also expects that mothers will individually gather expertise and skill and will work to achieve at least an approximation of normalcy in their so-called disordered individual child. In their simultaneous approximation and disruption of the normal and natural (Michalko 2002, 167–75), (m)others in my focus groups creatively embodied an alternative way to care about autism that critically mirrors back to us dominant culture's interpretations of both autism and autism mothers (168). The vocation of these (m)others was shaped not only by the power and seduction of normalcy but also by their relationship with their different child/adult and by their adoption of the form of attention that I call affirming care in their ethical orientation to the different child/adult in front of them as a life that they cannot help but attend to in ways that puncture the mastery of normalcy. In this critical and creative approach fashioned through the relationships of (m)others with autistic people, practices of affirming care rupture the compelling perception of the normal life as that which is "good" and reveal a glimpse of the concealed secrets of its exclusionary ground. (M)othering and care become dispersed sites of radically disruptive, political, loving, and affirming practices that collectively begin to rupture the paradox of care, forge solidarity between disability and feminist studies, and open new ways of being together that embrace embodied difference. These practices are undertaken in solidarity with disability justice activists and with other alternative practices of collective care (e.g., see Bailey and Mobley 2018; Berne 2015; Chataika and McKenzie 2013; and Piepzna-Samarasinha 2018) that move beyond (and perhaps have always moved beyond) the Global North's individualizing remedial care within the mother-child dyad.

The affirming care practices that (m)others described in my focus groups are radical in the sense that they begin from a location that differs both from Western scientific deficit understandings of autism and from the configuration of remedial care as tasked to mothers. Instead, practices of care were shaped by (m)others' lived experiences in relationship with their different autistic child/adult, as well as by the devalued ground of feminine and maternal sitpoints: love, affect, relationships, and the domestic (Garland-Thomson 2002; D. Smith 1999). When faced with paternalistic science and intensive Western cultural expectations of remedial mothering, (m)others pursued what they perceived would best carve out a "home" in a "misfit" world with and for their different child or adult. Recall Anna's story of a medical assessment that she approved for her twenty-nine-year-old son, David, so that he could gain access to resources within the mental health system. Through this process, Anna was gaslighted by professionals and labelled a "crazy" mother who "may have a problem with the [ableist] diagnosis of mental retardation" when she communicated to the assessors that they may have been missing some practical know-how about how to interact with nonspeaking people (on such gaslighting in systems, see Runswick-Cole, Fogg, and Douglas forthcoming). Based on her relationship with her nonspeaking son, Anna emphasized not only the importance of "a knowledge about working with [autistic people] and their strengths and abilities and sensitivities" but also the importance of a knowledge about the different ways of being social, such as using longer wait times between questions, that helped her son to gain access. Here, Anna attempted to meet scientific paternalism and authority as well as the historical coupling of femininity with madness by adopting an activist stance grounded in her experience and relationship with her autistic son (Douglas et al., "Mad Mothering," 2021; Douglas et al., "Making Memories," 2022; Garland-Thomson 2001). (M)others also paid attention to what their autistic children were telling them about how they learned differently and about their unique interactions with the world. Many (m)others shared stories about how they discovered through music that their child or adult offspring knew more than doctors were telling them was possible. Rosa, for example, said of her daughter, "She would pay attention if I sang to her instead of spoke." For the (m)others with whom I spoke, (m)othering and care came to mean, at least some of the time, ethically attending to and affirming the difference and uniqueness of their autistic child/adult while also resisting the paradox of care and its anguishing cultural imperative to "stop" autism (Yergeau 2018).

Focus group conversations opened an occasion to co-create a different kind of knowledge about autism and (m)othering, one that resists the paradox of care (E. Kim 2017; Runswick-Cole and Ryan 2019). In other words, (m)others in my focus groups uncoupled (m)othering from remedial care regimes and from autism mother identities governed by conventional autism science and by the "choice" to labour intensively. (M)others also described collective activist practices of affirming care that perhaps open "bridges" (Kelly 2017) across and between disability justice movements, autistic self-advocacy, (m)other activism, and feminist and disability studies as a way forward. These practices enact a "coming together of the 'disability commons'" (Runswick-Cole and Goodley 2018, 231) as (m)others push back against and offer alternatives to the legacies and ongoing harms, both for autistic people and for (m)others, of Western scientific, patriarchal, white supremacist, ableist, eugenic, neoliberal, capitalist forms of mothering, disability, and care. This undertaking is what I call unmothering autism (see also E. Kim 2017; and Runswick-Cole and Ryan 2019).

Conclusion

Is Neurodiversity's Mother Next?

I end this book, as I began, in the middle of an unfolding story about power, difference, (m)othering, and care in the context of radical struggles for disability justice (Ashburn and Edwards 2023; Brown, Ashkenazy, and Onaiwu 2017; Nishida 2022). I have made the case that the stories that we tell about autism, (m)othering, and care matter. Recall Cherokee and Greek author Thomas King's (2003, 2) statement that "the truth about stories is that that's all we are"; in other words, stories are culture-bearing and have the power to make – and therefore to remake – worlds. Despite gains made over decades by autistic and (m)other activists, the Western scientific story about autism and autism mothers prevails: autistic people's way of being is still reified and pathologized in much of mainstream autism research and everyday text (Fletcher-Watson et al., 2019; Re•Storying Autism Writing Collective 2022; Waltz 2023), and mothers, globally, continue to be held accountable (and blamed when we inevitably fail) for fixing autism through intensive labour that now begins before a child even arrives (Douglas, Runswick-Cole, et al. 2021; Waltz 2023). Finding a different way forward is vital.

My desire to disrupt knowledge production about autism, mothering, and care emerged from my different life together with my sons, Brennan and Jesse, and from my everyday encounters with text. I wanted to reconcile the paradox at the centre of our lives – that of loving and caring for and about an autistic child (and my own neurodivergent self!) in a world calling for sameness and identity through mothers' intensive normalizing labour. To do this disruptive work, I took a "backwards glance" (Ahmed 2006a, 2006b) at what might be behind the ubiquitous figure of "autism mother" –

both perceptually and historically – and behind her consuming desire to care through remedy. In part, this undertaking meant tracing and revaluing moments when alternative knowledge and affirming care glimmered – even if just fleetingly – some of the time for at least some (m)others of autistic children/adults living and loving together within the constraints of the mother-child dyad. My backward glance also dismantled the restrictive terms of the Global North's bourgeois mothering and its paradox of care. Far from natural, this social construction of mothering turns on a "god-trick," one that conceals its exclusionary ground and historical and geo-political specificity (Haraway 1991, 191; 2018, 15–16). I agree with Katherine Runswick-Cole and Daniel Goodley (2018), who argue that this form of parenting is oppressive both for (m)others and for disabled children (see also Douglas et al., "Making Memories," 2022). Dismantling the para-dox of care and the social construction of mothering needs more attention, and so this book invites care and disability justice scholars and activists, along with feminist, mothering, and disability studies researchers, as well as memoirists, scientists, service providers, professionals, and (m)others to open new possibilities for being together in difference beyond the para-dox of care within the mother-child dyad – perhaps engaging a backward glance of their own.

To begin to tell the story about autism, (m)othering, and care a little differently, I have inserted disruptive knowledge – critically and phenom-enologically oriented feminist and disability studies – into knowledge pro-duction and everyday text about autism and care. This disruptive approach begins in the partial and located "sitpoints" (Garland-Thomson 2002) of previously marginalized perspectives (Haraway 1991, 2018; D. Smith 1987, 1999) – in this case, of (m)others and autistic children/adults. I have shown that disruptive knowledge (including my own attempt to narrate ethically) is one important way to reveal and challenge exclusionary and violent late-modern, Western modes of power and subjectivity that persist in the lives of (m)others and autistic people (Dean 2002; Dehli 2008; Foucault 1982, 1991a, 2003). As a case in point, recall how this approach revealed the so-called natural duty of autism's mother therapist and warrior mother figures to labour around the clock and to shore up all their resources so that they might remedy their child by fighting autism – at times through violent means such as intensive behavioural therapies and even murder (Gibson and

Douglas 2018). The book disrupts the Western scientific, neoliberal, capitalist "critical exigence" to fix autism – indeed, all embodied difference (see Yergeau 2018, 4) – along with its assumptions about mothers and women as natural carers and about human development as universal progress toward autonomy, productivity, and conformity with non-autistic life.

I have argued for an ethic of disruption in knowledge production (especially in autism research and parent memoirs). This approach has meant not only adopting the philosophical stance of the skeptic and per-petually questioning the ground of knowing and being (Foucault 1982, 208) but also adopting a creative philosophical stance that seeks knowledge from the margins about the disruption of difference (Bailey and Mobley 2020; Collins 1987, 1990, 2015; Fritsch 2015, 2016; hooks 1987; Schalk and Kim 2018). I have made the case that an ethic of disruption requires a new quality of attention in knowledge production and everyday text, one that opens toward difference and care as fundamental to life, one that seeks other ways than remediation, fear, violence, mother blame, or grief to respond to the surprise of difference within the expected movements of everyday life (Foucault 1980a, 25; Titchkosky 2007, 64–65), one that is relational and desirous of difference without romanticizing our lives, one that is a site of resistance and love, and one that honours the fundamental alterity of us all, which can never be reduced to the same (Boler 1999; Levinas 1969). I have called this quality of attention affirming care. Other aspects of affirming care suggested by my work here, including (m)othering and disability justice as well as possibilities for solidarity between autistic and autism movements, are ripe for further study.

Through my disruptive approach, I have also told the "disability story of parents" (Dona M. Avery, quoted in Ryan and Runswick-Cole 2009, 43) a little differently from accounts that suggest straightforward disability or gender oppression, tracing not only mothers' complicity within oppressive care regimes but also, more importantly, for going forward differently, (m)others' resistance. I have called (m)others' subversion of ableist, patriarchal, neoliberal, capitalist, eugenic care regimes – a subversion of which this book is a part – unmothering autism (E. Kim 2017; Runswick-Cole and Ryan 2019). To unmother autism means to uncouple (m)othering from the curative care and violence that compel an autism-free future through autism mothers' intensive remedial labour in the mother-child dyad. It means to disperse (m)othering, autism, and care across a "disability commons" (Runswick-Cole and Goodley 2018). It means to move together – (m)others and autistic kin – against ableist regimes that govern and harm us all (albeit differently) both through our "freedom" to parent this way rather than that and through violent tactics like the overpolicing of brown and Black disabled people, including autistic people. It means to give greater consideration to theorizations of care that begin in the margins, including critical autism, (m)othering, Global South, Black, feminist-of-colour, disability studies, disability justice, and other alternative approaches (Bailey and Mobley 2020; hooks 1984; Schalk and Kim 2018; Yergeau 2018). And it means to release new "love stories" that affirm life together in difference in all its beauty and struggle (Douglas et al., "Re-storying Autism," 2021). I remind the reader here of the "lovely intimacy" with her son invoked by Estée Klar (2015, last para.) and of the love "that is fearsome, fearful, intrudes and demands response-ability" invoked by Martina Smith (2021, 112), which many (m)others I spoke with or encountered in everyday text described in their life with their different child/adult. My rereadings of everyday text and my conversations with (m)others in focus groups to unmother autism also revealed shared histories of resisting ableism and opened new pathways for solidarity between (m)others and autistic self-advocates as well as between feminist and disability studies, feminist mothering and care studies, and feminist science studies and other fields interested in advancing disability and gender justice.

As I come to the end of this book, I note two examples of what is newly unfolding in the continuing historical play of forces of domination and resistance around autism, (m)othering, and care. First, evident today is the momentum of the neurodiversity movement, the radical movement started by autistic self-advocates in the early 1990s to challenge ideas about the normal human and to refute the notion of care as corrective, a notion seen with Applied Behaviour Analysis and its aim to make autistic children "indistinguishable from their normal friends" (Lovaas 1987, 8). This movement's aims have been taken up in professional discourse and practice, including in "strengths-based" approaches to education and care (e.g., see T. Armstrong 2012). Celebrating rather than correcting difference marks a hopeful shift in the orientation of the professions. However, there may be danger here too, as the professionalization of neurodiversity discourse becomes detached both from autistic and neurodivergent voices and from grassroots political movements. Whether the voices of autistic and other neurodivergent people as well as their embodied struggles and access to supports will be reduced to the same (as in, "we are all neurodiverse"), with mothers' care reimagined through the marketization of neurodiversity (or neurodiversity's mother) is a story that remains to be written.

Second, evident on today's scene is how autism diagnosis – alongside the retraining of (m)others into dominant care regimes – has expanded to Black, Indigenous, and other groups of the Global South (de Sousa Santos 2018; Mohanty 2013). For example, within campaigns by parent advocacy organizations of the Global North, such as the Global Autism Public Health Initiative, launched by Autism Speaks (n.d.a), autism no longer appears solely as a white, Western, bourgeois disorder. Rather, the Western scientific governance of bodies and minds in the form of "urgently needed services" is now exported globally to developing nations through "caregiver skills training" programs in over seventy countries (Autism Speaks n.d.a). The heightened class, race, and gender inequities of this post-COVID-19 moment, which continue to task women with primary caregiving globally (Douglas et al., "Mad Mothering," 2021; Ringrose and Walkerdine 2008), have the effects of bolstering gendered care and enlisting a particular kind of mother and carer – autism's mother warrior – in the achievement of the neoliberal, autonomous, Western consumer-subject as the unquestioned standard of the normal human worldwide. This is a moment when we might glimpse the complex intertwining of race, gender, class, and geopolitics in the identity warrior mother within contemporary Western, capitalist, colonialist projects.[1]

In 2023, the Autism and Developmental Disabilities Monitoring (ADMM) Network (2023, 19) in the United States reported that "the percentage of 8-year-old children identified with ASD [autism spectrum disorder] was higher among Black, Hispanic, and Asian and/or Pacific Islander (A/PI) children compared to White children" for the first time. Although there is no comparable data for Canada, signs that autism may now be a legible diagnosis/identity for people of colour and Indigenous people in Canada are also emerging. The Cowessess First Nation in Saskatchewan, for example, recently partnered with the Autism Resource Centre (ARC) to address the underdiagnosis of autism within First Nations communities (Giesbrecht 2019). Recall that Black and Indigenous people have historically been more likely to receive diagnoses that label them unimprovable (e.g., mild intellectual disability and fetal alcohol spectrum disorder) than to receive the ironically privileged diagnosis of so-called improvable autism. Because the racist logics in diagnostic practices devalue alternate bodies, these communities have been cut off from vital pathways of support that require an autism diagnosis (Lindblom 2014; see also Antony et al. 2022). In this sense, expanding diagnostic practices and legal rulings such as Jordan's Principle (Chambers and Burnett 2017) may represent an opening of access.[2]

At the same time, there may be a danger here too. Powerful parent advocacy organizations such as ARC forward a biomedical understanding of autism that installs a Western, ableist, colonialist, capitalist version of the normal human as well as configuring mothering and care as individual, intensive, and remedial. Indigenous understandings of difference and care, as articulated, for example, by Chief Cadmus Delorme of the Cowessess First Nation, rub up against this dominant view: "When children have those special gifts, they actually have a unique relationship with the Creator, with the spiritual world ... A child who has a very unique perspective on the world, we can actually learn a lot from them" (quoted in Giesbrecht 2019, n.p.; see also Bevan-Brown 2013; Bruno et al. 2023; Durie 1998; and Ineese-Nash 2020). The telling of this story in everyday text has only just begun.[3] Will different Indigenous forms of (m)othering and collective care for and about an autistic Indigenous child or kin come to mean a reduction of difference to the same through ARC? Or will it mean the insertion of more hopeful practices grounded in Indigenous knowledges about difference, and all human beings and life as gift (Ineese-Nash 2020)? It is my hope that newly unfolding storylines – like the popularization of neurodiversity and the extension of autism diagnosis and identity beyond their white, bourgeois beginnings in the Global North – signal new, potentially more disruptive possibilities that might also begin to recuperate autism, (m)othering, and care from violent Western care regimes. Yet this story, too, remains to be written.

Years after I first sat down to write this book, my sons have grown. I have graduated from the social justice department where the telling of this story began and now lead an international multimedia story-making research project reimagining autism as desired difference, and teach educators and graduate students about affirming care, "mad" (m)othering, and critical autism and disability studies in education (e.g., see Douglas et al.,

"Re-storying Autism," 2021; Douglas et al., "Making Memories," 2022; and Re•Storying Autism Writing Collective 2022). I often hear stories from students, teachers, and practitioners, many of whom identify as autistic or neurodivergent, about their desire for more affirming practices and understandings of disability. Yet I still watch as my adult autistic son's unique and beautiful way of being – whether evident in his non-linear transition to adulthood or his need for solitude – are remade into disorder. Disturbing questions and comments about my "not enoughness" or "too muchness" as a (m)other continue (Bordo 2003, 161): "Maybe it's the high school you sent him to." "He just needs some tough love." I remain "mad" for advocating for a way forward in difference and through affirming care (Douglas et al., "Mad Mothering," 2021 Douglas et al., "Making Memories," 2022). In everyday text, too, trouble abounds. Stories of police violence toward autistic people who are in distress or who are just "walking along the train tracks," in the case of Indigenous autistic person Joshua Nixon (Simmons 2021), rub up against stories of parents fighting for access to intensive remedial therapies (Star Editorial Board 2022). These are just two jarring examples of how little has changed in everyday text. Stories such as these make me anxious each time my son leaves the house, though less so over time. Reconciling my contradictory experiences of the violence of everyday life with the intimate beauty of our family's life continues to be difficult.

Yet it is with a much more hopeful story about autism, (m)othering, and care that I wish to end here. This alternate story, as we have seen, emerges in those moments when alterity labelled autistic, in all its beauty and struggle, cannot be reduced to the same, despite powerful ableist, patriarchal, white supremacist, remedial care regimes. This book inserts the possibility of an ethic of disruption in knowledge production and the possibility of a new kind of memoir about disability and (m)othering, one that turns toward and affirms difference. Not only does this turn toward difference – "to listen to the sound of the 'what' that fleets" (Ahmed 2006b, 106) – reveal stories about unethical ableist, patriarchal, capitalist systems that entice autism mothers and carers, now globally, into working to approximate white, bourgeois, Western standards of normalcy, sometimes violently, in their autistic child. It also reveals what it might mean to live well in difference with autistic people and those who work with and care about them, many of whom are also multiply marginalized, including (m)others. These are the secrets that those of us who dwell in the margins and love autistic kin already glimpse – and practice at times – in our everyday life. This is an occasion for radical hope. Perhaps it is the unfinished or unspoken disability love stories of (m)others who affirm difference, advance disability and gender justice, and unmother autism in everyday life with autistic kin, that I most hope this book inserts into the world.

Notes

Acknowledgments

1 The full version of the artist statement can be found here: https://www.restorying autism.com/publications/8k2089h70ayq171mae7rovmtnz8u0j.

Introduction

1 In 1998, physician and researcher Andrew Wakefield published an article in *The Lancet* that blamed early childhood measles, mumps, and rubella vaccines for causing autism by harming children's immune systems. The article was later retracted by the journal when it was discovered that Wakefield's data had been falsified (Editors of *The Lancet* 2010).

2 I use the term "Global North" to describe the ongoing predominance of Western Enlightenment ways of being and knowing, such as white, male, nondisabled, bio-medical, and rational, regardless of geographical location. Within Canada, for example, a nation located in the geographic North, Indigenous, Black, and other Global South ways of being and knowing – what sociologist Boaventura de Sousa Santos (2018) calls epistemologies of the South – continue to be devalued and absented from know-ledge production and political and social life. Feminist scholar Chandra Talpade Mohanty (2003, 505–6; emphasis in original) sees this North-South divide as occurring between what she calls the "*One-Third World*" and the "*Two-Thirds World*." When I refer to Western European philosophies, I use the term "Western."

3 The neurodiversity movement rethinks neurology as diverse and fluid, akin to bio-diversity. For more on autistic self-advocacy and the neurodiversity movement, one grounded in disability rights and led by autistic people, see the work of autistic educator and author Nick Walker (2012), the Autistic Self Advocacy Network (https://autistic-advocacy.org), and Autistics United Canada (https://www.autisticsunitedca.org).

4 The language of "the stim" and "stimming" has been reclaimed by autistic self-advocates to mean the repetitive movements and/or sounds that many autistic and

other neurodivergent people describe as expressive of their way of being and considered to be both helpful for sensory regulation and enjoyable. This perception contrasts with clinical understandings of stimming as self-stimulatory behaviour, or a sign of disordered neurology (see Kapp et al. 2019).

5 On the continued and common use of restraint in schools, see the work of inclusive education scholars Nadine Bartlett and Taylor F. Ellis (2020) and disability studies scholar Robin Roscigno (2020).

6 My endeavour to understand a world where violence and exclusion against people perceived as different is ordinary – indeed, possible at all – and to reconcile this circumstance through an attentiveness to action, storytelling, and the possibility of the new is inspired in part by the philosophy of Hannah Arendt ([1954] 1994, [1958] 1998; see also Swift 2009). Arendt's philosophy gave me courage as I worked through an archive of popular media and lived experiences filled with violence. Arendt's work also inspired my pursuit of new possibilities for being together in difference, perceived as a relation that is between us (all of us). I depart from Arendt's thinking, however, about society and recuperating the ancient public-private divide and public realm of speech as the way forward for modernity. Consequently, Arendt does not come to play a major role in my overall argument.

7 I use the term "late modernity" to describe our contemporary moment as one when key structural features of modernity persist (e.g., capitalist production, colonialism, social institutions like the nuclear family, industrialization, urbanization, scientific rationality, and Western Enlightenment ideas about progress and the perfectibility of the human) even as features of postmodernity or liquid modernity take hold (e.g., neoliberal economics and ideology, the rise of identity and the self-fashioning individual, risk and the surveillance society, the erosion of social institutions like the welfare state, globalization, and the gig economy). See, for example, the work of sociologist Zygmunt Bauman (2004a, 2004b).

8 See also the work of disability justice advocates Patty Berne (2015), Mia Mingus (2011), and Lydia X.Z. Brown, E. Ashkenazy, and Morénike Giwa Onaiwu (2017), among others.

9 I use the term "neurodivergent" in a nonessentializing, nonreductive manner to refer to ways of being and claimed identities that depart from what is considered typical, normative, and good. For further reading on neurodivergence, see the work of autistic rhetoric scholar M. Remi Yergeau (2018); autistic scholar Nick Walker (https://neuroqueer.com/neurodiversity-terms-and-definitions/), and autistic activist Kassiane Asasumasu (http://timetolisten.blogspot.com), who coined the term.

10 See Ashburn and Edwards (2023), Carey, Block, and Scotch (2020), Douglas, Runswick-Cole et al., "Mad Mothering," (2021), Filax and Taylor (2014), Greenburg and Des Roches Rosa (2020), Re•Storying Autism Writing Collective (2022), Ryan (2021), Ryan and Runswick-Cole (2008, 2009), and Waltz (2020).

11 See also Hyun Kim (2012), Milton (2014), Nadesan 2005, Re•Storying Autism Writing Collective (2022), and Waltz 2013.

12 In some cases, electric shock continues to be used (see Re•Storying Autism Writing Collective 2022; also Broderick 2011; Dawson 2004; Gibson and Douglas 2018; Klar, Douglas, and McGuire 2016; Pyne 2020; Roscigno 2019; Sequenzia 2016; and Yergeau 2018).

13 Feminist sociologist Dorothy Smith (1999) describes how text coordinates and organizes the social and consciousness, as well as how the social is modified through the actual "everyday/everynight world" (5) of our interpretive practices while producing and interacting with texts: reading, writing, interpreting, feeling, resisting, disrupting, speaking back, or complying. Her work also describes how text is a generative site within the coordination and reproduction of power relations: "In coordinating particular local sequences of activity among participants, utterances [i.e., speech and writing] reaffirm, regenerate and modify social organization as it is projected toward the next occasion of action together" (145). I read Smith with an interpretive slant, which suggests that text enters our lives in practical, embodied, and lived ways and that its disruptive potential depends on how we take it up (or not) within everyday life.

14 It is with some care that I include (m)others' self-identification with the autism labels shared in focus groups and their use of these labels. I regard this self-identification as an activity that is related not only to the broader Western scientific activity of categorization, through which we know ourselves, our world, and one another (e.g., see Schutz 1970, 116–22), but also to the activity of distinguishing "types" of (m)others, autism, people, and so on as significant in some contexts, like research, rather than in others. The participation of immigrant and Asian (m)others in my study is notable since these mothers have been historically excluded from the identity category autism mother, raising the question of whether this participation might reflect the widening boundaries of autism diagnosis and the increased regulation of populations. It is also notable that Black, Indigenous, and queer (m)others (at least none identified as such) were absent from my focus groups, being (m)others who have also been excluded from the identity autism mother. The absence of these (m)others may also reflect my own dominant positioning in relation to the identity autism mother as a white, cisgender, middle-class researcher recruiting within autism mother networks in southwestern Ontario. These absences, too, may reflect some (m)others' (e.g., working-class) resistance to and, as Amy C. Sousa (2015) puts it, "strategic disengagement" from dominant autism (m)other networks. Also of note is the range of autism identifications and ages of offspring, implying the sustained activism of the (m)others in my groups, possibly indicative of which (m)others have access to participation in research as well as to sustained levels of activism (see Ryan and Runswick-Cole 2008).

15 For another example of the use of collage in focus groups, see Thomson et al. (2011).

16 For an example of an empirical social-scientific approach to autism and mothering, see the website of the Office of Women's Health Research Chair in Mental Health at York University, https://nkhanlou.info.yorku.ca.

17 On the social construction of mothering, see Douglas et al., "Mad Mothering," 2021; Douglas et al., "Making Memories," 2022; O'Reilly 2016; Rich 1986; Runswick-Cole and Goodley 2018; and Schalk and Kim 2020.

Chapter 1: Disruption as a Place to Begin

1 Following feminist disability studies scholar Rosemarie Garland-Thomson (2002), I use the term "sitpoint," rather than "standpoint" (on feminist standpoint theory, see Harding 2004, for example) to recognize disabled people's experiences as valuable and valid places to begin in knowledge production.

2 In other work, I focus more explicitly on ontology and a neomaterialist approach to autism and embodiment as well as on proliferating new stories beyond Western biomedicine through multimedia storytelling (see Douglas, Rice, and Siddiqui 2018; Douglas et al., "Re-storying Autism," 2021; Re•Storying Autism Writing Collective 2022; and Rice et al. 2020). In this book, I focus on power and on disrupting the Global North's knowledge regimes regarding autism, (m)othering, and care, which continue to hold sway and have been nearly totalizing.

3 I make an intentional distinction in the book between the use of the term Other (capitalized) and other (small case) to denote the difference between: 1), the production of the normative human through Western scientific and socio-cultural processes of labelling, devaluing, demarcating, and governing modernity's Others (women, Black, Indigenous, disabled); and 2), the ethical sense of the fundamental alterity of us all, a philosophical stance that guards against collapsing difference to the same (see Boler 1999; Levinas 1969).

4 For further reading on diffraction and interference and on neomaterialist ontology, see Re•Storying Autism Writing Collective (2022) and Rice, Bailey, and Cook (2022).

5 See, for example, Du Bois ([1903] 1994), Hochschild (1983), Hughes and Paterson (1997), Merleau-Ponty (1968), Paterson and Hughes (1999), D. Smith (1987, 1999), and Titchkosky (2003, 2007).

6 In "Disability Studies: A Field Emerged," Garland-Thomson (2013, 915) comments that recent major works in the field "mark the full emergence of a distinctive interdisciplinary field that has come to be called critical disability studies" (e.g., see Abberley 1987, 1998; Davis 1995, 2002; Finkelstein 1998; Garland-Thomson 1997, 2013; Goodley 2011; Goodley, Lawthom, and Runswick-Cole 2014; Michalko 2002; Oliver 1996; and Titchkosky 2003). Importantly, as an interdisciplinary field, the "subject matter" of disability studies, as disability studies scholar Simi Linton (1998, 2) puts it, is "not

simply the variations that exist in human behavior, appearance, functioning, sensory acuity, and cognitive processing, but, more crucially, the meaning we make of those variations." Another feature of this field is its ontological challenge of normative conceptions of the human that exclude alter embodiments. Disability studies scholars and activists understand disability not as a tragic individual phenomenon, as biomedicine would have it, but as a legitimate, albeit different, way of being/becoming in the world with something of value to teach us about our human life together (Davis 1995; Goodley 2011, 2014; Rice et al. 2018). Disability studies represents what Daniel Goodley (2011, xi) calls a "paradigm shift" away from writing and thinking about disability as a problem-object or "personal predicament" – how individuals cope, adapt to, or overcome such bodily tragedy – and toward the study of disability as a "social pathology," which includes understanding disability as a different, and viable, way of being in the world. For disability studies scholars, the disruption of disability becomes, in Rod Michalko's (2002, 168) words, "something to think with." Disability studies opens a space from which to disrupt the normative and ordinary and to ask critical questions about alterity and our shared life together, possibly even inserting something new (Titchkosky 2003, 36). With similar hope, Michalko (2002, 168) likens disability to a mirror that, when held up to society, can be revelatory of unquestioned assumptions, values, and practices that continue to marginalize and devalue alternative forms of embodiment. Disability studies scholars Sharon L. Snyder and David T. Mitchell (2006b, 192), too, speak of the disruptive potential of the field of disability studies, which "situates itself as a force of destabilization ... displacing the object of change onto unaccommodating environments, beliefs, disciplines, or research methods." Titchkosky (2007, 38) says, "A defining feature of disability studies scholarship ... is that it is establishing a tradition of inquiry that problematizes the ways in which disability is figured against an ahistorical, apolitical and even asocial background." Like Haraway (1991, 2018) and D. Smith (1999), who call for a new metaphor in feminist knowledge production, disability studies scholars call for historicizing the unmarked nondisabled body by beginning in disabled peoples' experience. This undertaking requires a rejection of the still prevalent notion in the natural and social sciences that disability is an object in and of itself. As disability studies scholar Lennard J. Davis (1995, 2) articulates, "Disability is not an object – a woman with a cane – but a social process that intimately involves everyone." Indeed, like feminist epistemologies, disability studies politicizes knowledge and shifts the ground of knowing to the historical, economic, cultural, and interactional/relational processes in which disability appears and becomes meaningful in everyday life.

7 Among many other sources of further reading, see Bailey (2018), Bell (2006), Bevan-Brown (2013), Brown, Ashkenazy, and Onaiwu (2017), Clare (2017), Erevelles (2011), Garland-Thomson (1997, 2013), Kafer (2013), McRuer (2006), Meekosha (2011), Nguyen (2018), Nishida (2022), Piepzna-Samarasinha (2018), Price (2015), Rice (2014, 2018), Schalk (2018), and Yergeau (2018).

Chapter 2: Autism's Refrigerator Mothers

1 On Kanner, see also Grinker (2007), Jack (2014), Murray (2008, 29–30), Nadesan (2005, 71–73), Silberman (2015), Silverman (2012, 32–42), Waltz (2013, 47–58), and Yergeau (2018).

2 Austrian pediatrician Hans Asperger also published descriptions of children in his care at the Vienna Hospital during the 1930s and '40s. He described a disorder similar to that identified by Kanner, which he called "autistic psychopathology" (Asperger 1991). The difference was that the children observed by Asperger more readily acquired language and typically became, as biographer Richard Pollak (1997, 249–50) recorded it, "successful" (if "egocentric") adults. Although Asperger's work may have been known to Kanner (Silberman 2015, 168), it was not published or translated in Europe or North America until the 1980s and for this reason is not part of the historical narrative of this chapter (see also McGuire 2016; Nadesan 2005; and Silberman 2015). Asperger's work emerged in Nazi Vienna and implicated psychiatry and Asperger himself in enabling the Nazi regime to draw a boundary between those children deemed untreatable, and thus sent to be murdered, and those children deemed intelligent and capable of some degree of normality, and thus (following these eugenic logics) treated in Asperger's clinic (Sheffer 2018).

3 For further reading about Bettelheim, see also Grinker (2007, 80–83), Jack (2014), McDonnell (1998), McGuire (2016), Murray (2008), Nadesan (2005, 97–99), Osteen (2008), Silverman (2012), and Waltz (2013).

4 *Warrandale* (A. King 1967) played a key role as the first of a series in a new form of *cinéma vérité* that King introduced: "actuality drama." It was, according to filmmaker, author, and critic Michael Koresky (2010, n.p.), considered a pioneering piece of art, and King was regarded as an artist of great depth. King's aim was to "capture life as it happened" and to chronicle "unadorned reality" in the form of "passionate stories," Koresky explains. This form of cinema was understood as showing great compassion for those who suffered the extremes of the human condition. It is troubling that the chronicling of histories of normalized violence against autistic individuals, alongside their exploitation as objects of innovative cinematic documentation, was deemed laudable and not seen as evidence of human rights violations.

5 Thank you to feminist social work scholar Margaret F. Gibson for permission to use our personal correspondence of May 18, 2014, about case studies (see also Silverman 2012, 72–73).

6 Case studies have been reclaimed in liberatory ways by a variety of disciplines, including the social sciences (i.e., ethnography and autoethnography), social work, education, and journalism. They differ from other narrative forms, such as scripture, myth, and folklore. At the same time, they are linked to Western colonialist practices of chronicling the distinctions between the normal and abnormal, such as the medical

case history, the cabinet of curiosities, and the freak show (Garland-Thomson 1996, 1997, 2001).

7 See founder of psychoanalysis Sigmund Freud's (1990) case study of "Dora" and "Little Hans," for example.

8 It is interesting to note that today's biogenetic approaches, although dominant, have not dispelled psychoanalysis or its version of mother blame from the world stage; it remains the dominant approach, for example, in both France and South Korea for autism treatment and research (Grinker 2007; H. Kim 2012).

Chapter 3: Returning the Psychoanalytic Gaze

1 Other examples of early autism mother narratives include *Dibs in Search of Self* (Axline 1964) and *The Child in the Glass Ball* (Junker 1964).

2 My analysis of Park's (1967) *The Siege: A Family's Journey into the World of an Autistic Child,* as well as Bruno Bettelheim's, Ole Ivar Lovaas's, and other experts' misogyny, has parallels to philosopher and historian of science Marga Vicedo's (2021) *Intelligent Love: The Story of Clara Park, Her Autistic Daughter, and the Myth of the Refrigerator Mother.* Like Vicedo, I trace scientific mother blame during this era and work to recuperate (m)others' simultaneous contributions to knowledge production *and* care as valuable, as well as the contributions of (m)others to histories of disability activism and to the neurodiversity movement in the Global North. I move beyond Vicedo and contribute a feminist and disability studies approach framed by interpretive and critical sociological approaches that also consider "the ways by which families, and particularly mothers, live alongside sometimes-hostile medical intervention in, about, and because of their families" (Nielsen 2022, para. 4). I also include new details about (m)others' contributions to disability activism from the 1940s to 2022 through their invoking of a "disability commons" (Runswick-Cole and Goodley 2018), or collective, alternative forms of care – what I call affirming care – that move beyond the mother-child dyad and Western individualist ontologies. This work includes a critical analysis of Applied Behaviour Analysis in solidarity with autistic self-advocates and an analysis of mounting evidence of harms (e.g., see Broderick 2011; Dawson 2004; Gibson and Douglas 2018; Pyne 2020; Roscigno 2019; Sequenzia 2016; and Yergeau 2018). I also include consideration of how, until very recently, the identities autism and autism mother have been unavailable to Indigenous, Black, and other people of colour (who have been misdiagnosed and governed through racist logics and diagnoses such as fetal alcohol spectrum disorder and emotional disorder) and how autism and autism mother (being subject to ableist, patriarchal governance) emerged as ironically privileged, white, middle-class identities (e.g., see Bevan-Brown 2013; L. Graham 2012; Lindblom 2014; and Roy and Balaratnasingam 2010).

Chapter 4: Autism's Mother Therapists

1   I am in solidarity with the neurodiversity movement, and I hold the meaning of autism open for the purposes of this book. I do not fix autism in brain-based difference, whether positive or negative. Instead, I orient to autism and embodied difference through an ethic of disruption – an orientation to disruption's creative possibilities for being and becoming together differently.

2   The concept of maternal deprivation derives from the work of developmental psychologists Mary D. Ainsworth (1964), Harry Harlow (1961), John Bowlby (1952), and others on psychological attachment beginning in the 1950s. Maternal attachment theory placed primacy on a mother's constant availability and care and identified grave effects, including physical illness and autism, that were said to be attributable to her absence, whether total or partial (Ehrenreich and English 2005, 249–54). Although historically linked to psychoanalysis, maternal attachment has been taken up mainly in developmental psychology, where ethological, rather than psychoanalytic, concepts have been influential (Blatt and Levy 2003, 103). Maternal attachment theory does not seem to have played a central role in everyday text about autism and mothers during this time, but continues to circulate versions of the "chilly" mother, childhood disorder, and autism today (e.g., see Jack 2014, 61–63; Koren-Karie et al. 2009; and Walkerdine and Lucy 1989, 47–63).

3   On the government initiative to close Thistletown Regional Centre, see Government of Ontario (2012). For further reading about deinstitutionalization as part of the larger disability and racial justice movement toward decarceration in our contemporary moment, see Ben-Moshe (2020).

4   Lovaas, a psychologist at the University of California, Los Angles, was also the engineer of the Feminine Boy project during this same time. Lovaas and his colleague George Rekers conducted similar experiments aimed at changing the behaviour of gender-nonconforming children, with the difference that a mother's disapproval, rather than electric shocks or slaps, was used. Conversion therapy for gender non-conformity has now been widely challenged under human rights laws (Pyne 2020). However, despite over thirty years of contestation by autistic self-advocates around human rights abuses associated with intensive behavioural therapies and with Lovaas's experiments, Applied Behaviour Analysis has grown into a burgeoning autism industry and is understood in many countries of the Global North as the gold standard of autism treatment (Broderick and Roscigno 2021; Gibson and Douglas, 2018).

5   Incidentally, this program would go on to become a self-proclaimed success, win awards, and establish the first integrated school program in Toronto. This outcome propelled its leaders to give workshops and to advocate for the establishment of such partnerships between parents and professional institutions in Ontario and beyond, including the United States (see L. Stone 1981).

6   For further reading on (m)others challenging scientific expertise, see Nathanson and Tuley (2009).

Chapter 5: Retraining Behaviourism

1   Early Intensive Behavioural Intervention (EIBI), or Applied Behaviour Analysis (ABA), is a behaviourist approach widely accepted today as the only evidence-based treatment for autism. It is funded as a gold-standard treatment in many parts of North America (see Gibson and Douglas 2018) and is used within autism agencies, schools, home therapy programs, and more. As an example of its reach, consider that the Ontario Ministry of Education issued "Policy/Program Memorandum 140" in 2007, which mandates the compulsory use of ABA in schools. According to the ministry, ABA "uses methods based on scientific principles of learning and behaviour to build useful repertoires of behaviour and reduce problematic ones" (Ontario Ministry of Education 2007, sec. 3, para. 1). It is significant to note that the use of ABA in Ontario is grounded in limited empirical evidence, including Ole Ivar Lovaas's (1987) much-cited study claiming that 47 percent of the autistic children who participated in his program at the University of California, Los Angeles, became "indistinguishable from their normal friends" through behaviourist treatment (quoted in Gibson and Douglas 2018, 3). Other possible evidence, such as the lived experience of autistic people and empirical, ethical, and moral evidence showing the harm of ABA, is not considered (e.g., see Anderson 2022; and Kedar 2012). This book offers a sustained critique and alternative.

Chapter 6: Autism's Warrior Mothers

1   This group is now called Autism Alliance of Canada (https://www.autismalliance.ca).

2   Some Indigenous scholars have recently described how neurodiversity is not a new concept invented by Western disability activists (e.g., see Grant Bruno, interviewed on *Behaviour Speak Podcast* 2022).

3   See, for example, the blogs of Amy Sequenzia (https://ollibean.com/author/amy-sequenzia/), Mel Baggs (https://ballastexistenz.wordpress.com/), and Michelle Dawson (http://www.sentex.net/~nexus23/naa_02.html).

4   On the "so-called red flags" of autism, including public health and advocacy campaigns that aim to "raise awareness about the signs of autism," see McGuire (2016, 67).

5   Stagliano's blog has been removed by the *Huffington Post* due to concerns about false health information.

6   For other examples of biomedical approaches in everyday text, see McCarthy (2008), Rones (2008), and Seroussi (1999).

7   For other examples, see Guernsey (2006), McCarthy (2008), and Seroussi (2000).

8 This mother expert role was incipient in earlier decades (see Kaufman 1976; and Maurice 1993).
9 The term "citizen scientist" was introduced by freelance writer Sara Solovitch (2001, 1) in *Wired* magazine, where she argues that the Internet has been instrumental in the advocacy movement of parents of disabled children, changing the shape of medical research: "United by the Net and emboldened by their numbers, parents of desperately ill children are funneling millions into research, building vast genetic databases, and rewriting the rules of the medical industry."

Chapter 7: Resisting Genomics and War

1 https://www.facebook.com/photo/?fbid=807353917416118.
2 https://www.facebook.com/AutismMothers/photos/a.442629202652/101565945 62632653.
3 https://www.facebook.com/autismfile/photos/pb.100064414344915.-2207520000./ 10152776178927769/.
4 This video continues to be edited by its owner. In some versions, the final statement has been changed to softer language: "Joining together to make a difference. Autism mothers worldwide." And there is now an invitation to autism mothers to "send your photos." Viewers are left with the statement "More to come ... "
5 https://www.facebook.com/GenerationRescue/.
6 See also the *CBS News* (2013) report about the documentary *Behind the Tragedy: Mother Murders Autistic Son,* produced by the Autism Media Channel, started by Polly Tommey in the United Kingdom.
7 https://www.esteerelation.com.
8 On Facebook, see https://www.facebook.com/fidgetsandfries, and on Instagram, see @fidgets.and.fries.

Conclusion: Is Neurodiversity's Mother Next?

1 For further reading on such global initiatives, see Titchkosky and Aubrecht (2015, 69), who draw from disability studies and postcolonial theory to trace and disrupt the World Health Organization's dissemination of "mental health" discourse, identified as a "colonizing force in postcolonial times," one that arises from and sustains Western colonial relations, exports "restrictive and exclusive versions of the human," and oppresses diverse bodies and minds in order to sustain exploitative colonial relations.
2 Jordan's Principle is a legal ruling in Canada meant to provide access to health care, products, supports, and services for all First Nations children and families, including those living on federal reserves, where the separation of families from community due to health care jurisdiction can interfere with children receiving health care in community (see Chambers and Burnett 2017).

3 See, for example, the 2024 Desiring Autism and Neurodivergence Symposium, which
   brought together autistic, neurodivergent, and nondisabled Indigenous and settler
   researchers, artists, activists, practitioners, and students from over ten nations to
   reimagine neurodivergence through critical, arts-based, intersectional, and decolonial
   perspectives, held at Queen's University, https://www.restoryingautism.com/
   maineventpagee.

Works Cited

Abberley, Paul. 1987. "The Concept of Oppression and the Development of a Social Theory of Disability." *Disability, Handicap and Society* 2 (1): 5–19. https://doi.org/10.1080/02674648766780021.

–. 1998. "The Spectre at the Feast: Disabled People and Social Theory." In *The Disability Reader: Social Science Perspectives*, ed. Tom Shakespeare, 79–93. London: Cassell.

Abraham, Carolyn. 2007. "Canadian Breakthrough Offers Hope on Autism." *Globe and Mail*, February 19. http://www.theglobeandmail.com/life/health-and-fitness/canadian-breakthrough-offers-hope-on-autism/article572698/.

–. 2008. "Research Paves Way for Predicting Autism." *Globe and Mail*, January 10.

–. 2010. "Genetic Finding Paves Way for Controversial Autism Testing." *Globe and Mail*, June 10.

–. 2011. "Goodbye, Thrifty Gene, and Hello to a New Prime Suspect behind the Global Upsurge in Obesity and Diabetes: The Womb." *Globe and Mail*, March 5.

Adler, Tina. 1994. "Comprehending Those Who Can't Relate: Researchers Seek the Neurobiological Roots of Our Social Side." *Science News*, April 16, 248–49.

Ahmed, Sara. 2004. *The Cultural Politics of Emotion*. New York: Routledge.

–. 2006a. "Orientations: Toward a Queer Phenomenology." *GLQ: A Journal of Lesbian and Gay Studies* 12 (4): 543–74. https://doi.org/10.1215/10642684-2006-002.

–. 2006b. *Queer Phenomenology: Orientations, Objects, Others*. Durham, NC: Duke University Press.

–. 2007. "A Phenomenology of Whiteness." *Feminist Theory* 8 (2): 149–68. https://doi.org/10.1177/1464700107078139.

–. 2010. *The Promise of Happiness*. Durham, NC: Duke University Press.

Ainsworth, Mary D. 1964. "Patterns of Attachment Behaviour Shown by the Infant in Interaction with His Mother." *Merrill-Palmer Quarterly of Behaviour and Development* 10 (1): 51–59. https://www.jstor.org/stable/23082925.

Alexiou, Gus. 2020. "Doctors Issuing Unlawful 'Do Not Resuscitate Orders' for Disabled Covid Patients 'Outrageous.'" *Forbes,* June 23. https://www.forbes.com/sites/gusalexiou/2020/06/23/unlawful-do-not-resuscitate-orders-for-disabled-covid-patients-outrageous/.

Althusser, Louis. 2001. *Lenin and Philosophy, and Other Essays.* Trans. Ben Brewster. New York: Monthly Review.

Anderson, Laura K. 2022. "Autistic Experiences of Applied Behavior Analysis." *Autism* 27 (3): 737–50. https://doi.org/10.1177/13623613221118216.

Antony, Celina, Madison Campbell, Stephanie Côté, Grant Bruno, Carolyn Tinglin, and Jonathan Lai. 2022. "Informing Care Pathways and Policies for Children and Youth with Indigenous Perspectives to Advance Canada's National Autism Strategy." *Frontiers in Psychiatry* 13: 1–16. https://doi.org/10.3389/fpsyt.2022.916256.

Arendt, Hannah. (1954) 1994. *Essays in Understanding, 1930–1954: Formation, Exile and Totalitarianism.* New York: Shocken Books.

–. (1958) 1998. *The Human Condition.* 2nd ed. Chicago: University of Chicago Press.

Armstrong, Pat, and Hugh Armstrong. 1984. *The Double Ghetto: Canadian Women and Their Segregated Work.* Toronto: McLelland and Stewart.

Armstrong, Thomas. 2012. *Neurodiversity in the Classroom: Strength-Based Strategies to Help Students with Special Needs Succeed in School and Life.* Alexandria, VA: ASCD.

Ashburn, Meghan, and Jules Edwards. 2023. *I Will Die on This Hill: Autistic Adults, Autism Parents and the Children Who Deserve a Better World.* London: Jessica Kingsley.

Asperger, Hans. 1991. "Autistic Psychopathology in Childhood." In *Autism and Asperger Syndrome,* ed. Uta Frith, 37–39. Cambridge, UK: Cambridge University Press.

Autism and Developmental Disabilities Monitoring (ADMM) Network. 2023. *Community Report on Autism 2023.* Atlanta, GA: Centres for Disease Control and Prevention. https://www.cdc.gov/ncbddd/autism/pdf/ADDM-Community-Report-SY2020-h.pdf.

Autism Canada. n.d. "Early Signs: Know What to Look For." https://autismcanada.org/about-autism/early-signs/.

Autism File Magazine. 2009a. "Autism Mothers – The Final Cut." *YouTube,* May 28. http://www.youtube.com/watch?v=sqiyND3RLW4.

–. 2009b. "Autism Mothers Unite Worldwide." Issue 33. https://www.facebook.com/photo.php?fbid=145784842768.

Autism Speaks. n.d. a. "Global Autism Public Health Initiative." https://www.autismspeaks.org/global-autism-public-health-initiative-gaph.

–. n.d.b. "Learn the Signs of Autism." https://www.autismspeaks.org/what-autism/learn-signs.

–. n.d.c. "What Causes Autism?" https://www.autismspeaks.org/what-causes-autism.

Autism Speaks Canada. n.d. "Early Indicators for Young Children." https://www.autismspeaks.ca/early-indicators-for-young-children/.

–. 2019. "Autism Speaks' MSSNG Project Reaches 10,000-Genome Milestone." May 6. https://www.autismspeaks.ca/autism-speaks-mssng-project-reaches-10000-genome-milestone/.

Autistics for Autistics (A4A). n.d. "Reforming National Autism Policies: A Report." https://a4aontario.com/wp-content/uploads/2021/01/A4A-National-Policy-Report-Recommendations-2021.pdf.

Autistic Self Advocacy Network. n.d. "Disability Community Day of Mourning." https://autisticadvocacy.org/projects/community/mourning/.

Axline, Virginia. 1964. *Dibs in Search of Self*. New York: Ballantine.

Baggs, Amanda. 2010. "Up in the Clouds and Down in the Valley: My Richness and Yours." *Disability Studies Quarterly* 30 (1). https://doi.org/10.18061/dsq.v30i1.1052.

Bailey, Moya, and Izzeta Autumn Mobley. 2018. "Work in the Intersections: A Black Feminist Disability Framework." *Gender and Society* 33 (1): 19–40. https://doi.org/10.1177/0891243218801523.

Barad, Karen. 2007. *Meeting the Universe Halfway: Quantum Physics and the Entanglement of Matter*. Durham: Duke University Press.

Barnett, Kristine. 2013. *The Spark: A Mother's Story of Nurturing, Genius and Autism*. Toronto: Vintage Canada.

Baron-Cohen, Simon. 1995. *Mindblindness: An Essay on Autism and Theory of Mind*. Cambridge, MA: MIT Press.

Baron-Cohen, Simon, Alan Leslie, and Uta Frith. 1985. "Does the Autistic Child Have a Theory of Mind?" *Cognition* 21 (1): 37–46. https://doi.org/10.1016/0010-0277(85)90022-8.

Barron, Judy, and Sean Barron. 1992. *There's a Boy in Here*. New York: Simon and Schuster.

Barthes, Roland. 1977. *Image, Music, Text*. Trans. Stephen Heath. New York: Hill and Wang.

Bartlett, Nadine, and Taylor F. Ellis. 2020. "Interrogating Sanctioned Violence: A Survey of Parents/Guardians of Children with Disabilities about Restraint and Seclusion in Manitoba's Schools." *Canadian Journal of Disability Studies* 9 (5): 122–55. https://doi.org/10.15353/cjds.v9i5.693.

Bascom, Julie, ed. 2012. *Loud Hands: Autistic People, Speaking*. Washington, DC: Autistic Press.

Battersby, Christine. 1998. *The Phenomenal Woman: Feminist Metaphysics and the Patterns of Identity*. New York: Routledge.

Bauman, Zygmunt. 2004a. *Identity: Conversations with Benedetto Vecchi*. Cambridge, UK: Polity.

–. 2004b. *Wasted Lives: Modernity and Its Outcasts*. Oxford: Polity.

Becker, Howard S. 1963. *Outsiders: Studies in the Sociology of Deviance*. New York: Free Press.

Behaviour Speak Podcast. 2022. "Episode 37: The Realities of Autism in First Nations." June 21. https://www.behaviourspeak.com/e/episode-37-the-realities-of-autism-in-first-nations-communities-in-canada-with-grant-bruno-phd-candidate/.

Bell, Chris. 2006. "Introducing White Disability Studies: A Modest Proposal." In *The Disability Studies Reader*, ed. Lennard J. Davis, 275–82. New York: Routledge.

Belli, Brita. 2010. "The Search for Autism's Missing Piece: Autism Research Slowly Turns Its Focus to Environmental Toxicity." *Environmental Magazine* 21: 24–32.

Ben-Moshe, Liat. 2020. *Decarcerating Disability: Deinstitutionalization and Prison Abolition*. Minneapolis: University of Minnesota Press.

Ben-Moshe, Liat, Chris Chapman, and Allison C. Carey. 2014. *Disability Incarcerated: Disability and Imprisonment in the United States and Canada*. New York: Palgrave Macmillan.

Ben-Moshe, Liat, and Sandy Magaña. 2014. "An Introduction to Race, Gender, and Disability: Intersectionality, Disability Studies, and Families of Color." *Women, Gender, and Families of Color* 2 (2): 105–14. https://doi.org/10.5406/womgenfamcol.2.2.0105.

Berlant, Lauren. 2011. *Cruel Optimism*. Durham, NC: Duke University Press.

Berne, Patty. 2015. "Disability Justice – A Working Draft." *Sins Invalid* (blog), June 10. https://www.sinsinvalid.org/blog/disability-justice-a-working-draft-by-patty-berne.

Bettelheim, Bruno. 1950. *Love Is Not Enough: The Treatment of Emotionally Disturbed Children*. Glencoe, IL: Free Press.

–. 1959. "Joey: A 'Mechanical Boy.'" *Scientific American*, June 1, 116–27. https://doi.org/10.1038/scientificamerican0359-116.

–. 1967. *The Empty Fortress: Infantile Autism and the Birth of the Self*. New York: Free Press.

Bevan-Brown, Jill. 2013. "Including People with Disabilities: An Indigenous Perspective." *International Journal of Inclusive Education* 17 (6): 571–83. https://doi.org/10.1080/13603116.2012.694483.

Bhattacharya, Tithi. 2017. "Introduction: Social Reproduction Theory." In *Social Reproduction Theory: Remapping Class, Recentering Oppression*, ed. Tithi Bhattacharya, 1–20. London: Pluto.

Blacher, Jan, and Erica Howell. 2007. "Unlocking the Mystery of Social Deficits in Autism: Theory of Mind as Key." *Exceptional Parent* 37 (8): 96–97.

Blatt, Sidney J., and Kenneth N. Levy. 2003. "Attachment Theory, Psychoanalysis, Personality Development and Psychopathology." *Psychoanalytic Inquiry* 23 (1): 102–50. https://doi.org/10.1080/07351692309349028.

Blum, Linda M. 2007. "Mother-Blame in the Prozac Nation: Raising Kids with Invisible Disabilities." *Gender and Society* 21 (2): 202–26. https://doi.org/10.1177/0891243206298178.

Boesveld, Sarah. 2014. "Murder-Suicide of B.C. Autistic Teen by His Mother Reignites Debate over Caregiver Support." *National Post,* April 25. https://nationalpost.com/news/murder-suicide-of-b-c-autistic-teen-by-his-mother-reignites-debate-over-caregiver-support.

Boler, Megan. 1999. *Feeling Power: Emotions and Education.* New York: Routledge.

Bordo, Susan. 1987. *The Flight to Objectivity: Essays on Cartesianism and Culture.* Albany: State University of New York Press.

–. 2003. *Unbearable Weight: Feminism, Western Culture and the Body.* Berkeley: University of California Press.

Botha, Monique, Robert Chapman, Morénike Giwa Onaiwu, Steven K. Kapp, Abs Stannard Ashley, and Nick Walker. 2024. "The Neurodiversity Concept Was Developed Collectively: An Overdue Correction on the Origins of Neurodiversity Theory." *Autism* 28 (6): 1591–94. https://doi.org/10.1177/1362361324123.

Bower, Bruce. 1981. "Autism: A World Apart." *Science News,* March 7, 154–55.

–. 1986. "Inside the Autistic Brain: Scientists Are Getting Down to Gray Matters Concerning a Tragic Developmental Disorder." *Science News,* September 6, 154–55.

–. 1989. "Remodeling the Autistic Child: Parents Join Clinicians to Transform the Tragedy of Autism." *Science News,* November 11, 312–13.

Bowlby, John. 1952. *Maternal Care and Mental Health.* Geneva: World Health Organization.

Braidotti, Rosi. 2013. *The Posthuman.* Cambridge, UK: Polity.

Braverman, Harry. 1998. *Labor and Monopoly Capital: The Degradation of Work in the Twentieth Century.* 25th anniversary ed. New York: Monthly Review.

Broderick, Alicia A. 2011. "Autism as Rhetoric: Exploring Watershed Rhetorical Moments in Applied Behavioral Analysis Discourse." *Disability Studies Quarterly* 31 (3). https://doi.org/10.18061/dsq.v31i3.1674.

Broderick, Alicia A., and Robin Roscigno. 2021. "Autism, Inc.: The Autism Industrial Complex." *Journal of Disability Studies in Education* 2 (1): 77–101. https://doi.org/10.1163/25888803-bja10008.

Brodie, Janine. 1995. *Politics on the Margins: Restructuring and the Canadian Women's Movement.* Halifax: Fernwood.

Brown, Lydia X.Z., E. Ashkenazy, and Morénike Giwa Onaiwu, eds. 2017. *All the Weight of Our Dreams: On Living Racialized Autism.* Lincoln, NE: Dragonbee.

Bruno, Grant, Titus A. Chan, Lonnie Zwaigenbaum, Emily Coombs, Indigenous Relations Circle, and David Nicholas. 2023. "Indigenous Autism in Canada: A Scoping Review." *Journal of Autism and Developmental Disorders:* 1–14. https://doi.org/10.1007/s10803-023-06045-z.

Bumiller, Kristin. 2008. "Quirky Citizens: Autism, Gender and Reimagining Disability." *Signs: Journal of Women in Culture and Society* 33 (4): 967–91. https://doi.org/10.1086/528848.

–. 2009. "The Geneticization of Autism: From New Reproductive Technologies to the Conception of Genetic Normalcy." *Signs: Journal of Women in Culture and Society* 43 (4): 875–99. https://doi.org/10.1086/597130.

Butler, Judith. 1997. "Performative Acts and Gender Constitution: An Essay in Phenomenology and Feminist Theory." In *Writing on the Body: Female Embodiment and Feminist Theory*, ed. Katie Conboy, Nadia Medina, and Sarah Stanbury, 401–17. New York: Columbia University Press.

–. 1998. "Foreword." In Maurice Natanson, *The Erotic Bird: Phenomenology in Literature*, ix–xvi. Princeton, NJ: Princeton University Press.

–. 2004. *Precarious Life*. London: Verso.

Callwood, June. 1976. "Crèche Recasts the Die for Emotionally Ill Babies." *Globe and Mail,* June 9, 7.

Campbell, Fiona Kumari. 2009. *Contours of Ableism: The Production of Disability and Abledness*. New York: Palgrave Macmillan.

Canadian Academy of Health Sciences (CAHS). 2022. *Autism in Canada: Considerations for Future Public Policy Development: Weaving Together Evidence and Lived Experience*. Ottawa: Oversight Panel on the Assessment on Autism, CAHS. https://cahs-acss.ca/wp-content/uploads/2022/04/CAHS-Summary-Report_EN.pdf.

Canadian Autism Spectrum Disorder Alliance. 2019. "Blueprint for a National Autism Spectrum Disorder Strategy: How the Canadian Government Can Lead." https://autismalliance.ca/wp-content/uploads/2019/03/Blueprint-for-a-National-ASD-Strategy.pdf.

Caplan, Paula J. 1998. "Mother-Blaming." In *"Bad" Mothers: The Politics of Blame in Twentieth-Century America*, ed. Molly Ladd-Taylor and Lauri Umansky, 127–44. New York: New York University Press.

Carey, Alison, Pamela Block, and Richard Scotch. 2020. *Allies and Obstacles: Disability Activism and Parents of Children with Disabilities*. Philadelphia: Temple University Press.

Carrega, Christina. 2020. "'He's Going to Be in a Better Place': Florida Mom Charged with the Murder of Son with Autism." *ABC News,* May 20. https://abcnews.go.com/US/florida-mom-charged-murder-son-autism/story?id=70848791.

CBS News. 2013 "Film Provides Glimpse into Life of Autistic Teen Killed by His Mother." August 13. https://www.cbsnews.com/news/film-provides-glimpse-into-life-of-autistic-teen-killed-by-his-mother/.

Chambers, Lori, and Kristin Burnett. 2017. "Jordan's Principle: The Struggle to Access On-Reserve Health Care for High-Needs Indigenous Children in Canada."

American Indian Quarterly 41 (2): 101–24. https://doi.org/10.5250/amerindiquar. 41.2.0101.

Chance, Paul. 1974. "'After You Hit a Kid, You Can't Just Get Up and Leave Him; You Are Hooked to That Kid.' A Conversation with Ivar Lovaas about Self-Mutilating Children and How Their Parents Make It Work." *Psychology Today* 7 (8): 76–84. https://doi.org/10.1037/e400562009-006.

–. 1987. "Saving Grace." *Psychology Today* 21 (12): 42–44. https://doi.org/10.1037/ e400892009-004.

Chapman, Chris, and Christine Kelly. 2015. "Adversarial Allies: Care, Harm, and Resistance in the Helping Professions." *Journal of Progressive Human Services* 26 (1): 46–66. https://doi.org/10.1080/10428232.2015.977377.

Chataika, Tsitsi, and Judy McKenzie. 2013. "Considerations of an African Childhood Disability Studies." In *Disabled Children's Childhood Studies: Critical Approaches in a Global Context*, ed. Tillie Curran and Katherine Runswick-Cole, 152–63. London: Palgrave Macmillan.

Cheung, Jessica. 2020. "Black People and Other People of Colour Make Up 83% of Reported COVID-19 Cases in Toronto." *CBC News*, July 20. https://www.cbc.ca/news/ canada/toronto/toronto-covid-19-data-1.5669091.

Clare, Eli. 2001. "Stolen Bodies, Reclaimed Bodies: Disability and Queerness." *Public Culture* 13: 359–65. https://doi.org/10.1215/08992363-13-3-359.

–. 2017. *Brilliant Imperfection: Grappling with Cure*. Durham, NC: Duke University Press.

Clarke, Juanne Nancarrow. 2012. "Representations of Autism in US Magazines for Women in Comparison to the General Audience." *Journal of Children and Media* 6, (2): 182–97. https://doi.org/10.1080/17482798.2011.587143.

Collins, Patricia Hill. 1987. "The Meaning of Motherhood in Black Culture and Black Mother-Daughter Relationships." *Sage* 4 (2): 3–10. https://doi.org/10.2307/ j.ctv1s2t0hn.15.

–. 1990. *Black Feminist Thought: Knowledge, Consciousness and the Politics of Empowerment*. New York: Routledge.

–. 2015. "The Social Construction of Black Feminist Thought." In *Women, Knowledge, and Reality: Explorations in Feminist Philosophy*, ed. Ann Garry and Marilyn Pearsall, 222–48. New York: Routledge, 2015.

Cooper, Carolyn. 2016. *Untethered: Growing Up with My Autistic Son*. Minneapolis, MN: Mill City Press.

Corelli, Rae. 1998. "Of Anguish and Mercy." *Maclean's*, November 23, 116.

Corker, Mairian. 1998. "Disability Discourse in a Postmodern World." In *The Disability Reader: Social Science Perspectives*, ed. Tom Shakespeare, 221–33. London: Cassell.

Corker, Mairian, and Tom Shakespeare, eds. 2002. *Disability/Postmodernity: Embodying Disability Theory*. London: Continuum.

Cornell, Bonnie. 1972. "Child's Mental Illness Hard to Diagnose." *Toronto Star,* November 16, 87.

Cosquer, Claire. 2019. "Altering Absence: From Race to Empire in Readings of Foucault." *Foucault Studies* 26: 1–20. https://doi.org/10.22439/fs.v0i26.5747.

Cowley, Geoffrey. 1995. "Blind to Other Minds." *Newsweek,* August 14, 67.

Crenshaw, Kimberle. 1989. "Demarginalizing the Intersection of Race and Sex: A Black Feminist Critique of Antidiscrimination Doctrine, Feminist Theory and Antiracist Politics." *University of Chicago Legal Forum* 140 (1): 139–67. https://chicagounbound.uchicago.edu/uclf/vol1989/iss1/8.

Darling, Rosalyn B. 2003. "Toward a Model of Changing Disability Identities: A Proposed Typology and Research Agenda." *Disability and Society* 18 (7): 881–95. https://doi.org/10.1080/0968759032000127308.

Darroch, Wendy. 1966. "Problem Children Learn How to Cope." *Toronto Daily Star,* May 31.

Davidson, Joyce, and Michael Orsini, eds. 2013. *Worlds of Autism: Across the Spectrum of Neurological Difference.* Minneapolis: University of Minnesota Press.

Davis, Lennard J. 1995. *Enforcing Normalcy: Disability, Deafness and the Body.* London: Verso.

–. 2002. *Bending over Backwards: Disability, Dismodernism and Other Difficult Positions.* New York: New York University Press.

–, ed. 2006. *The Disability Studies Reader.* 2nd ed. New York: Routledge.

Dawson, Michelle. 2004. "The Misbehavior of Behaviorists: Ethical Challenges to the Autism-ABA Industry." *No Autistics Allowed: Autism Society Canada Speaks for Itself* (blog), January 18. http://www.sentex.net/~nexus23/naa_aba.html.

Dean, Mitchell. 1999. *Governmentality: Power and Rule in Modern Society.* London: Sage.

–. 2002. "Liberal Government and Authoritarianism." *Economy and Society* 31 (1): 37–61. https://doi.org/10.1080/03085140120109240.

de Beauvoir, Simon. (1949) 2011. *The Second Sex.* Trans. Constance Borde and Sheila Malovany-Chevallier. New York: Vintage.

Dehli, Kari. 1994a. "Fictions of the Scientific Imagination: Researching the Dionne Quintuplets." *Journal of Canadian Studies* 29 (4): 85–110. https://doi.org/10.3138/jcs.29.4.86.

–. 1994b. "They Rule by Sympathy: The Feminization of Pedagogy." *Canadian Journal of Sociology* 19 (2): 195–216. https://doi.org/10.2307/3341344.

–. 2008. "Coming to Terms: Methodological and Other Dilemmas." In *The Methodological Dilemma: Creative, Critical, and Collaborative Approaches to Qualitative Research,* ed. Kathleen Gallagher, 46–66. London: Taylor and Francis.

De Rubeis, Silvia, and Joseph D. Buxbaum. 2014. "Genetic Advances in Autism: Leading the Way to Improved Care." *Exceptional Parent* 44 (4): 22–24.

Descartes, René. 1985. *The Philosophical Writings of Descartes*. Vol. 1. Trans. John Cottingham, Robert Stoothoff, and Dugald Murdoch. Cambridge, UK: Cambridge University Press.

de Sousa Santos, Boaventura. 2018. *The End of the Cognitive Empire: The Coming of Age of Epistemologies of the South*. Durham, NC: Duke University Press.

Dindar, Katja, Anne Lindblom, and Eija Kärnä. 2017. "The Construction of Communicative (In)competence in Autism: A Focus on Methodological Decisions." *Disability and Society* 32 (6): 868–91. https://doi.org/10.1080/096875 99.2017.1329709.

Dineen, Janice. 1991. "How Autistic Chloe Stunned the Medical World." *Toronto Star*, December 21, A1.

Diprose, Rosalyn. 2005. "A 'Genethics' That Makes Sense: Take Two." In *Ethics of the Body: Postconventional Challenges*, ed. Margrit Shildrick, Roxanne Mykitiuk, and Arthur L. Caplan, 237–58. Cambridge, MA: MIT Press.

Dolmage, Marilyn. 2011. "History Examined: One Woman's Story of Disability and Advocacy." In *Disability and Mothering: Liminal Spaces of Embodied Knowledge*, ed. Cynthia Lewiecki-Wilson and Jen Cellio, 203–9. Syracuse, NY: Syracuse University Press.

Doucet, Andrea. 2006. *Do Men Mother? Fathering, Care and Domestic Responsibility*. Toronto: University of Toronto Press.

Douglas, Patty. 2010. "'Problematising' Inclusion: Education and the Question of Autism." *Pedagogy, Culture and Society* 18 (2): 105–21. https://doi.org/10.1080/ 14681366.2010.488039.

–. 2013. "As If You Have a Choice: Autism Mothers and the Remaking of the Human." *Health, Culture and Society* 5 (1): 167–81. https://doi.org/10.5195/hcs.2013.137.

–. 2014. "Refrigerator Mothers." *Journal of the Motherhood Initiative for Research and Community Involvement* 5 (1): 94–114.

Douglas, Patty, and Estée Klar. 2019. "Beyond Disordered Brains and Mother Blame: Critical Issues in Autism and Mothering." In *The Routledge Companion to Motherhood*, ed. Lynn O'Brien Hallstein, Andrea O'Reilly, and Melinda Vandenbeld Giles, 205–14. London: Routledge.

Douglas, Patty, Michael Orsini, and Estée Klar. 2021. "5 Ways to Challenge Systemic Ableism during Autism Acceptance Month." *The Conversation*, April 21. https:// theconversation.com/5-ways-to-challenge-systemic-ableism-during-autism -acceptance-month-159122.

Douglas, Patty, Carla Rice, Margaret F. Gibson, Jan Hastie, and Raya Shields. Forthcoming. "Beyond 'Inclusionism': Unmaking and Remaking Autism and Inclusion through Creative Research." In *Practicing the Social*, ed. Carla Rice and Ingrid Mündel. Waterloo, ON: Wilfrid Laurier University Press.

Douglas, Patty, Carla Rice, and Christine Kelly. 2017. "Cripping Care: Care Pedagogies and Practices." *Review of Disability Studies* 13 (4): 1–10. https://www.rdsjournal. org/index.php/journal/article/view/779.

Douglas, Patty, Carla Rice, Katherine Runswick-Cole, Anthony Easton, Margaret F. Gibson, Julia Gruson-Wood, Estee Klar, and Raya Shields. 2021. "Re-storying Autism: A Body Becoming Disability Studies in Education Approach." *International Journal of Inclusive Education* 25 (4): 605–22. https://doi.org/10.1080/13603116. 2018.1563835.

Douglas, Patty, Carla Rice, and Areej Siddiqui. 2020. "Living Dis/artfully with and in Illness." *Journal of Medical Humanities* 41 (3): 395–410. https://doi.org/10.1007/ s10912-019-09606-5.

Douglas, Patty, Katherine Runswick-Cole, Penny Fogg, and Sara Ryan. 2022. "Making Memories, Making Madness: Mad (M)others of Disabled Children Write Back through Digital Storytelling." *Journal on Developmental Disabilities* 27 (2): 1–19. https://oadd. org/wp-content/uploads/2022/01/V27-N2-21-353-Douglas-et-al-v2.pdf.

Douglas, Patty, Katherine Runswick-Cole, Sara Ryan, and Penny Fogg. 2021. "Mad Mothering: Learning from the Intersections of Madness, Mothering and Disability." *Journal of Literary and Cultural Disability Studies* 15 (1): 39–56. https://doi. org/10.3828/jlcds.2021.3.

Du Bois, W.E.B. (1903) 1994. *The Souls of Black Folk.* New York: Dover.

Durie, Mason. 1998. *Whaiora: Maōri Health Development.* Oxford: Oxford University Press.

Editors of *The Lancet.* 2010. "Retraction – Ileal-Lymphoid-Nodular Hyperplasia, Non-specific Colitis, and Pervasive Developmental Disorder." *The Lancet,* February 6, 445. https://doi.org/10.1016/s0140-6736(10)60175-4.

Ehrenreich, Barbara, and Deirdre English. 2005. *For Her Own Good: Two Centuries of the Experts' Advice to Women.* Kindle ed. New York: Anchor Books.

Enright, Janet. 1989. "Families of Disabled Confronting Crisis." *Toronto Star,* May 23, D3.

Erevelles, Nirmala. 2011. *Disability and Difference in Global Contexts: Enabling a Transformative Body Politic.* New York: Palgrave Macmillan.

Fanon, Frantz. 1970. *Black Skin, White Masks.* London: Paladin.

Felepchuk, Erin. 2021. "Stimming, Improvisation, and COVID-19: (Re)negotiating Autistic Sensory Regulation during a Pandemic." *Disability Studies Quarterly* 41 (3). https://doi.org/10.18061/dsq.v41i3.8426.

Ferguson, Philip M. 2002. "A Place in the Family: An Historical Interpretation of Research on Parental Reactions to Having a Child with a Disability." *Journal of Special Education* 36 (3): 124–31. https://doi.org/10.1177/00224669020360030201.

Ferguson, Susan. 2019. *Women and Work: Feminism, Labour, and Social Reproduction.* Toronto: Between the Lines.

Filax, Gloria, and Dean Taylor, eds. 2014. *Disabled Mothers: Stories and Scholarship by and about Mothers with Disabilities*. Toronto: Demeter.

Fine, Michelle, and Adrienne Asch. 1988. *Women with Disabilities: Essays in Psychology, Culture and Politics*. Philadelphia: Temple University Press.

Finkelstein, Vic. 1998. "Emancipating Disability Studies." In *The Disability Reader: Social Science Perspectives*, ed. Tom Shakespeare, 28–49. London: Cassell.

Fisher, Pamela, and Daniel Goodley. 2007. "The Linear Medical Model of Disability: Mothers of Disabled Babies Resist with Counter-narratives." *Sociology of Health and Illness* 29 (1): 66–81. https://doi.org/10.1111/j.1467 -9566.2007.00518.x.

Fletcher-Watson, Sue, Jon Adams, Kabie Brook, Tony Charman, Laure Crane, James Cusack, Susan Leekam, Damian Milton, Jeremy R. Parr, and Elizabeth Pellicano. 2019. "Making the Future Together: Shaping Autism Research through Meaningful Participation." *Autism* 23 (4): 943–53. https://doi.org/10.1177/1362361318786721.

Foucault, Michel. 1972. *The Archaeology of Knowledge and the Discourse of Language*. Trans. A.M. Sheridan Smith. New York: Routledge.

–. 1980a. *The History of Sexuality*. Vol. 1, *An Introduction*. Trans. Robert Hurly. New York: Vintage.

–. 1980b. "Two Lectures." In *Power/Knowledge: Selected Interviews and Other Writings, 1972-1977*, ed. Colin Gordon, 78–108. New York: Vintage Books.

–. 1982. "Afterword: The Subject and Power." In *Michel Foucault: Beyond Structuralism and Hermeneutics*, ed. Hubert Dreyfus and Paul Rabinow, 208–26. Chicago: University of Chicago Press.

–. 1984. "Nietzsche, Genealogy, History." In *The Foucault Reader*, ed. Paul Rabinow, 76–99. New York: Pantheon.

–. (1965) 1988a. *Madness and Civilization: A History of Insanity in the Age of Reason*. Trans. Richard Howard. New York: Vintage.

–. 1988b. "Practicing Criticism." In *Politics, Philosophy, Culture: Interviews and Other Writings, 1977-1984*, ed. Lawrence Kritzman, 152–56. New York: Routledge.

–. 1991a. "Governmentality." In *The Foucault Effect: Studies in Governmentality*, ed. Gordon Burchell, Colin Gordon, and Peter Miller, 87–104. Chicago: University of Chicago Press.

–. 1991b. "Questions of Method." In *The Foucault Effect: Studies in Governmentality*, ed. Gordon Burchell, Colin Gordon, and Peter Miller, 73–86. Chicago: University of Chicago Press.

–. 1994. "Subjectivity and Truth." In *Ethics, Subjectivity and Truth*, ed. Paul Rabinow, 87–92. New York: New Press.

–. (1975) 1995. *Discipline and Punish: The Birth of the Prison*. 2nd ed. Trans. Alan Sheridan. New York: Vintage.

–. 2000. "For an Ethic of Discomfort." In *Power: The Essential Works of Foucault*, vol. 3, ed. James D. Faubian, 443–48. New York: New Press.

–. 2003. *Society Must Be Defended: Lectures at the College of France 1975–1976*. New York: Picador.

Freed, Dale A., and Phinjo Gombu. 1995. "Thistletown Shutdown Hits Parents of Disabled." *Toronto Star,* January 18, A1, A6.

Freeman, Victoria. 2019. *A World without Martha: A Memoir of Sisters, Disability and Difference*. Vancouver: Purich Books.

Freud, Sigmund. 1990. "Case Histories I: 'Dora' and 'Little Hans.'" In *The Pelican Freud Library*, vol. 8, ed. James Strachey, trans. Alix Strachey, with Angela Richards, Alan Tyson, and James Strachey. London: Pelican.

Friday, Terrine. 2010. "Mother Admits to Drowning Autistic Child." *National Post,* June 16. https://nationalpost.com/posted-toronto/mother-accused-of-drowning -child-pleads-guilty-to-manslaughter.

Fridriksson, Fridrik T., dir. 2010. *A Mother's Courage: Talking Back to Autism*. Reykjavík, Iceland: Frontier Filmworks/Klikk Production.

Frith, Uta. 1989. *Autism: Explaining the Enigma*. Oxford: Blackwell.

–. 1993. "Autism." *Scientific American,* June 1, 108–14.

Fritsch, Kelly. 2015. "Desiring Disability Differently: Neoliberalism, Heterotopic Imagination and Intra-Corporeal Reconfigurations." *Foucault Studies* 19: 43–66. https://doi.org/10.22439/fs.v0i19.4824.

–. 2016. "Cripping Neoliberal Futurity: Marking the Elsewhere and Elsewhen of Desiring Otherwise." *Feral Feminisms* 5 (Spring): 11–26. https://feralfeminisms. com/cripping-neoliberal-futurity/.

Galt, Virginia. 1995. "Community-Based Care No Help." *Globe and Mail,* February 15.

Garfinkel, Harold. 1967. *Studies in Ethnomethodology*. Englewood Cliffs, NJ: Prentice-Hall.

Garland-Thomson, Rosemarie, ed. 1996. *Freakery: Cultural Spectacles of the Extraordinary Body*. New York: New York University Press.

–. 1997. *Extraordinary Bodies: Figuring Physical Disability in American Culture and Literature*. New York: Columbia University Press.

–. 2001. *Re-shaping, Re-thinking, Re-defining: Feminist Disability Studies*. Washington, DC: Centre for Women Policy Studies.

–. 2002. "Integrating Disability, Transforming Feminist Theory." *NWSA Journal* 14 (3): 1–32. http://www.jstor.org/stable/4316922.

–. 2005. "Feminist Disability Studies." *Signs: Journal of Women in Culture and Society* 30 (2): 1557–87. https://doi.org/10.1086/423352.

–. 2011. "Misfits: A Feminist, Materialist Disability Concept." *Hypatia* 26 (3): 591–609. https://doi.org/10.1111/j.1527-2001.2011.01206.x.

–. 2013. "Disability Studies: A Field Emerged." *American Quarterly* 65 (4): 915–26. https://doi.org/10.1353/aq.2013.0052.

Genova, Lisa. 2012. *Love Anthony*. New York: Gallery Books.

Gernsbacher, Ann, Michelle Dawson, and H. Hill Goldsmith. 2005. "Three Reasons Not to Believe in an Autism Epidemic." *Current Directions in Psychological Science* 14 (2): 55–58. https://doi.org/10.1111%2Fj.0963-7214.2005.00334.x.

Gerwitsch, Aron. 1966. *Studies in Phenomenology and Psychology*. Evanston, IL: Northwestern University Press.

Gibson, Margaret F., ed. 2014. *Queering Motherhood: Narrative and Theoretical Perspectives*. Toronto: Demeter.

Gibson, Margaret F., and Patty Douglas. 2018. "Disturbing Behaviours: Ole Ivar Lovaas and the Queer History of Autism Science." *Catalyst: Feminism, Theory, Technoscience* 4 (2). https://doi.org/10.28968/cftt.v4i2.29579.

Giesbrecht, Lynn. 2019. "Cowesses Launches First Indigenous-Centred Autism Research Project." *Regina Leader Post,* May 24. https://leaderpost.com/news/saskatchewan/cowessess-launches-first-indigenous-centred-autism-research-project.

Gill, Virginia T., and Douglas W. Maynard. 1995. "On 'Labeling' in Actual Interaction: Delivering and Receiving Diagnoses of Developmental Disabilities." *Social Problems* 42 (1): 11–37. https://doi.org/10.2307/3097003.

Gilligan, Carol. 1993. *In a Different Voice: Psychological Theory and Women's Development*. Cambridge, MA: Harvard University Press.

Globe and Mail. 1960. "Thistletown Plans Expansion." January 22, 11.

–. 1961. "Crèche Hears Praise of Welfare Work." April 20, 14.

–. 1962. "Taught to be Children at This Day Nursery." October 8, 5.

–. 1965. "Centre's Controversial Director Has 90% Success with Patients." April 23, 8.

–. 1971. "Doctor Links Rubella with Infant Autism." May 20.

–. 1976. "National Society Formed: Group Will Seek Aid for Autistic." May 17, 14.

–. 1982. "Genetic Defect Linked to Autism." April 5.

Goffman, Erving. 1959. *The Presentation of Self in Everyday Life*. Garden City, NY: Doubleday.

–. 1961. *Asylums: Essays on the Social Situation of Mental Patients and Other Inmates*. London: Penguin.

–. 1963. *Stigma: Notes on the Management of Spoiled Identity*. Englewood Cliffs, NJ: Prentice Hall.

Goodley, Daniel. 2011. *Disability Studies: An Interdisciplinary Introduction*. London: Sage.

–. 2014. *Dis/ability Studies: Theorising Disablism and Ableism*. London: Routledge.

Goodley, Daniel, Rebecca Lawthom, and Katherine Runswick-Cole. 2014. "Posthuman Disability Studies." *Subjectivity* 7 (4): 342–61. https://doi.org/10.1057/sub.2014.15.

Gordon, Andrea. 2013. "Autism Linked to Gut Bacteria, Study Finds." *Toronto Star*, January 28. http://www.thestar.com/news/gta/2013/01/28/autism_linked_to_gut_bacteria_study_finds.html.

Gorril, Bruce. 1976. "Letters to the Editor: Autistic Children." *Globe and Mail*, June 17, 6.

Government of Ontario. 2012. "Improving Mental Health Services for Children and Youth." News release, March 19. http://news.ontario.ca/mcys/en/2012/03/improving-mental-health-services-for-children-and-youth-1.html.

–. 2019. *Recommendations for a New Needs-Based Ontario Autism Program: The Ontario Autism Program Advisory Panel Report*. https://www.children.gov.on.ca/htdocs/english/documents/specialneeds/autism/autismadvisorypanelreport_2019.pdf.

Graham, Linda. 2012. "Disproportionate Over-representation of Indigenous Students in New South Wales Government Special Schools." *Cambridge Journal of Education* 42 (2): 163–76. https://doi.org/10.1080/0305764X.2012.676625.

Graham, Mekada. 2007. "The Ethics of Care, Black Women and the Social Professions: Implications of a New Analysis." *Ethics and Social Welfare* 1 (2): 194–206. https://doi.org/10.1080/17496530701450372.

Gray, David E. 1993. "Perceptions of Stigma: The Parents of Autistic Children." *Sociology of Health and Illness* 15 (1): 102–20. https://doi.org/10.1111/1467-9566.ep11343802.

–. 2002. "'Everybody Just Freezes. Everybody Is Just Embarrassed': Felt and Enacted Stigma among Parents of Children with High Functioning Autism." *Sociology of Health and Illness* 24 (6): 734–49. https://doi.org/10.1111/1467-9566.00316.

–. 2003. "Gender and Coping: The Parents of Children with High Functioning Autism." *Social Science and Medicine* 56 (3): 631–42. https://doi.org/10.1016/S0277-9536(02)00059-X.

Greenburg, Carol, and Shannon Des Roches Rosa. 2020. "Two Winding Parent Paths to Neurodiversity Advocacy." In *Autistic Community and the Neurodiversity Movement: Stories from the Frontline*, ed. Steven K. Capp, 155–66. Singapore: Palgrave Macmillan.

Greenfeld, Josh. 1972. *A Child Called Noah: A Family Journey*. New York: Holt, Rinehart and Winston.

–. 1978a. *A Place for Noah*. New York: Holt, Rineheart and Winston.

–. 1978b. "A Place for Noah." *Psychology Today*, March, 92–99.

–. 1986. *A Client Called Noah: A Family Journey Continued*. New York: H. Holt.

Grinker, Roy R. 2007. *Unstrange Minds: Remapping the World of Autism*. New York: Basic Books.

Grosz, Elizabeth. 2005. *Time Travels: Feminism, Nature, Power.* Durham, NC: Duke University Press.

Gruner, Marian, and Christopher Sumpton, dirs. 2011. *The Autism Enigma.* Aired on CBC's *The Nature of Things,* December 8.

Gruson-Wood, Julia F. 2016. "Autism, Expert Discourses, and Subjectification: A Critical Examination of Applied Behavioral Therapies." *Studies in Social Justice* 10 (1): 38–58. https://doi.org/10.26522/ssj.v10i1.1331.

Guernsey, Diane. 2006. "Autism's Angels." *Town and Country,* August, 131–33.

Hacking, Ian. 2004. "Between Michel Foucault and Erving Goffman: Between Discourse in the Abstract and Face-to-Face Interaction." *Economy and Society* 33 (3): 277–302. https://doi.org/10.1080/0308514042000225671.

–. 2010. "Autism Fiction: A Mirror of an Internet Decade?" *University of Toronto Quarterly* 79 (2): 632–55. https://doi.org/10.3138/utq.79.2.632.

Hall, Kim Q., ed. 2011. *Feminist Disability Studies.* Bloomington: Indiana University Press.

Hall, Stuart. 1997. "Subjects in History: Making Diasporic Identities." In *The House That Race Built: Black Americans, U.S. Terrain,* ed. Wahneema Lubiano, 280–99. New York: Pantheon.

Hammond, Tiffany. 2023. *A Day With No Words.* New Egypt, NJ: Wheat Penny Press.

Hamraie, Aimi, and Kelly Fritsch. 2019, "Crip Technoscience Manifesto." *Catalyst: Feminism, Theory, Technoscience* 5 (1): 1–33. https://doi.org/10.28968/cftt.v5i1.29607.

Hankivsky, Olena. 2014. "Rethinking Care Ethics: On the Promise and Potential of an Intersectional Analysis." *American Political Science Review* 108 (2): 252–64. https://doi.org/10.1017/s0003055414000094.

Haraway, Donna. 1991. *Simians, Cyborgs and Women: The Reinvention of Nature.* London: Free Association Books.

–. 2016. *Staying with the Trouble: Making Kin in the Chthulucene.* Durham: Duke University Press.

–. 2018. *Modest_Witness@Second_Millennium.FemaleMan_Meets_OncoMouse: Feminism and Technoscience.* 2nd ed. New York: Routledge.

Harding, Sandra, ed. 2004. *The Feminist Standpoint Theory Reader: Intellectual and Political Controversies.* London: Routledge.

Harlow, Harry. 1961. "The Development of Affectional Patterns in Infant Monkeys." In *The Determinants of Infant Behaviour,* ed, Brian M. Foss, 75–97. London: Methuen.

Hays, Sharon. 1996. *The Cultural Contradictions of Motherhood.* New Haven, CT: Yale University Press.

Held, Virginia. 2006. *The Ethics of Care: Personal, Political and Global.* Oxford: Oxford University Press.

Heyworth, Kelly K. 2013. "Is It Something I Did?" *babytalk,* April, 30–33.

Higashida, Naoki. 2016. *The Reason I Jump: The Inner Voice of a Thirteen-Year-Old Boy with Autism.* Toronto: Vintage Canada.

Hochschild, Arlie R. 1983. *The Managed Heart: Commercialization of Human Feeling.* Berkeley: University of California Press.

Hodge, Nick, Patty Douglas, Madeleine Kruth, Nicola Martin, Stephen Connolly, Kendra Gowler, and Cheryl Smith. 2023. "Contemplating Teacher Talk through a Critical Autism Studies Lens." In *The Routledge International Handbook of Critical Autism Studies,* ed. Damian Milton and Sara Ryan, 242–54. London: Routledge.

Hook, Derek. 2005. "Affecting Whiteness: Racism as Technology of Affect." International Journal of Critical Psychology 16: 74–99. http://eprints.lse.ac.uk/956/.

hooks, bell. 1984. *Feminist Theory: From Margin to Center.* Boston: South End.

–. 2000. *Feminism Is for Everybody: Passionate Politics.* Cambridge, MA: South End.

–. 2004. *The Will to Change: Men, Masculinity, and Love.* Portland, OR: Beyond Words/Atria Books.

Hopper, Doris. 1976. "A Kiss for Mom Is Breakthrough for Neil." *Toronto Star,* July 9.

Hughes, Bill, Linda McKie, Debra Hopkins, and Nick Watson. 2005. "Love's Labors Lost? Feminism, the Disabled People's Movement and an Ethic of Care." *Sociology* 39 (2): 259–75. https://doi.org/10.1177%2F0038038505050538.

Hughes, Bill, and Kevin Paterson. 1997. "The Social Model of Disability and the Disappearing Body: Towards a Sociology of Impairment." *Disability and Society* 12 (3): 325–40. https://doi.org/10.1080/09687599727209.

Hune-Brown, Nicholas. 2016. "The Autism Wars." *Toronto Life,* December 6. https://torontolife.com/city/life/autism-wars/.

Hunt, Paul. 1998. "A Critical Condition." In *The Disability Reader: Social Science Perspectives,* ed. Tom Shakespeare, 7–19. London: Cassell.

Husserl, Edmund. (1954) 1970. *The Crisis of European Sciences and Transcendental Phenomenology.* Trans. David Carr. Evanston, IL: Northwestern University Press.

Ilg, Francis, and Louise B. Ames. 1960. "Slow Child May Be Fast." *Toronto Daily Star,* April 12.

–. 1961. "Parents Needn't Feel Guilty about Emotional Ills." *Toronto Daily Star,* November 29.

Ineese-Nash, Nicole. 2020. "Disability as a Colonial Construct: The Missing Discourse of Culture in Conceptualizations of Disabled Indigenous Children." *Canadian Journal of Disability Studies* 9 (3): 28–51. https://doi.org/10.15353/cjds.v9i3.645.

Jack, Jordynn. 2014. *Autism and Gender: From Refrigerator Mothers to Computer Geeks.* Urbana: University of Illinois Press.

Jimenez, Marina. 2009. "The Somali Autism Puzzle." *Globe and Mail,* April 7.

Jones, Allison. 2016. "Ontario Restores Some Funding for Children with Autism Following Backlash." *CityNews,* June 28. https://toronto.citynews.ca/2016/06/28/ontario-restores-some-funding-for-children-with-autism-following-backlash/.

Jones, Sandra C., and Valerie Harwood. 2009. "Representations of Autism in Australian Print Media." *Disability and Society* 24 (1): 5–18. https://doi.org/10.1080/09687590802535345.

Jordan, Glenn, dir. 1979. *Son-Rise: A Miracle of Love.* Los Angeles, CA: Rothman/Wohl Productions.

Junker, Karen S. 1964. *The Child in the Glass Ball.* New York: Abingdon.

Kafer, Alison. 2013. *Feminist, Queer, Crip.* Bloomington: Indiana University Press.

–. 2016. "Un/safe Disclosures: Scenes of Disability and Trauma." *Journal of Literary and Cultural Disability Studies* 10 (1): 1–20. https://doi.org/10.3828/jlcds.2016.1.

Kanner, Leo. 1943. "Autistic Disturbances of Affective Contact." *Nervous Child* 2 (3): 217–50. https://doi.org/10.4135/9781526483232.n5.

Kanner, Leo, and Leon Eisenberg. 1955. "Notes on the Follow-Up Studies of Autistic Children." In *Psychopathology of Childhood,* ed. Paul H. Hoch and J. Zubin, 227–39. New York: Grune and Stratton.

Kapp, Steven K., Robyn Steward, Laura Crane, Daisy Elliot, Chris Elphick, Elizabeth Pellicano, and Ginny Russell. 2019. "'People Should Be Allowed to Do What They Like': Autistic Adults' Views and Experiences of Stimming." *Autism* 23 (7): 1782–92. https://doi.org/10.1177/1362361319829628.

Kaufman, Barry N. 1976. *Son-Rise.* New York: Harper and Row.

Kedar, Ido. 2012. *Ido in Autismland: Climbing Out of Autism's Silent Prison.* Self-published.

Kediye, Fatima, Angela Valeo, and Rachel C. Berman. 2009. "Somali-Canadian Mothers' Experiences Parenting a Child with Autism Spectrum Disorder." *Journal for the Association of Research on Mothering* 11 (1): 211–23. https://jarm.journals.yorku.ca/index.php/jarm/article/view/22520.

Keller, Evelyn Fox. 1995. *Refiguring Life: Metaphors of Twentieth-Century Biology.* New York: Columbia University Press.

Kelly, Christine. 2013. "Building Bridges with Accessible Care: Disability Studies, Feminist Care Scholarship, and Beyond." *Hypatia* 28 (4): 784–800. https://doi.org/10.1111/j.1527-2001.2012.01310.x.

–. 2016. *Disability Politics and Care: The Challenge of Direct Funding.* Vancouver: UBC Press.

–. 2017. "Care and Violence through the Lens of Personal Support Workers." *International Journal of Care and Caring* 1 (1): 97–113. https://doi.org/10.1332/239788217x14866305589260.

–. 2018. "A Future for Disability: Perceptions of Disabled Youth and Nonprofit Organizations." *Social Theory and Health* 16: 44–59. https://doi.org/10.1057/s41285-017-0042-5.

Kephart, Beth. 1998. *A Slant of Sun: One Child's Courage*. New York: Norton.

Khanlou, Nazilla, Nasim Haque, Nida Mustafa, Luz Maria Vazquez, Ann Mantini, and Jonathan Weiss. 2017. "Access Barriers to Services by Immigrant Mothers of Children with Autism in Canada." *International Journal of Mental Health and Addiction* 15: 239–59. https://doi.org/10.1007/s11469-017-9732-4.

Kilee Patchell-Evans Autism Research Group. n.d. "Research Interests." http://kpearg.com/researchInterests.html.

Kim, Eunjung. 2017. *Curative Violence: Rehabilitating Disability, Gender, and Sexuality in Modern Korea*. Durham, NC: Duke University Press.

Kim, Hyun U. 2012. "Autism across Cultures: Rethinking Autism." *Disability and Society* 27 (4): 535–45. https://doi.org/10.1080/09687599.2012.659463.

King, Allan, dir. 1967. *Warrandale*. Toronto: Allan King Associates.

King, Thomas. 2003. *The Truth about Stories: A Native Narrative*. Toronto: Anansi.

Kirby, Sandra, Lorraine Greaves, and Colleen Reid. 2010. *Experience, Research, Social Change: Methods beyond the Mainstream*. 2nd ed. Toronto: University of Toronto Press.

Kirby-McIntosh, Laura. n.d. "History of the Ontario Autism Coalition." https://ontarioautismcoalition.com/history/.

Kirkwood, Leone. 1967. "The Autistic Child's Haunted World." *Globe and Mail*, May 18, W1.

–. 1972. "U.S. Program Helps Train Parents as Therapists for Autistic Children." *Globe and Mail*, June 2, 12.

Kittay, Eva Feder. 1999. *Love's Labor: Essays on Women, Equality and Dependency*. New York: Routledge.

Klar, Estée. 2008. "The Burden of Proof." *Joy of Autism* (blog), January 15. https://static1.squarespace.com/static/5c2795ace17ba3d4ccac0e2e/t/5d13c4c9021d530001aac455/1561576688144/The_Joy_of_Autism_part1.pdf.

–. 2015. "Mental Ability and the Discourse of Disease: Another Comment on the Globe and Mail Article on 'Treating the Brain and the Immune System in Tandem.'" *Joy of Autism* (blog), January 19. https://static1.squarespace.com/static/5c2795ace17ba3d4ccac0e2e/t/5d13b54e04c48b0001ae0cef/1561572688577/Estée+Klar+Estée+Klar+-+My+autistic+son+and+I+explore+issues+and+meanings+of+autism+in+our+lives.pdf.

Klar, Estée, Patty Douglas, and Anne McGuire. 2016. "Autism Strategy Masks Societal Exclusion of Autistic Ontarians." *Ottawa Citizen*, April 19. http://ottawacitizen.com/opinion/columnists/klar-douglas-and-mcguire-autism-strategy-masks-societal-exclusion-of-autistic-ontarians.

Kohl, Helen. 1979. "The Strange Ones: Autistics Can Be Brought into Our World." *Toronto Star,* April 7, 10–12.

Koren-Karie, Nina, David Oppenheim, Smadar Dolev, and Nurit Yirmiya. 2009. "Mothers of Securely Attached Children with Autism Spectrum Disorder Are More Sensitive Than Mothers of Insecurely Attached Children." *Journal of Child Psychology and Psychiatry and Allied Disciplines* 50 (5): 643–50. https://doi.org/10.1111/j.1469-7610.2008.02043.x.

Koresky, Michael. 2010. "Eclipse Series 24: The Actuality Dramas of Allan King." *Current,* September 21. http://www.criterion.com/current/posts/1599 -eclipse-series-24-the-actuality-dramas-of-allan-king.

Kröger, Teppo. 2009. "Care Research and Disability Studies: Nothing in Common?" *Critical Social Policy* 29 (2): 398–420. https://doi.org/10.1177%2F0261018309105177.

Ladd-Taylor, Molly, and Lauri Umansky. 1998. "Introduction." In *"Bad" Mothers: The Politics of Blame in Twentieth-Century America*, ed. Molly Ladd-Taylor and Lauri Umansky, 1–28. New York: New York University Press.

Lalvani, Priya. 2019. *Constructing the (M)other: Narratives of Disability, Motherhood, and the Politics of Normal.* New York: Peter Lang.

Landsberg, Michelle. 1965a. "Children in a Nightmare World of Tangled Emotions." *Globe and Mail,* April 22, W1.

–. 1965b. "Dispute over Treatment Hinders Facilities." *Globe and Mail,* April 24, 18.

Landsman, Gail. 2009. *Reconstructing Motherhood and Disability in the Age of "Perfect" Babies.* New York: Routledge.

Larner, Wendy. 2000. "Neo-liberalism: Policy, Ideology, Governmentality." *Studies in Political Economy* 63 (1): 5–25. https://doi.org/10.1080/19187033.2000.11675231.

LeVasseur, Jeanne J. 2003. "The Problem of Bracketing in Phenomenology." *Qualitative Health Research* 13 (3): 408–20. https://doi.org/10.1177%2F1049732302250337.

Levinas, Emmanuel. 1969. *Totality and Infinity.* Trans. Alphonso Lingus. Pittsburgh: Duquesne University Press.

–. 1989. "Ethics as First Philosophy." In *The Levinas Reader*, ed. Sean Hand, 75–87. Oxford: Blackwell.

–. 1998. *Entre Nous: Thinking-of-the-Other.* Trans. Barbara Harshaw and Michael Smith. New York: Columbia University Press.

Levinson, Jack. 2010. *Making Life Work: Freedom and Disability in a Community Group Home.* Minneapolis: University of Minnesota Press.

Lewiecki-Wilson, Cynthia, and Jen Cellio, eds. 2011. *Disability and Mothering: Liminal Spaces of Embodied Knowledge.* Syracuse, NY: Syracuse University Press.

Lindblom, Anne. 2014. "Under-detection of Autism among First Nations Children in British Columbia, Canada." *Disability and Society* 29 (8): 1248–59. https://doi.org/10.1080/09687599.2014.923750.

Linton, Simi. 1998. *Claiming Disability: Knowledge and Identity.* New York: New York University Press.

Lloyd, Genevieve. 1993. *The Man of Reason: "Male" and "Female" in Western Philosophy.* 2nd ed. London: Routledge.

Lorde, Audre. 1988. *A Burst of Light: Essays.* Ithaca, NY: Firebrand Books.

–. 2007. *Sister Outsider: Essays and Speeches.* Berkeley, CA: Crossing.

Lovaas, Ole Ivar. 1977. *The Autistic Child: Language Development through Behavior Modification.* New York: Irvington.

–. 1981. *Teaching Developmentally Disabled Children: The Me Book.* Baltimore, MD: University Park Press.

–. 1987. "Behavioral Treatment and Normal Educational and Intellectual Functioning in Autistic Children." *Journal of Consulting and Clinical Psychology* 55 (1): 3–9. https://doi.org/10.1037//0022-006x.55.1.3.

MacFabe, Derrick. 2012. "Short-Chain Fatty Acid Fermentation Products of the Gut Microbiome: Implications in Autism Spectrum Disorders." *Microbial Ecology in Health and Disease* 23 (1). https://www.tandfonline.com/doi/full/10.3402/mehd.v23i0.19260.

Maclean's. 1996. "Montreal Tragedy." November 18, 23.

Malacrida, Claudia. 2019. "Mothering and Disability: From Eugenics to Newgenics." In *Routledge Handbook of Disability Studies*, ed. Nick Watson, Alan Roulstone, and Carol Thomas, 467–78. London: Routledge.

Mallett, Rebecca, and Katherine Runswick-Cole. 2012. "Commodifying Autism: The Cultural Contexts of 'Disability' in the Academy." In *Disability and Social Theory: New Developments and Directions*, ed. Daniel Goodley, Bill Hughes, and Lennard J. Davis, 33–51. Basingstoke, UK: Palgrave Macmillan.

Manning, Corrine. 2011. "From Surrender to Activism: The Transformation of Disability and Mothering at Kew Cottages, Australia." In *Disability and Mothering: Liminal Spaces of Embodied Knowledge*, ed. Cynthia Lewiecki-Wilson and Jen Cellio, 183–202. Syracuse, NY: Syracuse University Press.

Matthews, Gwyneth F. 1983. *Voices from the Shadows: Women with Disabilities Speak Out.* Toronto: Women's Press.

Maurice, Catherine. 1993. *Let Me Hear Your Voice: A Family's Triumph over Autism.* New York: Alfred A. Knopf.

Maynard, Douglas W. 2005. "Social Actions, Gestalt Coherence, and Designations of Disability: Lessons from and about Autism." *Social Problems* 52 (4): 499–524. https://doi.org/10.1525/sp.2005.52.4.499.

McCarthy, Jenny. 2007. *Louder Than Words: A Mother's Journey in Healing Autism.* New York: Penguin.

–. 2008. *Mother Warriors: A Nation of Parents Healing Autism against All Odds.* New York: Plume.

McDonnell, Jane T. 1993. *News from the Border: A Mother's Memoir of Her Autistic Son*. New York: Ticknor and Fields.

–. 1998. "On Being the 'Bad' Mother of an Autistic Child." In *"Bad" Mothers: The Politics of Blame in Twentieth-Century America*, ed. Molly Ladd-Taylor and Lauri Umansky, 220–29. New York: New York University Press.

McGovern, Cammie. 2006. "Boy Wonder: Once We Stopped Trying to 'Fix' Our Autistic Son, We Started to Appreciate the World as He Saw It." *Reader's Digest*, August, 137–40.

–. 2021. *Hard Landings: Looking into the Future for a Child with Autism*. New York: Avery.

McGuire, Anne. 2011. "Representing Autism: A Sociological Examination of Autism Advocacy." *Atlantis: Critical Studies in Gender, Culture and Social Justice* 35 (2): 62–71.

–. 2016. *War on Autism: On the Cultural Logic of Normative Violence*. Ann Arbor: University of Michigan Press.

McGuire, Anne, and Rod Michalko. 2011. "Minds between Us: Autism, Mindblindness and the Uncertainty of Communication." *Educational Philosophy and Theory* 43 (2): 162–77. https://doi.org/10.1111/j.1469-5812.2009.00537.x.

McRuer, Robert. 2006. "We Were Never Identified: Feminism, Queer Theory, and a Disabled World." *Radical History Review* 94: 148–54. https://doi.org/10.1215/01636545-2006-94-148.

Meekosha, Helen. 2011. "Decolonising Disability: Thinking and Acting Globally." *Disability and Society* 26 (6): 667–82. https://doi.org/10.1080/09687599.2011.602860.

Merleau-Ponty, Maurice. 1962. *Phenomenology of Perception*. Trans. Colin Smith. London: Routledge.

–. 1968. *The Visible and the Invisible*. Trans. Alphonso Lingus. Evanston, IL: Northwestern University Press.

Merriam-Webster Dictionary. n.d. "Campaign." http://www.merriam-webster.com/dictionary/campaign.

Merryday, Leigh. 2012. "So You're Wondering If Your Child Might Be Autistic." *Flappiness Is* (blog), January 1. http://flappinessis.com/so-youre-wondering-if-your-child-might-be-autistic/.

Michalko, Rod. 1999. *The Two-in-One: Walking with Smokie, Walking with Blindness*. Philadelphia: Temple University Press.

–. 2002. *The Difference that Disability Makes*. Philadelphia: Temple University Press.

Milton, Damian. 2012. "On the Ontological Status of Autism: The 'Double Empathy Problem.'" *Disability and Society* 27 (6): 883–87. https://doi.org/10.1080/09687599.2012.710008.

–. 2014. "Autistic Expertise: A Critical Reflection on the Production of Knowledge in Autism Studies." *Autism* 18 (7): 794–802. https://doi.org/10.1177%2F136 2361314525281.

Milton, Damian, Susy Ridout, Marianthi Kourti, Gillian Loomes, and Nicola Martin. 2019. "A Critical Reflection on the Development of the Participatory Autism Research Collective (PARC)." *Tizard Learning Disability Review* 24 (2): 82–89. https://doi.org/10.1108/tldr-09-2018-0029.

Milton, Damian, Susy Ridout, Nicola Martin, Richard Mills, and Dinah Murray, eds. 2020. *The Neurodiversity Reader: Exploring Concepts, Lived Experience and Implications for Practice*. Shoreham-by-Sea, UK: Pavillion.

Mingus, Mia. 2011. "Changing the Framework: Disability Justice." *Leaving Evidence* (blog), February 12. https://leavingevidence.wordpress.com/2011/02/12/ changing-the-framework-disability-justice/.

Ministry of Children, Community and Social Services. 2016. "Ontario Investing $333 Million to Improve Autism Services: New Autism Program to Reduce Waitlists and Provide Better Services for Families." News release, March 29. https://news. ontario.ca/mcys/en/2016/03/ontario-investing-333-million-to-improve-autism -services.html?_ga=1.204636824.982121985.1459442482.

Mitchell, Bob, and Jim Wilkes. 2009. "Accused Mother 'Loved Son So Much.'" *Toronto Star,* October 27. https://www.thestar.com/news/crime/2009/10/27/accused_ mother_loved_son_so_much.html.

Mitchell, David T. 2002. "Narrative Prosthesis and the Materiality of Metaphor." In *Disability Studies: Enabling the Humanities*, ed. Brenda J. Brueggemann, Sharon L. Snyder, and Rosemarie Garland-Thomson, 15–30. New York: Modern Language Association of America.

Mitchell, David T., and Sharon L. Snyder. 2003. "The Eugenic Atlantic: Race, Disability and the Making of an International Eugenic Science, 1800–1945." *Disability and Society* 18 (7): 843–64. https://doi.org/10.1080/0968759032000127281.

–. 2015. *The Biopolitics of Disability: Neoliberalism, Ablenationalism and Peripheral Embodiment*. Ann Arbor: University of Michigan Press.

Mitchell, Lisa M. 2001. *Baby's First Picture: Ultrasound and the Politics of Fetal Subjects*. Toronto: University of Toronto Press.

Mohanty, Chandra Talpade. 2003. "'Under Western Eyes' Revisited: Feminist Solidarity through Anticapitalist Struggles." *Signs: Journal of Women and Culture in Society* 28 (2): 499–535. https://doi.org/10.1086/342914.

Morgan, David. 1997. *Focus Groups as Qualitative Research*. 2nd ed. Thousand Oaks, CA: Sage.

Morris, Jenny. 1991. *Pride against Prejudice: A Personal Politics of Disability*. London: Women's Press.

–. 1993. "Feminism and Disability." *Feminist Review* 43: 57–70. https://doi. org/10.1057/fr.1993.4.

–. 2001. "Impairment and Disability: Constructing an Ethics of Care that Promotes Human Rights." *Hypatia* 16 (4): 1–16. https://doi.org/10.1111/j.1527-2001.2001. tb00750.x.

Moser, Don. 1965. "Screams, Slaps and Love: A Surprising, Shocking Treatment Helps Far-Gone Mental Cripples." *Life,* May 7, 90A–90D, 91–96, 101.

Mothering. 1998. "Does the MMR Vaccine Contribute to Autism?" September, 51.

Murphy, Michelle. 2015. "Unsettling Care: Troubling Transnational Itineraries of Care in Feminist Health Practices." *Social Studies of Science* 45 (5): 717–37. https:// doi.org/10.1177%2F0306312715589136.

Murray, Stuart. 2008. *Representing Autism: Culture, Narrative, Fascination.* Liverpool, UK: Liverpool University Press.

Nadesan, Majia Holmer. 2005. *Constructing Autism: Unraveling the "Truth" and Understanding the Social.* London: Routledge.

Natanson, Maurice. 1970. *The Journeying Self: A Study in Philosophy and Social Role.* Reading, UK: Addison-Wesley.

Nathanson, Jessica, and Laura Camille Tuley. 2009. *Mother Knows Best: Talking Back to Experts.* Toronto: Demeter.

Ne'eman, Ari. 2010. "The Future (and the Past) of Autism Advocacy, or Why the ASA's Magazine, *The Advocate,* Wouldn't Publish This Piece." *Disability Studies Quarterly* 30 (1). https://doi.org/10.18061/dsq.v30i1.1059.

–. 2018. "The CDC Just Announced One in 59 Children Are Autistic. Here's Why That's Not Evidence of an Epidemic." *Vox,* April 30. https://www.vox.com/the-big -idea/2018/4/28/17295398/cdc-autism-rates-epidemic-diagnosis-vaccines-myth.

Nguyen, Xuan Thuy. 2018. "Critical Disability Studies at the Edge of Global Development: Why Do We Need to Engage with Southern Theory?" *Canadian Journal of Disability Studies* 7 (1): 1–25. https://doi.org/10.15353/cjds.v7i1.400.

Nielsen, Kim E. 2022. "Book Review: *Intelligent Love: The Story of Clara Park, Her Autistic Daughter, and the Myth of the Refrigerator Mother,* by Marga Vicedo." *Journal of Family History* 47 (3). https://doi.org/10.1177/03631990221084934.

Nishida, Akemi. 2022. *Just Care: Messy Entanglements of Disability, Dependency, and Desire.* Philadelphia: Temple University Press.

Noddings, Nel. 2013. *Caring: A Relational Approach to Ethics and Moral Education.* Berkeley: University of California Press.

O'Brien, Catherine. 2009. "Mothers Unite for World Autism Day: If You Want to Be Heard, You Have to Get Noticed." *Mail Online,* April 3. http://www.dailymail. co.uk/home/you/article-1164799/Mothers-unite-World-Autism-Day-8216-If -want-heard-noticed-8217.html.

Oliver, Michael. 1996. *Understanding Disability: From Theory to Practice*. New York: St. Martin's Press.

O'Malley Halley, Jean. 2007. *Boundaries of Touch: Parenting and Adult-Child Intimacy*. Urbana: University of Illinois Press.

Onaiwu, Morénike Gina. Forthcoming. *Neurodiversity en Noir: A Collection of Black Neurodiverse Voices*. London: Jessica Kingsley.

Ontario Association for Emotionally Disturbed Children. 1964. *A Brief to the Honourable W.G. Davis, Minister of Education, Province of Ontario, Concerning the Improvement of Educational Facilities for Emotionally Disturbed Children*. Toronto: Ontario Association for Emotionally Disturbed Children.

Ontario Ministry of Education. 2007. "Policy/Program Memorandum 140." May 17. http://www.edu.gov.on.ca/extra/eng/ppm/140.html.

Opai, Keri. 2017. "A Time and Space for Takiwātanga." *Altogether Autism Journal* 2: 13. https://www.altogetherautism.org.nz/wp-content/uploads/2023/11/2017 -Issue-2-Untapped-Autistic-Potential.pdf.

O'Reilly. Andrea, ed. 2007. *Maternal Theory: Essential Readings*. Bradford, ON: Demeter.

–, ed. 2016. *Matricentric Feminism: Theory, Activism and Practice*. Bradford. ON: Demeter.

Orsini, Michael. 2022. "Who Needs to (Un)know? On the Generative Possibilities of Ignorance for Autistic Futures." *International Journal of Qualitative Studies in Education*. https://doi.org/10.1080/09518398.2022.2098399.

Osteen, Mark, ed. 2008. *Autism and Representation*. New York: Routledge.

O'Toole, Corbett J. 2004. "The Sexist Inheritance of the Disability Movement." In *Gendering Disability*, ed. Bonnie G. Smith and Beth Hutchison, 294–300. New Brunswick, NJ: Rutgers University Press.

Panitch, Melanie. 2008. *Disability, Mothers and Organization: Accidental Activists*. New York: Routledge.

Paré, Ambroise. 1982. *On Monsters and Marvels*. Trans. Janis L. Pallister. Chicago: University of Chicago Press.

Park, Alice. 2017. "This Is How Much of Autism Is Genetic." *Healthday News*, September 27. https://www.health.com/syndication/how-much-of-autism-is-genetic.

Park, Clara Claiborne. 1967. *The Siege: A Family's Journey into the World of an Autistic Child*. Harmondsworth, UK: Penguin.

Parsell, Diana. 2004. "Assault on Autism." *Science News*, November 9, 311–12.

Paterson, Kevin, and Bill Hughes. 1999. "Disability Studies and Phenomenology: The Carnal Politics of Everyday Life." *Disability and Society* 14 (5): 597–610. https://doi.org/10.1080/09687599925966.

Piepzna-Samarasinha, Leah Lakshmi. 2018. *Care Work: Dreaming Disability Justice*. Vancouver: Arsenal Pulp.

Pollak, Richard. 1997. *The Creation of Dr. B: A Biography of Bruno Bettelheim*. New York: Simon and Schuster.

Portelli, John, and Christina P. Konecny. 2013. "Neoliberalism, Subversion and Democracy in Education." *Encounters/Encuentros/Rencontres on Education* 14: 87–97. https://doi.org/10.24908/eoe-ese-rse.v14i0.5044.

Price, Margaret. n.d. "Access Invocation." *Margaret Price: Rhetoric, Disability, Knitting, Skating, Tiny Dogs* (blog). https://margaretprice.wordpress.com/access-statement -for-presentations/.

–. 2015. "The Bodymind Problem and the Possibilities of Pain." *Hypatia* 30 (1): 268–84. https://doi.org/10.1111/hypa.12127.

Puar, Jasbir K. 2007. *Terrorist Assemblages: Homonationalism in Queer Times*. Durham, NC: Duke University Press.

–. 2017. *The Right to Maim: Debility, Capacity, Disability*. Durham, NC: Duke University Press.

Public Health Agency of Canada. 2018. *Autism Spectrum Disorder among Children and Youth in Canada 2018: A Report of the National Autism Spectrum Disorder Surveillance System*. https://www.canada.ca/en/public-health/services/publications/ diseases-conditions/autism-spectrum-disorder-children-youth-canada-2018. html.

–. 2019. *Autism Spectrum Disorder: Highlights from the 2019 Canadian Health Survey on Children and Youth*. https://www.canada.ca/content/dam/phac-aspc/documents/ services/publications/diseases-conditions/autism-spectrum-disorder-canadian -health-survey-children-youth-2019/autism-spectrum-disorder-canadian-health -survey-children-youth-2019.pdf.

Pyne, Jake. 2020. "'Building a Person': Legal and Clinical Personhood for Autistic and Trans Children in Ontario." *Canadian Journal of Law and Society* 35 (2): 341–65. https://doi.org/10.1017/cls.2020.8.

Rabinow, Paul, and Nikolas Rose. 2003. "Introduction: Foucault Today." In *The Essential Foucault: Selections from the Essential Works of Foucault, 1954–84*, ed. Paul Rabinow and Nikolas Rose, vii–xxxv. New York: New Press.

Rapp, Rayna. 2011. "A Child Surrounds This Brain: The Future of Neurological Difference According to Scientists, Parents and Diagnosed Young Adults." In *Sociological Reflections on the Neurosciences*, ed. Martyn Pickersgill and Ira Vankeulen, 3–26. London: Emerald.

Rapp, Rayna, and Faye Ginsburg. 2011. "Reverberations: Disability and the New Kinship Imaginary." *Anthropological Quarterly* 84 (2): 379–410. https://doi. org/10.1353/anq.2011.0030.

Renzetti, Elizabeth. 2011. "The Anatomy of Evil." *Globe and Mail*, July 30.

Re•Storying Autism Writing Collective: Raya Shields, Steacy Easton, Julia Gruson-Wood, Margaret F. Gibson, Patty N. Douglas, and Carla M. Rice. 2022. "Storytelling

Methods on the Move." *International Journal of Qualitative Studies in Education.* https://doi.org/10.1080/09518398.2022.2061625.

Rice, Carla. 2014. *Becoming Women: The Embodied Self in Image Culture.* Toronto: University of Toronto Press.

Rice, Carla, Eliza Chandler, Kirsty Liddiard, Jen Rinaldi, and Elisabeth Harrison. 2018. "The Pedagogical Possibilities for Unruly Bodies." *Gender and Education* 30 (5): 663–82. https://doi.org/10.1080/09540253.2016.1247947.

Rice, Carla, Elisabeth Harrison, and May Friedman. 2019. "Doing Justice to Intersectionality in Research." *Cultural Studies Critical Methodologies* 19 (6): 409–20. https://doi.org/10.1177/1532708619829779.

Rice, Carla, Andrea LaMarre, Nadine Changfoot, and Patty Douglas. 2020. "Making Spaces: Multimedia Storytelling as Reflexive, Creative Praxis." *Qualitative Research in Psychology* 17 (2): 222–39. https://doi.org/10.1080/14780887.2018.1442694.

Rich, Adrienne. 1986. *Of Woman Born: Motherhood as Experience and Institution.* New York: Norton.

Richardson, Diane. 2005. "Desiring Sameness? The Rise of a Neoliberal Politics of Normalisation." *Antipode* 37 (3): 515–35. https://doi.org/10.1111/j.0066-4812. 2005.00509.x.

Richardson, Sarah S., Cynthia R. Daniels, Matthew W. Gillman, Janet Golden, Rebbeca Kukla, Christopher Kuzawa, and Janet Richards. 2014. "Society: Don't Blame the Mothers." *Nature*, August 13, 131–32. https://doi.org/10.1038/512131a.

Rimland, Bernard. 1964. Infantile Autism: The Syndrome and Its Implications for a Neural Theory of Behaviour. New York: Appleton-Century-Crofts.

–. 1978. "Inside the Mind of the Autistic Savant." *Psychology Today* 12 (3): 69–80.

–. 1993. "Forward." In Catherine Maurice, *Let Me Hear Your Voice: A Family's Triumph over Autism*, xiii–xvii. New York: Alfred A. Knopf.

Ringrose, Jessica, and Valerie Walkerdine. 2008. "Regulating the Abject: The TV Make-Over as Site of Neo-liberal Invention toward Bourgeois Femininity." *Feminist Media Studies* 8 (3): 227–46. https://doi.org/10.1080/14680770802217279.

Rodas, Julie Miele. 2018. *Autistic Disturbances: Theorizing Autism Poetics from the DSM to Robinson Crusoe.* Ann Arbor: University of Michigan Press.

Rodier, Patricia M. 2000. "The Early Origins of Autism." *Scientific American*, February 1, 56–63.

Rones, Nancy. 2008. "What Autism Does to a Mother." *Redbook,* April 9. https://www.redbookmag.com/life/mom-kids/advice/a2866/autism-and-motherhood/.

Roscigno, Robin. 2019. "Neuroqueerness as Fugitive Practice: Reading against the Grain of Applied Behavioural Analysis Scholarship." *Educational Studies* 55 (4): 405–19. https://doi.org/10.1080/00131946.2019.1629929.

–. 2020. "Semiotic Stalemate: Resisting Restraint and Seclusion through Guttari's Micropolitics of Desire." *Canadian Journal of Disability Studies* 9 (5): 156–84. https://doi.org/10.15353/cjds.v9i5.694.

Rose, Nikolas. 1985. *The Psychological Complex: Psychology, Politics and Society in England, 1960–1939.* London: Routledge and Kegan Paul.

–. 1996. "Governing 'Advanced' Liberal Democracies." In *Foucault and Political Reason: Liberalism, Neo-liberalism, and Rationalities of Government*, ed. Andrew Barry, Thomas Osborne, and Nikolas Rose, 37–64. Chicago: University of Chicago Press.

–. 1999. *Governing the Soul: The Shaping of the Private Self.* 2nd ed. London: Free Association Books.

–. 2007. *The Politics of Life Itself: Biomedicine, Power and Subjectivity in the Twenty-First Century.* Princeton, NJ: Princeton University Press.

Rosen-Sheidley, Beth, Chantalle Wolpert, and Susan Folstein. 2004. "Genetic Counseling for Autism Spectrum Disorders." *Exceptional Parent* 34 (3): 63–67.

Ross, Marvin. 1989. "Physiological Links to Autism Increase." *Globe and Mail*, March 18, D4.

Roy, Meera, and Sivasankaran Balaratnasingam. 2010. "Missed Diagnosis of Autism in an Australian Indigenous Psychiatric Population." *Psychology and Counseling* 18 (6): 534–37. https://doi.org/10.3109/10398562.2010.498048.

Ruddick, Sara. 1995. *Maternal Thinking: Toward a Politics of Peace.* Boston: Beacon.

Rudikoff, Sonya. 1972. "Why Some Children Don't Speak." *Commentary*, October 1, 58–67.

Runswick-Cole, Katherine. 2014. "'Us' and 'Them': The Limits and Possibilities of a 'Politics of Neurodiversity' in Neoliberal Times." *Disability and Society* 29 (7): 1117–29. https://doi.org/10.1080/09687599.2014.910107.

Runswick-Cole, Katherine, Patty Douglas, Penny Fogg, Susan Alexander, Stephanie Erhat, Jennifer Eves, Barbara Shapely-King, and Incy Wood. Forthcoming. "'When Father Christmas Is the Gaslighter': How Special Education Systems Make (M)others 'Mad.'" *Journal of Literary and Cultural Disability Studies.*

Runswick-Cole, Katherine, and Daniel Goodley. 2018. "The 'Disability Commons': Re-thinking Mothering through Disability." In *The Palgrave Handbook of Disabled Children's Childhood Studies*, ed. Katherine Runswick-Cole, Tillie Curran, and Kirsty Liddiard, 231–46. Houndmills, UK: Palgrave.

Runswick-Cole, Katherine, Rebecca Mallett, and Sami Timimi, eds. 2016. *Re-thinking Autism: Diagnosis, Identity and Equality.* London: Jessica Kingsley.

Runswick-Cole, Katherine, and Sara Ryan. 2019. "Liminal Still? Unmothering Disabled Children." *Disability and Society* 34 (7): 1125–39. https://doi.org/10.1080/09687599.2019.1602509.

Rutter, Michael. 2000. "Genetic Studies of Autism: From the 1970s into the Millennium." *Journal of Abnormal Child Psychology* 28 (1): 3–14. https://doi.org/10.1023/A:1005113900068.

Ryan, Sara. 2021. *Love, Learning Disabilities and Pockets of Brilliance: How Practitioners Can Make a Difference to the Lives of Children, Families and Adults.* London: Jessica Kingsley.

Ryan, Sara, and Katherine Runswick-Cole. 2008. "Repositioning Mothers: Mothers, Disabled Children and Disability Studies." *Disability and Society* 23 (3): 199–210. https://doi.org/10.1080/09687590801953937.

–. 2009. "From Advocate to Activist? Mapping the Experiences of Mothers of Children on the Autism Spectrum." *Journal of Applied Research in Intellectual Disabilities* 22 (1): 43–53. https://doi.org/10.1111/j.1468-3148.2008.00438.x.

Saini, Michael, Kevin P. Stoddart, Margaret F. Gibson, Rae Morris, Deborah Barrett, Barbara Muskat, David Nicholas, Glenn Rampton, and Lonnie Zwaigenbaum. 2015. "Couple Relationships among Parents of Children and Adolescents with Autism Spectrum Disorder: Findings from a Scoping Review of the Literature." *Research in Autism Spectrum Disorders* 17: 142–57. https://doi.org/10.1016/j.rasd.2015.06.014.

Schalk, Sami. 2018. *Bodyminds Reimagined: (Dis)ability, Race, and Gender in Black Women's Speculative Fiction.* Durham, NC: Duke University Press.

Schalk, Sami, and Jina B. Kim. 2020. "Integrating Race, Transforming Feminist Disability Studies." *Signs: Journal of Women in Culture and Society* 46, (1): 31–55. https://doi.org/10.1086/709213.

Scherer, Stephen. 2012. "Is There an Autism Epidemic?" *Toronto Star* (blog), November 9. http://thestar.blogs.com/autismproject/2012/11/is-there-a.html.

Schill, Florence. 1957a. "Research Indicated: Treatment Is Lacking for Disturbed Children." *Globe and Mail,* January 16, 13.

–. 1957b. "They Need Help: 2-Year-Old Diagnosed as Autistic." *Globe and Mail,* January 23, 11.

Schreibman, Laura, and Robert L. Koegel. 1975. "Autism: A Defeatable Horror." *Psychology Today* 8 (10): 61–67.

Schutz, Alfred. 1962. *Collected Papers 1: The Problem of Social Reality,* ed. Maurice Natanson. The Hague: Martinus Nijhoff.

–. (1932) 1967. *The Phenomenology of the Social World.* Trans. George Walsh and Fredrick Lehnert. Evanston, IL: Northwestern University Press.

–. 1970. *On Phenomenology and Social Relations.* Ed. Helmut Wagner. Chicago: University of Chicago Press.

Science News. 1977. "Mother-to-Be's Anxiety Linked to Autism." December 3, 374.

Scientific American. 1972. "Rubella and Autism." December, 42. https://sciam-cms.s3.amazonaws.com/sciam/cache/file/664311B5-0A05-4D8D-9592BFC708B14D25.pdf.

Scott, Joan W. 1991. "The Evidence of Experience." *Critical Inquiry* 17 (4): 773–97. https://doi.org/10.1086/448612.

Segal, Julius, and Zelda Segal. 1992. "Living with an Autistic Child." *Parents,* June, 88–94.

Sequenzia, Amy. 2016. "Autistic Conversion Therapy." *Autism Women's Network* (blog), April 27. http://autismwomensnetwork.org/autistic-conversion-therapy/.

Seroussi, Karyn. 2000. *Unraveling the Mystery of Autism and Pervasive Developmental Disorder: A Mother's Story of Research and Recovery.* New York: Simon and Schuster.

Shakespeare, Tom. 2006. *Disability Rights and Wrongs.* New York: Routledge.

Shamsie, Jalal, ed. 1977. *Experience and Experiment: A Collection of Essays.* Toronto: Leonard Crainford.

Sheffer, Edith. 2018. *Asperger's Children: The Origins of Autism in Nazi Vienna.* New York: Norton.

Sibley, Kassiane. 2017. "Radical Neurodivergence Speaking." *Time to Listen* (blog), November 1. http://timetolisten.blogspot.ca/.

Silberman, Steve. 2015. *Neurotribes: The Legacy of Autism and the Future of Neurodiversity.* New York: Avery.

Silverman, Chloe. 2012. *Understanding Autism: Parents, Doctors and the History of a Disorder.* Princeton, NJ: Princeton University Press.

Silvers, Anita. 1995. "Reconciling Equality to Difference: Caring (f)or Justice for People with Disabilities." *Hypatia* 10 (1): 30–55. https://doi.org/10.1111/j.1527 -2001.1995.tb01352.x.

–. 1998. "A Fatal Attraction to Normalizing: Treating Disabilities as Deviations from 'Species-Typical' Functioning." In *Enhancing Human Traits: Ethical and Social Implications,* ed. Erik Parens, 95–123. Washington, DC: Georgetown University Press.

Simmons, Galen. 2021. "Stratford Police Cleared in Violent Arrest of Autistic Indigenous Man." *London Free Press,* February 9. https://lfpress.com/news/ local-news/no-charges-to-be-laid-against-stratford-officers-involved-in -2015-arrest-of-autistic-indigenous-man.

Simon, Roger. 2000. "The Paradoxical Practice of Zakhor: Memories of 'What Has Never Been My Fault or Deed.'" In *Between Hope and Despair: Pedagogy and the Remembrance of Historical Trauma,* ed. Roger Simon, Sharon Rosenberg, and Claudia Eppert, 9–25. Latham, MD: Rowman and Littlefield.

Simplican, Stacy Clifford. 2015. "Care, Disability and Violence: Theorizing Complex Dependency in Eva Kittay and Judith Butler." *Hypatia* 30 (1): 217–33. https://doi. org/10.1111/hypa.12130.

Simpson, David E., dir. 2002. *Refrigerator Mothers.* Chicago: Kartemquin Films.

Simpson, Leanne Betasamosake. 2017. *As We Have Always Done: Indigenous Freedom through Radical Resistance.* Minneapolis: University of Minnesota Press.

Sinclair, Jim. 1993. "Don't Mourn for Us." *Our Voice: The Newsletter of Autism* 1 (3). http://www.autreat.com/dont_mourn.html.

Singer, Judy. 2017. *Neurodiversity: The Birth of an Idea*. Self-published.

Singh, Jennifer S. 2016. *Multiple Autisms: Spectrums of Advocacy and Genomic Science*. Minneapolis: University of Minnesota Press.

Skinner, Burrhus F. 1963. "Operant Behaviour." *American Psychologist* 18 (8): 503–15. https://doi.org/10.1037/h0045185.

Skinner, Michael, Mohan Manikkan, and Carlos Guerrero-Bosagna. 2011. "Epigenetic Trans-generational Actions of Environmental Factors in Disease Etiology." *Trends in Endocrinology and Metabolism* 21 (4): 214–22. https://doi.org/10.1016/j.tem.2009.12.007.

Smith, Bonnie G., and Beth Hutchinson, eds. 2004. *Gendering Disability*. New Brunswick, NJ: Rutgers University Press.

Smith, Dorothy. 1987. *The Everyday World as Problematic: A Feminist Sociology*. Toronto: University of Toronto Press.

–. 1992. "Sociology from Women's Experience: A Reaffirmation." *Sociological Theory* 10 (1): 88–98. https://doi.org/10.2307/202020.

–. 1999. *Writing the Social: Critique, Theory and Investigations*. Toronto: University of Toronto Press.

Smith, Martina. 2021. "Political Love and SpaceTime Disturbances: Reimagining Parenting and Disabled Childhoods beyond Neoliberal and Developmental Discourses." PhD diss., University of Sheffield. https://etheses.whiterose.ac.uk/29592/.

Snow Patrol. 2004. "Run." Track 7 on *Final Straw*. London: Polydor Records.

Snyder, Sharon L., and David T. Mitchell. 2006a. "Eugenics and the Racial Genome: Politics at the Molecular Level." *Patters of Prejudice* 40 (4–5): 399–412. https://doi.org/10.1080/00313220601020122.

–. 2006b. *Cultural Locations of Disability*. Chicago: University of Chicago Press.

Solomon, Andrew. 2008. "The Autism Rights Movement." *New York Magazine*, May 25. http://nymag.com/news/features/47225/.

–. 2012. *Far From the Tree: Parents, Children and the Search for Identity*. New York: Scribner.

Solomon, Robert. 1988. *Continental Philosophy since 1750: The Rise and Fall of the Self*. Oxford: Oxford University Press.

Solovitch, Sarah. 2001. "The Citizen Scientists." *Wired*, September 1. http://archive.wired.com/wired/archive/9.09/disease.html.

Sousa, Amy C. 2011. "From Refrigerator Mothers to Warrior-Heroes: The Cultural Identity Transformation of Mothers Raising Children with Intellectual Disabilities." *Symbolic Interaction* 34 (2): 220–43. https://doi.org/10.1525/si.2011.34.2.220.

–. 2015. "'Crying Doesn't Work': Emotion and Parental Involvement of Working Class Mothers Raising Children with Developmental Disabilities." *Disability Studies Quarterly* 35 (1). https://doi.org/10.18061/dsq.v35i1.3966.

Stagliano, Kim. 2010a. *All I Can Handle: I'm No Mother Teresa.* New York: Skyhorse.

–. 2010b. "Vaccine Safety: Why Parents Are Concerned." *Huffington Post* (blog), October 17. Retracted in the interest of public health. http://www.huffingtonpost.com/kim-stagliano/89-of-parents-rank-vaccin_b_759305.html.

Stapleton, Betty. 1965. "Warrandale Reaches the Unreachables." *Toronto Daily Star,* December 15, 57.

Star Editorial Board. 2022. "Seeking Clarity on Ontario's Autism Therapy." *Toronto Star,* October 3. https://www.thestar.com/opinion/editorials/2022/10/03/seeking-clarity-on-ontarios-autism-therapy.html.

Stehli, Annabel. 1991. *The Sound of a Miracle: A Child's Triumph over Autism.* New York: Doubleday.

Stiker, Henri-Jacques. 1999. *A History of Disability.* Trans. William Sayers. Ann Arbor: University of Michigan Press.

Stoddart, Kevin, ed. 2005. *Children, Youth and Adults with Asperger Syndrome: Integrating Multiple Perspectives.* London: Jessica Kingsley.

Stoler, Ann. 1995. *Race and the Education of Desire: Foucault's History of Sexuality and the Colonial Order of Things.* Durham, NC: Duke University Press.

Stone, F. 1999. "Inside the World of Autism: Alone with My Thoughts." *Today's Parent* 16 (10): 110–17.

Stone, Linda. 1981. "Therapy Penetrates Silence of Autistic." *Globe and Mail,* April 23, T1.

Stote, Karen. 2015. "Genocide." *Eugenics Archive,* January 30. https://eugenicsarchive.ca/discover/encyclopedia/54cbb7a4b40f65dda4000001.

St. Pierre, Elizabeth A. 2014. "A Brief and Personal History of Post Qualitative Research: Toward 'Post Inquiry.'" *Journal of Curriculum Theorizing* 30 (2): 2–19. https://journal.jctonline.org/index.php/jct/article/view/521.

Swift, Simon. 2009. *Hannah Arendt.* London: Routledge, 2009.

Talaga, Tanya. 2013. "Autism Breakthrough at Sick Kids." *Toronto Star,* July 11. https://www.thestar.com/news/world/2013/07/11/genetic_risks_found_in_half_of_autistic_children_new_study_shows.html.

Tamboukou, Maria. 1999. "Writing Genealogies: An Exploration of Foucault's Strategies for Doing Research." *Discourse: Studies in the Cultural Politics of Education* 20 (2): 201–17. https://doi.org/10.1080/0159630990200202.

Thomas, Carol. 1999. *Female Forms: Experiencing and Understanding Disability.* Buckingham, UK: Open University Press.

–. 2006. "Disability and Gender: Reflections on Theory and Research." *Scandinavian Journal of Disability Research* 8 (2–3): 177–85. https://doi.org/10.1080/15017410600731368.

–. 2007. *Sociologies of Disability and Illness: Contested Ideas in Disability Studies and Medical Sociology*. Basingstoke, UK: Palgrave Macmillan.

Thomas, Charles C. 1960. "Medicine: Child Is Father." *Time*, July 25. http://content.time.com/time/subscriber/article/0,33009,826528,00.html.

Thomas, Trudelle. 2003. "Misfit Mothers: Memoirs by Mothers of Children with Disabilities." *Journal of the Association for Research on Mothering* 5 (1): 186–97.

Thomson, Rachel, Mary Jane Kehily, Lucy Hadfield, and Sue Sharpe. 2011. *Making Modern Mothers*. Bristol, UK: Policy.

Time. 1948. "Medicine: Frosted Children." April 26, 77–78.

–. 1968. "Psychiatry: Chicago's Dr. Yes." July 5. https://content.time.com/time/subscriber/printout/0,8816,941622,00.html.

Titchkosky, Tanya. 2000. "Disability Studies: The Old and the New." *Canadian Journal of Sociology* 25 (2): 197–224. https://doi.org/10.2307/3341823.

–. 2003. *Disability, Self and Society*. Toronto: University of Toronto Press.

–. 2007. *Reading and Writing Disability Differently: The Textured Life of Embodiment.* Toronto: University of Toronto Press.

–. 2011. *The Question of Access: Disability, Space, Meaning.* Toronto: University of Toronto Press.

Titchkosky, Tanya, and Catherine Aubrecht. 2009. "The Anguish of Power: Remapping Mental Diversity with an Anticolonial Compass." In *Breaching the Colonial Contract: Anti-colonialism in the US and Canada*, ed. Arlo Kemf, 179–99. Dordrecht: Springer.

–. 2015. "Who's MIND, Whose Future? Mental Health Projects as Colonial Logics." *Social Identities: Journal for the Study of Race, Nation and Culture* 21 (1): 69–84. https://doi.org/10.1080/13504630.2014.996994.

Titchkosky, Tanya, and Rod Michalko. 2012. "The Body as the Problem of Individuality: A Phenomenological Disability Studies Approach." In *Disability and Social Theory: New Developments and Directions*, ed. Daniel Goodley, Bill Hughes, and Lennard J. Davis, 127–42. New York: Palgrave Macmillan.

Toronto Daily Star. 1958. "A Fine Start." November 5.

–. 1960. "$9,081 Atkinson Grant Aids West end Crèche." February 13.

–. 1961. "Crèche Will Continue Treatment at Centre." April 20, 52.

–. 1969. "Parents of Autistic Hear from Experts." July 24, 29.

Toronto Star. 1972. "Parents Seeking Help for Handicapped Children." April 25, 61.

–. 1973. "The Girl Who Began Life in Mental Homes – at 18 Months." March 17, 21.

–. 1985. "Alberta Researcher Searching for Cause of Autism." September 28.

–. 1996. "Autistic Son Dies, Mother Charged." November 8, A8.

Traustadottir, Rannveig. 1991. "Mothers Who Care: Gender, Disability and Family Life." *Journal of Family Issues* 12 (2): 211–28. https://doi.org/10.1177/0192513 91012002005.

Tremain, Shelley. 2010. "Biopower, Styles of Reasoning, and What's Still Missing from Stem Cell Debates." *Hypatia* 25 (3): 577–609. https://www.jstor.org/stable/40928638.

–, ed. 2015. *Foucault and the Government of Disability.* Revised ed. Ann Arbor: University of Michigan Press.

Tronto, Joan. 1993. *Moral Boundaries: A Political Argument for an Ethic of Care.* New York: Routledge.

Tsing, Anna Lowenhaupt. 2015. *The Mushroom at the End of the World: On the Possibility of Life in Capitalist Ruins.* Woodstock: Princeton University Press.

Tuck, Eve, and Wayne K. Wang. 2012. "Decolonization Is Not a Metaphor." *Decolonization: Indigeneity, Education and Society* 1 (1): 1–40.

Tupou, Jessica, Sally Curtis, Dorothy Taare-Smith, Ali Glasgow, and Hannah Waddington. 2021. "Māori and Autism: A Scoping Review." *Autism* 25 (7): 1844–58. https://doi.org/10.1177/13623613211018649.

Underwood, Kathryn, Arlene Haché, and Patty Douglas. 2021. *IECSS Policy Brief No. 11: Submission to the Day of Discussions on Alternate Care.* https://www.torontomu.ca/content/dam/inclusive-early-childhood-service-system/findings/publications/PolicyBriefNo.11_EN_SubmissiontotheDayofGeneralDiscussiononchildren%27s rightsandalternativecare-Disabilityandchildhood_June16,2021_updatedFINAL.pdf.

Union of the Physically Impaired Against Segregation (UPIAS). 1975. *Fundamental Principles of Disability.* https://disability-studies.leeds.ac.uk/wp-content/uploads/sites/40/library/UPIAS-fundamental-principles.pdf.

Unland, Karen. 1997. "Woman Spared Jail in Autistic Son's Death." *Globe and Mail,* July 3, A7.

Vandenbeld Giles, Melinda, ed. 2014. *Mothering in the Age of Neoliberalism.* Toronto: Demeter.

Van Manen, Max. 1990. *Researching Lived Experience: Human Science for an Action Sensitive Pedagogy.* Albany: State University of New York Press.

Vicedo, Marga. 2021. *Intelligent Love: The Story of Clara Park, Her Autistic Daughter, and the Myth of the Refrigerator Mother.* Boston: Beacon.

Walcott, Rinaldo. 2020. "We Must Work toward an Abolitionist Future for Our World." *Maclean's,* June 4. https://www.macleans.ca/opinion/we-must-work-toward-an-abolitionist-future-for-our-world/.

Walden, Rachel. 2012. "Autism: Origins Unknown, but Women Still Get the Blame." *Women's Health Activist* 37 (6): 11.

Walker, Nick. 2012. "Throw Away the Master's Tools: Liberating Ourselves from the Pathology Paradigm." In *Loud Hands: Autistic People, Speaking*, ed. Julie Bascom, 225–37. Washington, DC: Autistic Press.

–. 2021. *Neuroqueer Heresies: Notes on the Neurodiversity Paradigm, Autistic Empowerment, and Postnormal Possibilities*. Fort Worth, TX: Autonomous Press.

Walkerdine, Valerie. 1984. "Developmental Psychology and the Child-Centred Pedagogy: The Insertion of Piaget into Early Childhood Education." In *Changing the Subject: Psychology, Social Regulation and Subjectivity*, ed. Julian Henriques, Wendy Holloway, Cathy Urwin, Couze Venn, and Valerie Walkerdine, 148–98. London: Routledge.

–. 2006. "Playing the Game: Young Girls Performing Femininity in Video Game Play." *Feminist Media Studies* 6 (4): 519–37. https://doi.org/10.1080/14680770 600990036.

Walkerdine, Valerie, and Helen Lucy. 1989. *Democracy in the Kitchen: Regulating Mothers and Socialising Daughters*. London: Virago.

Wallis, Claudia. 2006. "Inside the Autistic Mind." *Time*, May 7.

Waltz, Mitzi. 2013. *Autism: A Social and Medical History*. New York: Palgrave.

–. 2014. "Book Review: *Worlds of Autism: Across the Spectrum of Neurological Difference*, edited by Joyce Davidson and Michael Orsini." *Disability and Society* 29 (8): 1337–38. https://doi.org/10.1080/09687599.2014.934064.

–. 2020. "The Production of the Normal Child: Neurodiversity and the Commodification of Parenting." In *Neurodiversity Studies: A New Critical Paradigm*, ed. Hannah Bertisldotter Rosqvist, Nick Chown, and Anna Stenning, 15–26. New York: Routledge.

–. 2023. "Critical Autism Parenting." In *The Routledge International Handbook of Critical Autism Studies*, ed. Damian Milton and Sara Ryan, 194–202. London: Routledge.

Watts, Ivan Eugene, and Nirmala Erevelles. 2004. "These Deadly Times: Reconceptualizing School Violence by Using Critical Race Theory and Disability Studies." *American Educational Research Journal* 41 (2): 271–99. https://doi.org/10.3102/00028312041002271.

Wendell, Susan. 1989. "Toward a Feminist Theory of Disability." *Hypatia* 4 (2): 104–24. https://doi.org/10.1111/j.1527-2001.1989.tb00576.x.

–. 1996. *The Rejected Body: Feminist Philosophical Reflections on Disability*. New York: Routledge.

Weusten, Josje. 2011. "Narrative Constructions of Autism: Reading Embodied Language beyond Binary Oppositions." *Journal of Literary and Cultural Disability Studies* 5 (1): 53–69. https://doi.org/10.3828/jlcds.2011.4.

White, Nancy J. 1997. "Parents Face Court for Leaving Boy Behind." *Toronto Star*, September 21, A8.

Williams, Donna. 2009. *Nobody Nowhere: The Remarkable Autobiography of an Autistic Girl*. London: Jessica Kingsley.

Williams, Fiona. 2001. "In and beyond New Labour: Towards a New Political Ethics of Care." *Critical Social Policy* 21 (4): 467–93. https://doi.org/10.1177/026101830 102100405.

–. 2011. "Towards a Transnational Analysis of the Political Economy of Care." In *Feminist Ethics and Social Policy: Towards a New Global Political Economy of Care*, ed. Rianne Mahon and Fiona Robinson, 21–38. Vancouver: UBC Press.

Wilson, Robert A. n.d. "Eugenics." *Eugenics Archive.* https://www.eugenicsarchive. ca/encyclopedia?id=5233ce485c2ec500000000a9.

Wing, Lorna. 1981. "Asperger's Syndrome: A Clinical Account." *Psychological Medicine* 11 (1): 115–29. https://doi.org/10.1017/s0033291700053332.

–. 1988. "The Continuum of Autistic Characteristics." In *Diagnosis and Assessment in Autism*, ed. Gary B. Mesibov and Eric Scholpler, 91–110. New York: Plenum.

Woods, Richard, Damian Milton, Larry Arnold, and Steve Graby. 2018. "Redefining Critical Autism Studies: A More Inclusive Approach." *Disability and Society* 33 (6): 974–79. https://doi.org/10.1080/09687599.2018.1454380.

Woods, Richard, and Krysia Emily Waldock. 2020. "Critical Autism Studies." In *Encyclopedia of Autism Spectrum Disorders*, 2nd ed., ed. Fred R. Volkmar, 1–9. New York: Springer. https://doi.org/10.1007/978-1-4614-6435-8_102297-2.

World Health Organization. 2013a. "Comprehensive and Coordinated Efforts for the Management of Autism Spectrum Disorders." April 8. https://apps.who.int/ gb/ebwha/pdf_files/eb133/b133_4-en.pdf.

–. 2013b. *Mental Health Action Plan 2013–2020*. http://www.who.int/mental_health/ publications/action_plan/en/.

Wright, Lisa. 1995. "Thistletown Closing Feared." *Toronto Star,* January 19.

Wu, C. 1995. "Sometimes a Bigger Brain Isn't Better." *Science News,* August 19, 116.

Wynter, Sylvia. 1992. "Rethinking 'Aesthetics': Notes Toward a Deciphering Practice." In *Ex-isles: Essays on Caribbean Cinema*, ed. Mbye B. Cham, 237–79. Trenton, NJ: Africa World.

Yaffe, Barbara. 1977. "Autistics: Society's Forgotten Ones. Adults with No Future?" *Globe and Mail,* July 27.

Yergeau, M. Remi. 2013. "Clinically Significant Disturbance: On Theorists Who Theorize Theory of Mind." *Disability Studies Quarterly* 33 (4). https://doi. org/10.18061/dsq.v33i4.3876.

–. 2018. *Authoring Autism: On Rhetoric and Neurological Queerness*. Durham, NC: Duke University Press.

Young, Iris Marion. 1980. "Throwing Like a Girl: A Phenomenology of Feminine Body Comportment Motility and Spatiality." *Human Studies* 3 (2): 137–56. https:// doi.org/10.1007/bf02331805.

–. 2002. "Forward." In *Disability/Postmodernity: Embodying Disability Theory*, ed. Mairian Corker and Tom Shakespeare, xii–xiv. London: Continuum.

Zaleski, Jeff, Paul Gediman, Charlotte Abbott, and Sarah Gold. 1999. "Book Review: *Unraveling the Mystery of Autism and Pervasive Developmental Disorder: A Mother's Story of Research and Recovery,* by Karyn Seroussi." *Publishers Weekly,* December 13, 71.

Zournazi, Mary. 2003. *Hope: New Philosophies for Change.* New York: Routledge.

Zurcher, Ariane. 2012. "Tackling That Troublesome Issue of ABA and Ethics." *Emma's Hope Book* (blog), October 10. https://emmashopebook.com/tag/the-ethics-of -aba/.

Index

"disability story of parents," 33, 66–67, 100, 112, 143–44, 216, 224. *See also* autism mother narratives; "disability commons"; parent advocacy
disability studies: background to, 31, 60–64; on care and caring, 65–66, 68–72, 209; critical approaches, 61–62, 233n6; interdisciplinarity, 11–12, 61–64, 140; intersectionality, 64, 66–67, 71–72; on intervention logic, 13–14; on social interaction, 53–54
"discursive explosion," 21, 22, 35, 63, 110, 153
"disordered mind" theory, 139
disruption ethic, 7–8, 177, 214
disruptive knowledge: approaches, 40–42, 46–52, 54, 102; disability and disabled bodies, 223–24, 233n6. *See also* affirming care
DNA testing, 166
"double empathy," 19
"double-burden," women's care work, 71, 201
"double-consciousness," 39, 53
Du Bois, W. E. B., 39, 52–53

Early Intensive Behavioural Intervention (EIBI). *See* behaviour modification therapy
educational approaches, 131, 133. *See also* behaviour modification therapy
Edwards, Jules, 69
Ehrenreich, Barbara, 83, 88
embodied difference, 7–8, 9, 16, 25, 208–9, 237n1
embodied knowledge/consciousness, 39, 41–42, 102, 184–85
Emma's Hope Book (Zurcher) blog, 146

empathy, normative, 19, 114, 140, 144
empiricism, 45
empowerment, feminine, 177, 178–79, 185, 188–89, 205
The Empty Fortress: Infantile Autism and the Birth of the Self (Bettelheim), 86–87, 103, 113
English, Deirdre, 83, 88
Enright, Janet, 136
Environmental Magazine, 170
environmental risk factors, 6–7, 154–55, 167, 169–70, 190
environmentalism, 158–59
epidemic rhetoric, 156, 161–62. *See also* warrior mothers
epigenetics, 167, 169, 170
epistemologies: alternative, 40–41, 230n2; of difference and identity, 217; feminist and disability studies, 233n6; situated vs relativistic, 46–47; Western Enlightenment, 41, 42, 45–48. *See also* science
essentialism, 62, 73, 144
ethic of disruption, 13–16, 168, 224. *See also* affirming care
ethical narration, 10–11, 143–44, 151, 190–91, 213. *See also* autism mother narratives
ethnomethodology, 44, 158
eugenics, 30–31, 79, 164–65, 235n2
evidence-based treatment claim. *See* Applied Behaviour Analysis (ABA)
evolutionary view. *See* Theory of Mind (ToM)
experiential knowledge. *See* "sitpoints"

Facebook, 178–79, 180, 193, 194
factory time and productivity, 134
facts of social life, 44, 158–59

Ilg, Francis, 89–90, 96
immigrant (m)others, 205, 210, 211
impairment-disability binary, 61–62
independent living movement, 66, 69–70
Indigenous knowledge, 64, 157, 227
Indigenous (m)others and children, 51, 94, 226, 228, 236*n*2
individualism/individualization, 6, 62, 64, 68, 167, 181
"infantile autism" diagnosis, 77, 79, 81, 91, 96, 109
Infantile Autism: The Syndrome and Its Implications for a Neural Theory of Behaviour (Rimland), 113, 115, 116
Institute of Child Behavior (San Diego), 116
institutional care, 136–37
instrumental reason, 42–44, 203
intellectual disability, 227
intelligence testing, 104–5
"intelligent love," 105–6, 120, 236*n*2
Intelligent Love: The Story of Clara Park, Her Autistic Daughter, and the Myth of the Refrigerator Mother (Vicedo), 236*n*2
Intensive Behavioural Intervention (IBI). *See* Applied Behaviour Analysis (ABA)
intensive mothering: defined, 28, 71; autism mother ideal, 27, 141; maternal expertise, 172–75; naturalization of, 136, 192–93; normal development and, 105–6, 131–35; normative identity-making, 27–29; privatization of care, 119; white, middle-class ideal, 120–21. *See also* mother therapists; mother-child dyad

interdependency, 70, 73, 74
interdisciplinary approaches, 39–40, 233*n*6
Internet advocacy and campaigns, 161–62, 169, 172, 177, 178–82, 239*n*9
interpretive approaches in sociology, 33, 52–55, 58–60, 74
interpretive schemes, taken-for-granted, 14, 184–85
intersectionality, 65–67, 193–94

Jack, Jordyn, 26, 104, 173, 201
Jordan's Principle, 227, 239*n*2
Joy of Autism (blog), 191
Just Care: Messy Entanglements of Disability, Dependency and Desire (Nishida), 68, 69

Kanner, Leo, 79–80, 86, 90, 96, 104–5, 115, 208
Kaufman, Barry, 133, 142
Kaufman, Raun (son), 133, 142
Kaufman, Suzy (mother), 133, 142
Kelly, Christine, 72, 150–51
Kephart, Beth, 142
Khor, Tony, 187
Kilee Patchell-Evans Autism Research Group, 42–44
Kim, Eunjung, 31
Kim, Jina B., 64
King, Allan, 82
King, Thomas, 11, 222
"kinship imaginary," 217–18, 229
Kirby-McIntosh, Laura, 17
Kirkwood, Leone, 95
Kittay, Eva Feder, 73
Klar, Adam (son), 191, 192
Klar, Estée, 191–92, 225

knowledge production: ethic of
disruption, 13–16, 40–41, 47–48,
223–24, 228; from the margins,
11–12; as partial and situated, 32–33,
40–42, 46–47; subjugated
experiences, 32, 47–48. *See also*
science
Koegel, Robert L., 129, 131, 132,
137–38
Kohl, Helen, 140
Konecny, Christina P., 41, 56
Korean culture, 31
Koresky, Michael, 235*n*4

Ladd-Taylor, Molly, 90
The Lancet, 230*n*1
Landsberg, Michelle, 95
Landsman, Gail, 104, 174–75
language, role of, 183–85, 205, 235*n*2
learning styles, 208–9
Leslie, Alan, 114
*Let Me Hear Your Voice: A Family's
Triumph over Autism* (Maurice),
124–25
LeVasseur, Jeanne, 58–59
Levinas, Emmanuel, 11
Lewiecki-Wilson, Cynthia, 102
Lewis, Leona, 179, 181, 185
Life (magazine), 121–22
lifeworlds, 60
liminal spaces, 102–3, 177
"line of fault," 11–12
Linton, Simi, 233*n*6
Little Light Daycare, 174
Lorde, Audre, 16, 73
*Louder Than Words: A Mother's Journey
into Healing Autism* (McCarthy), 3
Lovaas, Ole Ivar: authoritarian
discipline, 26; behavioural

experiments, 18, 121–22, 135,
238*n*1; conversion therapy, 237*n*4;
on parent therapists, 123, 125, 138
love: autistic/non-normative, 208;
"dispolitical" care work, 214–15; in
global campaigns, 181–82;
"intelligent," 105–6, 120, 236*n*2;
intimacy, 191, 192–93, 225; mother
expert and, 173–75
Love Anthony (novel) (Genova), 154
"lovely intimacy," 191, 192–93, 225
Lucy, Helen, 138

Ma'at care/Egyptian philosophy, 73
MacFabe, Derrick, 43
machine imagery, 87–88
"mad" mothering, 6, 220, 227–28
magnetic resonance imaging
(MRI), 114
Mahler, Margaret, 91
Mail Online, 178
Malacrida, Claudia, 31, 164–65
Māori understandings, 29, 50
marketization, 131, 171–72, 173, 176,
188–89
Marx, Karl: on factory production, 134
masculinity, 186, 187, 188
"masking," 53
maternal attachment theory, 237*n*2
"maternal commons," 198. *See also*
"disability commons"
maternal expertise, 34–35, 104, 105–7,
125–27, 142, 205–7. *See also* warrior
mothers
maternal instinct, 83–84, 87–88, 93, 174
maternal knowledge/care proximity, 201
"maternal texts," 143, 148–49. *See also*
autism mother narratives
"maternal thinking," 105–6

normal development, 131–35, 201–2, 213–16, 217. *See also* mother therapists
normalcy: as achievement, 129–30; as "embodied *practice*," 128; gendered duty of (m)others, 80–81, 137, 211–12; productivity and, 134, 141; seduction of, 203
normalization therapies: autism industry, 158; autism mother complicity, 101–2; imperative and resistance, 99, 151–52, 217; (m)others' critiques, 214, 217; rehabilitation logic, 49–50, 81, 158, 203–4; scientific guidance and, 127–28; spectre of failure, 136–37, 187, 189, 190; of violence, 8–9, 235*n*4. *See also* behaviour modification therapy; intensive mothering
normativity, 16, 27–29, 49–50, 58–60, 121–22, 161–62, 233*n*6
nuclear family ideal, 30–31, 68, 120

objectification, 41–42, 45, 60, 128, 233*n*6
O'Malley Halley, Jean, 92
On Monsters and Marvels (Paré), 86
Ontario Association for Emotionally Disturbed Children, 99, 112
Ontario Autism Coalition, 27
Ontario Autism Program, 16–17
Ontario government: deinstitutionalization, 118, 119, 237*n*3; funding controversies, 16–18; Ministry of Children, Community and Social Services, 16–17; Ministry of Education, 238*n*1
ontologies, 45, 89, 96, 233*n*6
Orsini, Michael, 63

Orthogenic School, Chicago, 25, 81–82, 88
(m)othering and care: collective, 29, 68; disability and feminist studies on, 65–66; disabled children: paradox of care and, 150–52, 174, 175; individualization of, 31. *See also* "disability commons"
Other/other distinction, 46–47, 233*n*3
O'Toole, Corbett J., 64

Panitch, Melanie, 99, 101, 102
paradox of care: defined, 27–32, 162; disruptions to, 149–51, 209–10; (m)others' challenges to, 203–4, 223; scientific self-governance and, 84, 93–94, 128–29, 131–32, 138. *See also* affirming care
Paré, Ambroise, 86
parent advocacy: autism fathers, 26; biomedical views, 70–71, 159, 227–28; biomedicalization of autism through, 70–71; "crusadership," 101, 111–12; gaslighting of mothers, 51, 91, 155, 220; globalization of, 28, 157, 226; intensive mothering, 112–13; Internet campaigns, 161–62, 169, 172, 178–83, 239*n*9; self-advocacy and, 65–66; women of colour, 121. *See also* autism mothers
Parenthood (television show), 153
Parents (magazine), 115–16, 133
Parents Today (magazine), 136
Park, Clara Claiborne: affirming care, 103–5; embodied communication, 106–8; "games" at home, 92, 124; "intelligent love," 120; maternal treatment, 84, 85, 92, 93; neurodiversity advocacy, 110; *The Siege,* 84, 103, 146–47, 236*n*2

Park, Elly (daughter), 103–8
participatory research, 198
paternalism, 25–26, 73, 83, 84, 89, 126.
  See also scientific expertise
pathologization, 7, 58, 86–87, 192–93,
  222
patriarchal motherhood. *See* intensive
  mothering; mother blame
patriarchy, 28, 56
pediatrics, 90, 235n2
pharmaceutical industry, 166
phenomenology: on approach, 33, 198;
  Black, 39; bracketing, 58–60; lived
  experiences, 54–55; queer, 55–56; on
  texts and meanings, 14, 20, 132, 177
Piepzna-Ṣamarasinha, Leah Lakshmi,
  10, 64
policing/police violence, 7–8, 10, 157,
  193–94, 228
political economy of care, 120
popular media and science, 10, 81–82,
  118, 153–54
Portelli, John, 41, 56
positron emission tomography
  (PET), 114
power, theories of, 48–49, 51–53,
  56–57, 60, 182. *See also*
  governmentality/governance
pregnancy and risk, 166, 167, 169–70
preventative care, 130–31, 169–71, 172
privatization of care, 134–35, 175–76
problem-solution dialectic, 173, 191,
  192–93, 198–99, 216. *See also*
  paradox of care
propionic acid (PPA)-injected rats,
  42–44
pseudoscience, 26, 113, 116
psychiatry, 77–78, 79–80, 85, 201–2,
  235n2

psychoanalysis: autism mother
  narratives and, 103–8; disordered
  love, 174; maternal treatment, 82–85;
  mother blaming, 33–34, 89–94, 98,
  112, 116–17, 236n8; on mother-infant
  relationship, 90–91; postwar, 82–83,
  86–89, 90–92; resistance, 112
psychogenic views/trapped child, 82–83,
  115, 116–17, 125, 145, 215
psychology: behavioural therapies, 18–
  19, 34, 116, 237n4; child
  development, 49–50, 80–81, 85,
  90–91; "disordered mind" theory,
  139; maternal attachment theory,
  237n2; on neurocognitive
  impairment, 113–14, 116–18.
  See also behaviourism; biological
  views; mother therapists
Psychology Today (magazine), 129,
  137–38
Puar, Jasbir, 22
Publisher's Weekly, 141

Quebec Society for Autistic
  Children, 137
*Queer Phenomenology: Orientations,
  Objects, Others* (Ahmed), 55

"racial hygiene," 31. *See also* eugenics
racism/racial discrimination: autism
  identity/diagnosis, 94, 193, 226–27,
  236n2; wild child metaphors,
  139–40
Rapp, Rayna, 217
*The Reason I Jump: The Inner Voice of a
  Thirteen-Year-Old Boy with Autism*
  (Higashida), 164, 175
*Recommendations for a New Needs-
  Based Ontario Autism Program: The*

support groups, parent, 205. *See also* "disability commons"

Suzuki, David, 158–59, 160

TEACCH (North Carolina) autism program, 124

Teaching Developmentally Disabled Children: The Me Book (Lovaas), 125

technology of affect, 89–94, 101, 130–32

television shows, 15, 16, 96–97, 153, 158–59

testimonial reading, 144

texts, everyday, 19–21, 74, 102, 177, 232*n*13

Theory of Mind (ToM), 19, 114, 139, 208

There's a Boy in Here (Barron), 135, 150

Thistletown Regional Centre (Toronto), 81, 83, 118, 119, 124, 237*n*3

Time (magazine), 5, 79

Titchkosky, Tanya, 4, 6, 10, 12, 13, 32; on disability and disruption, 54, 102, 209–10, 233*n*6; on phenomenology, 60

Today's Parent (magazine), 23, 133

Tommey, Polly, 178, 239*n*6

Toronto: autism advocacy, 111; focus groups, 23, 32, 35; (m)other networks, 22–23; school integration program, 237*n*5; service agency experiences, 199, 204

Toronto Daily Star, 95

Toronto Society for Autistic Children, 124

Toronto Star, 89, 118, 135, 137, 140

tragedy narratives, 3–7, 13, 67–68, 96, 110, 135, 190

trauma response, 96–97

Traustadottir, Rannveig, 100

Tronto, Joan, 73

Tuck, Eve, 157

Understanding Autism: Parents, Doctors, and the History of a Disorder (Silverman), 65

Union of the Physically Impaired Against Segregation (UPIAS) (UK), 61, 64

United States: autism spectrum disorder incidence, 226; parent advocacy, 26

University of California at Los Angeles, 121, 237*n*4, 238*n*1. *See also* Lovaas, Ole Ivar

University of Guelph, 160

University of Western Ontario, 160

unmothering autism: described, 31–32, 162, 220–21, 224–25; critical approaches, 48–52; interpretive approaches, 52–55. *See also* affirming care

"unmothering disability" concept, 31

vaccine concerns, 3, 168, 169, 170–71, 178, 202, 230*n*1

Van Manen, Max, 24–25, 198

Vicedo, Marga, 236*n*2

victimization language, 6, 140–41

Vienna Hospital, 1930s and 40s, 235*n*2

violence: of behaviourist approaches, 18, 70, 138, 146, 148; modern modes of power, 223–24; normalizing care regimes, 51, 70, 144; ordinary normalized, 231*n*6, 235*n*4; parental complicity, 69; policing/police violence, 7–8, 10, 157, 193–94, 228;